Praise for *The Girl Who Saw Heaven*

"An absolutely beautiful story. Ari's near-death experience is a gift for all of the world, showing the connectedness we share with our loved ones beyond death. Highly recommended!"

—EBEN ALEXANDER, MD, former Harvard
neurosurgeon and author of *Proof of Heaven*,
The Map of Heaven, and *Living in a Mindful Universe*

"This unbelievable story will break your heart, enthrall you, and challenge your views of an afterlife, but in the end, Ari's glorious shared death experience will inspire and affirm your faith. Read it and be transformed. Required reading for anyone who's going to die!"

—WILLIAM J. PETERS, author of *At Heaven's Door* and
founder of the Shared Crossing Project

"*The Girl Who Saw Heaven* is unique, inspiring, and healing. It's a story for your heart and your soul that you'll remember for the rest of your life. Ari has a spiritual assignment to share it with as many grieving adults and children as possible. Her story fills people with comfort, hope, and tears of joy! I'm one of only a few people who heard Ari's account originally, and I'm delighted you'll finally know it too. Please read it yourself and share it with others—they'll thank you deeply for doing so."

—BILL GUGGENHEIM, coauthor of *Hello from Heaven!*

"A relatable yet eye-opening account for anyone coping with grief. Lisa Reburn's carefully researched and beautifully written book thrusts the reader into a complicated yet compelling story. *The Girl Who Saw Heaven* highlights the power of relying on your faith and the Lord without feeling preachy or stiff and leaves you with hope and peace."

—CHRISTINE KILLIMAYER, WHNT news anchor and executive producer of the Emmy-nominated documentary *10 Years After the Storm*

The
Girl Who
Saw
Heaven

*A Fateful Tornado
and a Journey of Faith*

Lisa Reburn

and Alex Tresniowski

Simon & Schuster Paperbacks
New York London Toronto Sydney New Delhi

100 YEARS
SIMON &
SCHUSTER
PAPERBACKS

An Imprint of Simon & Schuster, LLC
1230 Avenue of the Americas
New York, NY 10020

First Simon & Schuster trade paperback edition August 2024

SIMON & SCHUSTER PAPERBACKS and colophon are registered trademarks of
Simon & Schuster, LLC

Simon & Schuster: Celebrating 100 Years of Publishing in 2024

For information about special discounts for bulk purchases, please contact Simon &
Schuster Special Sales at 1-866-506-1949 or business@simonandschuster.com.

The Simon & Schuster Speakers Bureau can bring authors to your live event.
For more information or to book an event, contact the Simon & Schuster Speakers
Bureau at 1-866-248-3049 or visit our website at www.simonspeakers.com.

Interior design by Carly Loman

Manufactured in the United States of America

10 9 8 7 6 5 4 3 2 1

Library of Congress Cataloging-in-Publication Data has been applied for.

ISBN 978-1-9821-8952-5
ISBN 978-19821-8953-2 (pbk)
ISBN 978-1-9821-8954-9 (ebook)

*To Ari, for allowing me to join you on your very personal
journey and for giving me a better picture of the
immediacy of the transition from this life to Heaven.*

*To Susan, for challenging me to be a better person as I observed
you constantly maintaining the very picture of strength from
such an uncommon place of humility and self-sacrifice.*

*And to each of you who will read Ari's story and think about loved
ones in your own life who have passed away, may the firm hope that
Ari has of a living Heaven also be yours. When you hear words like,
"They are in a better place," my hope is that you will recall Ari's
experience as a little kindergartener watching her family, carefree and
pain-free, immediately walking away from the tragedy that ended their
earthly lives and walking toward the indescribable beauty and love
of Heaven, where she knows she will see them again, soon enough.*

This book was written for you.

Everyone who calls on the name of the Lord will be saved.

—Romans 10:13 (NIV)

The Girl Who Saw Heaven

CHAPTER ONE

We knew it was coming, and yet we didn't know.

The afternoon of April 27, 2011, Kenny Casey was on his way to fix a broken water pipe. Lean, soft-spoken, and sixty-two, Kenny was a longtime resident of Arab—a small, mistakenly named town near where the Tennessee River dips into Alabama, about seventy miles north of Birmingham. Kenny had a bad hip and a stiff back from forty years in the concrete business, but he could still build or fix just about anything, and when storms came through, which was often, Kenny was always ready to drive somewhere and fix something that wasn't working.

That particular day began with squalls and thunderstorms blowing in from East Texas, and warnings from meteorologists that tornadoes were likely on the way—which, in the South, during tornado season, was not that unusual. Tornadoes were just what happened in Alabama in the spring. Kenny set out in his blue Chevy extended-cab pickup and headed for Arab Water Works, the utility company on Cullman Road and the site of the broken pipe. On the way, he switched on the radio—WXJC AM, 850 on the dial—so he could listen to the weather.

A tornado, he heard, was headed straight for Arab.

Kenny knew he didn't have much time. Tornadoes move quickly, sometimes sixty miles an hour on the ground, fast enough to out-race a car. Most likely, Kenny had time to make one good decision and stick to it. He decided to turn the truck around and drive to the home of his mother-in-law in Arab's rural Ruth community, a quarter mile from his own home, to make sure she was okay.

When he got there, the storm caught up to him.

Fist-sized chunks of hail fell from the sky and shattered his windshield. Boards and branches flew past him like paper. Kenny rushed his uncle, niece, and mother-in-law into the home's concrete-topped storm shelter tucked into a dirt hill beside the road. He stepped aside to let a truck race past him. Just before pulling shut the shelter's heavy wooden door, Kenny took one last look at the darkening sky.

What he saw could only make sense in a dream.

"Huge trees were flying through the air like bowling pins," he says.

Then he heard the sound.

People talk about the sound without knowing quite how to de-scribe it. Deafening. Sickening. Unearthly. "Sort of like standing next to an airplane turbine engine when you first crank it up, only a hundred times louder," Kenny says. "It sounded like the world was exploding."

A fleeting glimpse of the thing was all he allowed himself before yanking shut the shelter door, joining his family in the cramped space and beginning his prayers.

Our Father, who art in heaven . . .

Fifteen seconds later, it was over.

Kenny opened the shelter and emerged into an eerie stillness. "Graveyard quiet," he recalls.

He never saw the tornado's black funnel, but he knew from hearing it that it had traveled over the nearby holler and through a large, wooded field—land where he and three other families had their homes.

Right then, he says, "I knew my house was gone."

He got in his truck and drove down the road, but broken trees blocked his way a hundred yards from the field. From there, he had to go on foot. His hip was sore now, but adrenaline pushed him forward and he crawled his way around mangled tree trunks and across the field.

Finally, he was in it—the barren, flattened footprint of the storm.

He stood there and surveyed the tornado's grim toll. An eighty-year-old tree had been uprooted and dropped on his house, leaving nothing but a stew of wood and bricks. A stand of oak trees bordering the field had been mowed like grass, some yanked up, some sheared at the base. A hundred-year-old family barn behind his house, reduced to a bramble of planks. A two-ton pickup truck flipped over on its top, like a toy.

Around him, nothing stirred. No breath of wind or crack of wood. The familiar was now strange and new. The world was flat and Kenny could see for hundreds of yards in almost any direction, though he couldn't tell which direction was which. Time had stopped and the air smelled of dirt and grass and gas leaking from broken lines. A place of life was now a wasteland, stripped of everything.

"I was thinking, 'There's no way anyone could have survived,'" Kenny says.

In the distance, a flicker of movement.

Kenny limped his way toward it. In the middle of a field, in a clump of high grass, he saw something tremble.

It was a child.

"Her eyes were closed and she was barely moving, but she was starting to come around," Kenny says. "She was moaning like she was really hurt. I knew right away who it was."

She was Ari Hallmark, the six-year-old daughter of Kenny's friend Shane Hallmark and Shane's wife, Jennifer.

Kenny, his hip and back nearly giving out, found the strength to lift Ari in his arms and cradle her. He held her like she was his own child, with her head on his shoulder, and later he said no one could have taken her out of his arms even if they'd tried. He knew Ari needed medical help, so he started walking, but he didn't know where to go—all the landmarks he was used to were gone.

Instead, Kenny followed the sound of sirens. He carried Ari for nearly a mile, past the pockmarks of homes sucked whole into the air, until he made it up to Ruth Road. There he saw a bright red fire truck, and a fireman running toward them. Only then did Kenny surrender Ari.

"Wait," he said before the fireman took her away.

Kenny pulled off his red sweatshirt and gently wrapped it around Ari's neck, stabilizing her head. Then, as the fireman rushed away with the child, and as a hard rain poured down on the desolate scene, Kenny slumped to the ground, put his head in his hands, and prayed the little girl would live.

He had no idea how badly she was hurt. All he knew was the tornado had thrown her across the black sky like a rag doll and set her down more than two hundred yards away from where she sheltered. Two football fields away. What she'd gone through in that time, Kenny couldn't possibly know.

In fact, what happened to Ari in those terrible moments was something almost completely incomprehensible. Something beyond the storm, beyond all imagining.

Beyond, even, the confines of earth.

This is the story of Ari Hallmark and what happened to her.

My name is Lisa Reburn and I've known Ari since shortly after the Super Tornado Outbreak of 2011, one of the deadliest and most devastating meteorological events in recorded history—what Birmingham-based TV meteorologist James Spann called "an unspeakable American tragedy." It was the storm that brought Ari and me together. I first met her at the only five-casket church visitation I've ever attended.

A visitation is an informal gathering of friends and family the night before the funeral, and the caskets held most of Ari's family.

Like Ari, I'm a Southern girl, born in North Alabama. I grew up in the city of Florence, along the Tennessee River, and about two dozen of my relatives—aunts, uncles, cousins, grandparents—all lived within three blocks of my family's home. On Sundays after church you'd find nearly all of us at my grandmother's house, gathered around the same tables, digging into home-cooked candied yams, fried okra, black-eyed peas, chicken and dressing, and my aunt Helen's warm chocolate pie.

Today, I'm a retired educator who worked in the Florida and Alabama public school systems for nearly twenty-four years, before earning my PhD and working eleven more years in higher education. One of my focuses has been on students who are blind or visually impaired. Occasionally, I have worked with young people during their times of grief.

On April 27, 2011, I was driving a few miles west of Arab, rushing home to Florence, when most of the early tornadoes struck. Somehow, I avoided a direct hit and made it home through blinding rain and battering winds. Over the next few days, I learned the tornadoes had taken the lives of more than *three hundred people*—at least ten times more than even the most pessimistic meteorologist could have imagined.

Two days after the outbreak, I answered a call from Susan Garmany, a paraprofessional at a school in Arab. Susan and I had worked together one day a week for three years, assisting a student who was blind. In the call, Susan told me that her six-year-old granddaughter, Ari, was in the hospital, badly injured and in the intensive care unit.

Susan told me Ari was screaming, not from pain, but from a much deeper wound, and she just wouldn't stop. Susan wasn't sure what to do, and she asked for my advice.

The next day, Susan called me again to help with Ari. I stayed close to both Ari and Susan for the next several weeks, then months, then years. In the decade since I first met them, Susan and Ari have become more than just my friends—they are family to me, and I to them.

It was about a month and a half after the tornado that I learned Ari had an unusual story to tell—a story that went beyond the storm. She first described it when she was in the hospital, mainly through drawings, and after that she only sporadically brought it up. Whenever she did tell the story, it was detailed and consistent. It was also a story that, as she grew older, she became more determined to share, because she believed its message would be of great help and solace to others.

It is, very simply, the most incredible story I have ever heard.

"This is how good I can remember it," Ari explained not long after the storm, when she was still six years old. "We were all in the tiny bathroom together and we had just seen the tornado in Maw Maw's backyard. We heard glass breaking and things banging real loud around the house. I felt the house vibrating and I remember it starting to go sideways before the whole house just completely turned around. Then it was moving and I was up in the tornado with cows flying around me. I could hear Pepper barking and cows mooing really loud. I saw Maw Maw pointing at something. She said, 'Oh, look at that. What's that? Let's go see.'"

So begins Ari's description of her incredible experience on April 27, 2011. In the midst of the cataclysmic storm, as 175 mph winds tore her grandparents' home off its foundation and flung it into the sky, Ari had a profoundly beautiful, peaceful, and life-changing experience in Heaven. She saw her maternal grandfather who died a few years before the tornado (and before she was old enough to remember him) and she saw angels. She saw Jesus gently receive her baby cousin from her mother's arms and hold him. She saw a burst of light brighter than anything she'd ever witnessed, and streets that sparkled with gold, "like mirror lights were coming off them." Ari saw colors that have no names on earth.

And when the storm somehow laid her down on a patch of grass in the field, broken but not shattered, Ari returned with a beautiful, inspirational message. At the heart of that message is a very simple idea:

"You're going to see your loved ones who passed away again," says Ari, now eighteen. "This is not your last time with them. Your time on earth is temporary and you should be at peace with where your loved ones are when they pass. You can miss them. But you don't have to hurt all the time. You will see them again."

In a way, Ari's extraordinary experience began six months *before* the tornado hit. Back then, Ari lived the mostly typical life of a Christian child in the South. Her grandfather was a Baptist preacher, though she never got to hear him preach. Ari's parents took her to church every Sunday starting when she was two, and in the car on the way home they'd talk to her about God and Jesus. Grace before meals, prayers at night, verses from the Bible, contemporary Christian music on the radio—slowly, Ari built a relationship with Christ.

Then, about six months before the storm, Ari "started having the dreams," says her grandmother, Susan, who now lives with Ari in the Ruth community in Arab. "She had them over and over and it was always the same thing—a voice in her dreams telling her that both of her parents were going to die at the same time."

For months, Ari cried uncontrollably every time her parents dropped her off at school, because "I was sure I was going to lose them and I wanted to spend every possible moment with them while I still had them," Ari says. Many people, including Ari's kindergarten teacher, Laura Byars, tried to comfort her, but nothing helped. By Christmas, Ari had lost weight, and there were dark circles under her eyes. She had been crying for more than two months, *every day*.

Then, the tornado struck.

The details of the tornado, and the destruction it caused, often seem inconceivable to me, too cruel and random to make any sense of, and especially hard to make peace with.

In all, sixty-two tornadoes touched down in Alabama on April 27, 2011, part of a three-day weather event that included more than 360 confirmed tornadoes tearing through parts of twenty-one states. More than twenty of the tornadoes in Alabama were considered "killer" tornadoes, meaning they led directly to deaths, and three of them reached the very highest rating on the Enhanced Fujita Scale—EF5, an exceedingly rare designation for tornadoes (there hadn't been a single one in the country in three years). EF5s feature winds over 200 mph, strong enough to pick up cars, trucks, and even trains and carry them one mile through the air. This unprecedented three-day storm, in turn, was part of the single worst month for tornadoes anywhere in the United States in all of American history—the National Oceanic and Atmospheric Administration confirmed a staggering *757 tornadoes* in April 2011, beating the old monthly record by more than two hundred.

The 2011 Super Outbreak caused more than $11 billion in damage to buildings, roads, homes, and other structures and systems in the US, making it the costliest tornado outbreak of all time. It also seriously injured more than three thousand people.

No single day that April was deadlier than April 27. An inconceivable *316 people* were lost that day, most of them Alabamians.

Yet as grim as these statistics are, they do not come close to telling the real story of April 27, 2011.

That story cannot be told with numbers, nor can the suffering within it be measured by any scale. Ari's is only one of the thousands and thousands of heartbreaking stories that could be told about those three fateful days, and I never allow myself to forget that. But Ari's experience is the one I know best, and to me it defies categorization and transcends simple storytelling.

There have been some, however, who have tried to stop Ari from sharing this story. People who, because of tragic circumstances, entered Ari's life and made it harder than it had to be. People who argued that Ari's desire to talk about Heaven wasn't "normal"—that she should be forced to pursue more ordinary activities "like softball." People who said, "Young kids don't need to be going around talking about death all the time," as if the best thing for Ari, emotionally and spiritually, would be to take everything she endured and stuff it away and pretend it didn't happen.

These people, however, did not, and never even tried to, know Ari. Nor did they listen to the people who did—or to Ari herself.

The truth is that Ari has always wanted to share her story because she wants people "to hear about my time in Heaven and be inspired by it," she says now. "Back when I was six, I couldn't really know the effect my story would have on people. But now I really believe this is a message people want and need to hear."

As a native of Alabama I have lived with the threat of deadly tornadoes all my life. It is something everyone who grows up in the American South learns how to handle. It does not help to be afraid of tornadoes, though it's essential to have a healthy respect for them—to understand and appreciate what they do.

Put simply, tornadoes take. They take sturdy homes off their foundations and churn them into bits. They take whole forests that have grown and nourished wildlife for decades and flatten them into oblivion. They take livestock and tractors as easily as they take the roofs off schools and stores, and they take strong, thick carpenter nails hammered into hardwood by generations past and yank them loose, destroying the sacred things they once held together. They take away loved ones, leaving despair and pain. Tornadoes take.

But people?

People *give*.

As much as anything, Ari's story is about how the grace of God was manifest in Arab, Alabama, through the community of people who came together to help a wounded but truly remarkable child. It is a story of the triumph of faith and humanity over the hardest of hardships and the unbreakable bonds of love that connect families, and sometimes strangers. Among the ruins are many resurrections; among the horrors, countless blessings. God is present in all these moments, just as He is in the most remarkable of all the events Ari describes—the beautiful journey that took her to a place beyond the storm.

That is why I feel so strongly about Ari's story—because there is so much love and wisdom and comfort, and ultimately hope, to be found in it.

And because I am certain that, as you get to know Ari, you will be as impressed and inspired by her courage and spirit as I have been.

SIXTEEN DAYS OUT

April 11, 2011
Vestavia Hills, Alabama

It began, simply enough, as air.

Air caught between the higher atmospheric pressure near the earth's surface and the lower pressure in the surrounding atmosphere, a tension of warring meteorological forces that spun the air into wind.

Winds that grew stronger over the tropical waters of the Gulf of Mexico and began whirling in a counterclockwise circle, propelling themselves out of the Gulf and toward the US coast, where electrical energy and booming shock waves transformed them into thunderstorms.

A long, sturdy, rolling line of thunderstorms, weak as they swept over Mississippi, but intensifying as they crossed the border into central Alabama late in the afternoon of April 11.

Thunderstorms that rumbled fourteen miles northeast into Vestavia Hills, a quiet Birmingham suburb, where, at 7:29 p.m. (central time), their peak winds were measured at 100 mph—powerful enough to earn them a new meteorological designation.

The storms were now a tornado.

A tornado that touched down somewhere behind the Vestavia Hills Police Department building on Montgomery Highway, and from there ripped through the playground and picnic table area in nearby Byrd Park, snapping or uprooting thirty towering pine trees, knocking over numerous large hardwoods on the grounds of the Vestavia Country Club, and dislodging drywall fasteners on a home next to the club, one of several houses damaged by the winds or falling trees.

And then—the tornado was over. It lasted one minute. It had a small impact area—one hundred yards wide by a half mile long. Its 100 mph winds made it an EF1 tornado, the second-least-dangerous type on the EF Scale, which rates tornadoes from zero to five based on wind strength and damage. The EF1 on April 11 did not, luckily, kill a single soul, and it was seen, for the most part, as a relatively minor weather event.

Only later would meteorologists look back on the tornado and see it as something else altogether—a harbinger of what was yet to come.

CHAPTER TWO

Something was wrong on the sonogram.

Jennifer Hallmark lay on the imaging table in her doctor's office in Arab, scared to death. She was there for a scheduled exam after a long, challenging year of trying to get pregnant, a year that included receiving hormone injections as part of a fertility treatment, as well as any number of store-bought pregnancy tests, invasive exams, embarrassing talks with new doctors, genetics testing, X-rays, charts, thermometers, calendars, quite a bit of cash, and a fair amount of unsolicited advice from close friends, relatives, and even a few strangers—all a part of the price that Jennifer and her husband, Shane, were willing to pay to start a family.

Besides this difficulty getting pregnant, Jennifer was, as far as she knew, perfectly healthy. In fact, she was unusually fit. A different doctor once pushed down on her stomach and said he'd never felt so much abdominal muscle on a woman before (Jennifer did one hundred sit-ups every night, feet under the couch, without fail). Blond, fair, and pretty, Jennifer was twenty-four years old and two years into her marriage to Shane, who, like her, was excited about having a family, even if he was a bit more anxious than she was about the reality of raising a child.

And now the doctor said there was a "mass" on the sonogram.

Other frightening words followed: polyps, cysts, blighted ovum, potentially cancerous.

"Jennifer, you need surgery," the doctor said.

An appointment was made with a surgeon. Jennifer's parents, Susan and Mike Garmany, went with her to the hospital; so did Shane and his parents, Phillip and Ann Hallmark. Jennifer was scared. She had no idea what was wrong with her or what was going to happen. Susan tried to soothe her daughter and stayed with her while a nurse inserted an IV and prepped her for surgery. Then it was time, and Shane and the family retreated silently to a waiting room.

Just ten minutes later, a nurse appeared.

"Y'all need to come back here," she said.

In the operating room, they found Jennifer crying.

"What in the world?" Susan yelled out as she rushed to her daughter's side. "What is it? What's wrong?"

"Mom," Jennifer said through tears, "I'm pregnant."

It was true. Before the surgery, as part of regular procedure, the doctor gave Jennifer a pregnancy test. To everyone's surprise, the test came up positive. There was no mass. There was, in fact, a baby.

And the baby was Ari.

The city was supposed to be called "Arad" with a *d*.

This was the intention of Stephen Tuttle Thompson, the first settler to build a house on the land that would become Arab. It was Stephen who, in 1882, applied to the US Postal Service to open a post office in the town, which was then known as Thompson's Village, after Stephen's father, Joseph Thompson. The form required three possible names for the city, and Stephen listed Ink, Bird, and Arad—the last of which was the biblical name Stephen had given his son. Apparently, Arad was also the name Stephen preferred for the town, given the unusual first two choices.

Sure enough, postal officials did select Arad.

But a staffer misread the name on Stephen's application as "Arab" with a *b*. The mistake was never corrected and the name stuck, and Arab, Alabama, all thirteen and a half square miles of it, was incorporated in 1892.

Arab (pronounced *AY-rab*) sits on the modest elevation of Brindlee Mountain in the southernmost part of the Appalachian Plateau, the strip of rugged land that runs from New York to Alabama along the western wall of the Appalachian Mountain range. Indigenous Americans from the Cherokee Nation lived there in the early 1800s before the mostly Scotch-Irish settlers arrived on packhorses and in wagon trains from the Carolinas, Tennessee, and Georgia. These settlers traveled on a new federal pathway called Bear Meat Cabin Road, which was little more than a crudely cleared trail with tree stumps cut just short enough so they wouldn't break the axles on the wagons.

Over the years, Arab grew: the first gristmill in 1885; the first school in 1902; the first drugstore in 1926 (patronized eight years later by the infamous Bonnie and Clyde); the first successful newspaper, the *Arab Tribune*, in 1958. Jennifer Hallmark's maternal ancestors trace back to well before these years; in fact, they settled the land before it even had a name. Jennifer's great-great-great-grandmother was a full-blooded Cherokee from the Deer Clan— the keepers and caregivers of deer, as legend has it. Susan still has an old photograph that shows her ancestor wearing a necklace with the image of a deer burned into a small piece of rounded leather. The clan's legacy is a deep, abiding love of and respect for nature and animals; members were taught to apologize to deer prior to killing them, and to explain the necessity of doing so.

Jennifer came from farming people, and her maternal great-grandfather owned large stretches of land on which he grew cotton. Her mother, Susan, remembers joining the other kids in the family to pick cotton for a few weeks "to earn money for new school clothes"—hot, hard work during the brutal Alabama summers. Susan also remembers her granddaddy letting the kids pile on top of the day's fluffy cotton haul for afternoon drives through the fields in the old cotton truck, a memory that still makes her smile. In winters her family joined many other Southerners who moved temporarily to Michigan, so the men could work in the car factories until they got to go back home in the spring to plant their crops.

Susan's paternal grandparents were sharecroppers. Despite being born three months premature—he fit in the palm of his mother's hand and spent his first several months swaddled inside a shoebox behind the family's potbellied stove—Susan's grandfather grew up strong and had thirteen children. The youngest boy, Bobby, grew up to marry a girl he'd known since grade school, Marlene, and they had five children of their own, one of whom was Susan.

Bringing up their children in the 1950s, Susan's parents never had much extra money, but they did have all the food and family they needed. They grew okra, beans, peas, and tomatoes in their garden, though one of Susan's favorite snacks was her mother's peanut butter "suitcases"—"one slice of bread with peanut butter on it, folded over." The girls picked blueberries and huckleberries for pies and cobbler, while Susan's brothers hunted deer and squirrels and brought home plenty of catfish. "Back then, boys were fishing by five years old, hunting by eight," Susan says. "My momma would tell them, 'Don't you load that gun until you see something,' but my brothers didn't pay her any mind."

Like her mother, Susan met her future husband, Mike, in school, when he began following her up and down the hallways of their high school. Susan, shy and reserved, kind of liked that Mike followed her around the way he did. Mike was shy and quiet, too, the result of being born tongue-tied, and his older brother had to do most of the talking for him, since few people could understand him. When Mike turned ten, a doctor clipped his tongue and after that he spoke normally, but retained his quiet demeanor.

Shy or not, Mike did summon the courage during a high school typing class to take the long walk all the way from the back of the classroom to the front, where, right under the teacher's nose, he approached Susan at her desk and asked to borrow a pencil.

"Why do you need a pencil in typing class?" she responded.

That inauspicious first conversation did not stop Mike. He kept chasing Susan down the halls until, one afternoon, Susan slowed down just enough to let him catch her. When she was sixteen and he was seventeen, they married in the yard outside the house her father and uncle built; the local pastor, Albert E. Patterson, officiated. Early on, Mike worked the night shift at Dunlop Tires, where his father was a manager, while Susan finished up high school during the days.

"I would leave him letters in the morning before classes and he would leave me letters at night," Susan says. "That was the only way we could share things because we barely saw each other."

They had a child, Jason, in 1977, and another son, Josh, in 1981.

In between, in 1979, their daughter, Jennifer, was born.

"The best baby you could ever want," Susan remembers. "Didn't cry or fuss much, slept in her own room at two weeks." Pretty, blond, and naturally athletic, young Jennifer loved playing sports and climbing trees more than the traditional pastimes for girls, and she preferred the company of her two brothers to that of her female friends. She always insisted on joining in when her father and the boys were playing at something, and she was good at basketball and ran faster than most boys her age. Whenever her father took jobs mowing weeds in vacant lots, Jennifer was quick enough on her feet to catch the rabbits that scampered out (she always set them free after a while).

"I mean, she was feminine and she could doll up and look beautiful, but she just didn't like wearing dresses all that much," says Susan. "I'd put her in a dress for church and that was a battle. With me, I started wearing makeup when I was in the sixth grade. Jennifer waited until the tenth grade to finally try some lipstick."

Everyone could tell that Jennifer was exceptionally smart and strong-willed, even though, as her mother says, "She never quite put her best foot forward in school. Jennifer was an adventurous free spirit who didn't like the responsibility that came with being smart, so a lot of the time she would act like she wasn't."

One of the only future goals Jennifer ever talked about was her desire to be a mother and have a family of her own.

Jennifer first met Shane Hallmark at the Walker Building Supply store just north of town and up the road from the Kirkpatrick Concrete company on US Route 231. Jennifer's younger brother, Josh, worked there with Shane, stocking and selling tools, fixtures, paints, lumber, and electrical and plumbing supplies. Jennifer showed up one evening to give her brother a ride home, and the next day Shane pulled Josh aside and asked about the pretty blonde who came to see him.

"That's my sister," Josh told him.

After that, Shane didn't fool anyone about how sweet he was on Jennifer, while those around her could tell she liked him, too.

"We all knew," Susan says.

The word around town was that Shane was a solid, decent man, and Jennifer's father, Mike, thought so, too.

"That Shane is a good boy," he told Susan one day. "He's got good manners and he's respectful."

Handsome, healthy, tan, and muscular, Shane had perfectionistic tendencies, and he worked hard to keep the world around him as neat as possible. He didn't mind having friends over to his home, but the instant they got up and said good night, Shane would haul out the vacuum and clean every inch of the carpets. He loved drag racing and tinkering with his cars' engines, but he also had a collection of model cars that he cherished. As soon as he was done enjoying them, though, he would get down to the business of cleaning and waxing each tiny car before putting it back in its precise spot in a glass case. At thirteen, Shane developed alopecia universalis, a condition that caused the loss of every bit of his hair, including his eyelashes (his hair never came back). Jennifer thought that only added to his striking appearance and pristine demeanor.

When he showed up for his first date with Jennifer, Shane wore pressed blue jeans, a well-ironed T-shirt, and sneakers that shone like fresh white snow. "Not a wrinkle on him," says Susan.

Jennifer, on the other hand, was known to make a mess or two.

She loved dogs and on occasion would try to sneak one into Shane's pristinely clean house for a quick but inevitably fur-shedding visit. Shane, however, always caught on—and years later Jennifer's unsuccessful stowaway attempts became part of the Hallmark family lore. (Ari *loved* those stories and became a dog-sneaker, too.)

Because Shane didn't have an ounce of meanness to him, he found a middle ground with Jennifer, who in turn tolerated his compulsive cleaning. In fact, Jennifer was pleased with how spotless he kept their cars and trucks. As a couple, they complemented each other in different ways, and rarely found anything to argue over.

"I never knew of them fussing," says Susan. "They fit together really well. It was like they finished each other."

Shane and Jennifer eloped to get married, and a year later they hosted a more formal ceremony at a lodge on the Parches Cove Hunting Preserve, on the edge of the Tennessee River, in the very small town of Union Grove.

Shane wore a perfectly ironed purple shirt and a black cap. Jennifer had her blond hair swept up in a soft, glamourous style, wore pearl drop earrings with floating crystals, and chose a lovely long dress that made her look like Cinderella. Jennifer's father, Mike, was the minister. During the ceremony a bald eagle swept into the river and came up with a fish in its talons, a moment the photographer just missed capturing. It was, the guests all agreed, a beautiful wedding and a wonderful start for the happy couple. It wouldn't be long, most figured, before their little family grew.

After the scare with the sonogram, Jennifer was able to enjoy the good news that she was pregnant. She'd waited a long time for this moment to come. When she was young she liked to joke that she wanted to have a big belly just like her granddaddy. Sure enough, when Jennifer was nine months along, she and her grandfather posed for a photo, big belly to big belly, both smiling ear to ear.

On a fall day in 2004, Shane drove Jennifer to Crestwood Medical Center, thirty miles up US Route 231 in Huntsville, for what was supposed to be a normal delivery. But there was another complication—the labor took too long and the baby's vital signs began to drop. The doctor performed an emergency cesarean and didn't even allow Jennifer's mother to be with her during the surgery. Thankfully, everything went well, and Ari Hallmark arrived in the world. She was eight pounds, with wispy blond hair and delicate features—perfect in every way. Jennifer held her beautiful daughter and beamed, while Shane "looked just a little overwhelmed by it all," remembers Susan. "He was so happy, but he was also like, 'Oh my, what did I get myself into?'"

Six weeks later, just after Christmas, Jennifer felt a terrible pain in her abdomen. She doubled over in agony and couldn't stand up straight. Horrified, Shane rushed her to the hospital. Jennifer was diagnosed with a postnatal gallbladder infection that led to pancreatitis, a potentially deadly condition, and she had to check back into the hospital for two weeks. The news was a shock for everyone.

"How could our perfectly healthy daughter be so sick that she might die?" cried Susan.

In those two weeks Jennifer could not eat or drink at all and was hooked to an IV around the clock. Shane stayed by her side in her hospital room as much as they let him. Susan, meanwhile, took care of Ari, and brought her to the hospital to see Jennifer when it was allowed.

Still, it was an unfortunate separation for Ari and Jennifer so soon after the birth. "Ari cried a lot," says Susan. "She was restless and she didn't understand what was happening, and it was an awfully long time to be separated from her momma at such a young age."

Jennifer recovered and came back home, but just a few months later she doubled over in pain again. The pancreatitis was back, and Jennifer had to return to the hospital, separating her from Ari for another two weeks.

"Both times, Jennifer could have died," Susan says. "That's how serious it was. But she's tough and she pulled through."

After that, life for the Hallmarks settled down. Ari grew up to be a tomboy and a free spirit, just like her mother—strong-willed, feisty, happy to go her own way. She was her mother's daughter in so many ways: she cracked her knuckles just like Jennifer did, and she hated anyone touching the inside folds of her arms, just like Jennifer had.

"Sometimes I even called her Jennifer by mistake," says Susan. "And the older she got the more she looked like her mom, so blond and pretty. It was like I was looking at a mini Jennifer."

This was, for Jennifer, exactly what she'd envisioned for her life since she was young—a happy, healthy family of her own. And now she was living it, with handsome Shane and lovely Ari, in her own little corner of the American Dream.

TWELVE DAYS OUT

April 15, 2011
Boones Chapel, Autauga County, Alabama

The first amateur radio report came in at 11:02 a.m.—hail "the size of quarters" in downtown Birmingham.

Not much later, an EF1 tornado with 100 mph winds touched down and damaged trees in the Nanafalia community west of Birmingham.

From there, the winds picked up, surging to 150 mph at 1:45 p.m., when an EF3 tornado struck the town of Geiger. Yet another EF3 raged through Greene County at 3:16 p.m., snapping hundreds of trees, battering homes, and crushing a power transmission tower.

The storm system, already in its second day, was not nearly finished. Just before 5:00 p.m., several witnesses reported seeing the third EF3 tornado of the day hit the Boones Chapel area in Autauga County. Dozens of single-family and mobile homes were damaged or destroyed, and a double-wide trailer was picked up and thrown across State Route 69, killing its one occupant. The brutal tornado rode the ground and wreaked havoc for nearly eight miles, leveling a path that was eight football fields wide.

The chaos was not unexpected. The event began a day earlier, on April 14, and lasted through April 16, a fifty-two-hour period that saw 178 tornadoes touch down in fifteen states—forty-five of them in Alabama on April 15, the most to ever appear in the state on a single day.

When the storms finally wound down and did their last bits of recorded damage—an eighteen-wheeler hydroplaning and jack-knifing on I-65, signs in a shopping center blowing away in Wadley— a total of four Alabamians had tragically lost their lives.

Across fifteen states—38 deaths, 588 injuries.

It went down in the books as one of the worst storms in the history of Alabama—and yet, years later, those three days of ferocious storms would come to be known, improbably, as "the Forgotten Outbreak."

The outbreak would be "forgotten" only because of what would happen just twelve days later, on April 27, 2011.

CHAPTER THREE

Baby Ari was a happy and thriving child, but the early periods of separation from her mother had an effect on her. She grew accustomed to sleeping with her grandmother and she cried whenever Jennifer tried to put her to bed in her own room. "It was really tough for Shane and Jennifer when Ari was little," says Jennifer's sister-in-law, Mandy Garmany. "Sometimes Jennifer just gave up—just literally fixing a bottle for Ari and saying, 'You drink until you can't drink no more, girl, 'cause I don't know what else to do for you.'"

Luckily this rough spell didn't last, and by the time Ari was a toddler she became "herself"—a normal, sprightly, exceptionally cheerful little girl. "If you look at pictures of her back then, she always had a big, beautiful smile on her face," her grandmother remembers. "Always grinning about something, just a happy little child."

At first the Hallmarks lived in Shane's home on Frontier Road in Arab while Shane continued working at Walker Building Supply. Around then, Susan Garmany's husband, Mike, lost his job as manager at Dunlop Tires when the company moved its plant out of the country. Mike had worked there for thirty years. The state paid for him to earn a trucking license, but he disliked being away from home for long stretches and stopped driving after a year. His son

Josh suggested they pursue something Josh had dreamed of doing since he was a teenager—run a chicken farm.

Mike liked the idea, and together he and Susan used the inheritance money Susan's father left her when he passed away as a down payment on a working fifteen-acre farm with four large chicken houses on New Friendship Road in Union Grove, a short drive from Arab. They called the place the G&H Farms, for Garmany and Hallmark. Mike managed the farm while Josh worked there full-time. Shane worked afternoons and weekends when he was off from his job at Walker's, though Mike and Josh hoped to make the business profitable enough to hire Shane full-time.

But Mike never got the chance. In 2005, he unexpectedly passed away of a heart attack, just one month shy of his forty-eighth birthday. He was memorialized at the Gilliam Springs Baptist Church as a wonderful, hardworking Christian man, and laid to rest in the Gilliam Springs Cemetery. "I had a very blessed life with Mike and I have nothing but good memories," says Susan. "I had him for thirty years, and they were very good years."

Susan and Josh decided to keep the farm going. Knowing it had been Mike's desire to bring Shane aboard, Susan used Mike's life insurance money to pay off the farm's debts and hire Shane, who quit his job at Walker's to join G&H full-time. Together, Josh and Shane did all the farmwork, rising every day at 6:00 a.m. and getting up in the middle of the night whenever an alarm alerted them to some or another problem in the chicken houses. Meanwhile, Susan could not bear to go back to the house where she and Mike had lived and raised their children. The day after Mike passed away she put up a For Sale sign and hired a contractor to build her a new home on the half-acre plot Shane and Josh carved out for her on the farm. It was a lovely spot, atop a small hill and overlooking New Friendship Road, and while her house was being built Susan moved in with Shane and Jennifer for six months and helped take care of Ari, who called her Nanny.

During this time, Shane and Jennifer bought a plot of land very near the chicken farm in Union Grove and, with materials generously sold to him at cost by the owner of Walker Building Supply, Shane started construction on a new home for his young family. When the contractors finished Susan's new house, Shane and Jennifer moved into it with her for another six months until Shane completed their new home in Union Grove. For that one year, Susan, Shane, Jennifer, and Ari all lived together, a team of four, helping each other build their new houses and new lives.

Once Shane and Jennifer moved into their own home, Susan remained a huge part of their lives. On Tuesday evenings, in what became a family ritual, Shane and Jennifer took Ari out to dinner and a movie (they were both decent cooks, but neither much enjoyed it, so they ate out three times a week). On the way to the restaurant, they'd pass Susan's new house and Ari would always say, "Poor Nanny, let's take Nanny with us," and so they'd stop and pick up Susan and bring her along. Ari also liked to sleep over at Susan's home whenever she could. That was the way things usually worked in and around Arab—families pretty much stuck together, through whatever challenges came their way.

For the first four years of Ari's life, Jennifer stayed home to raise her. Jennifer's sister-in-law, Mandy, did the same with her two young daughters, AnnaClaire and Addison (everyone called her Addi).

"That was a blessing for both of us," says Mandy. "Jennifer and I and the kids spent a lot of time together, and it helped me to have basically my best friend with me. Because the guys, they worked pretty much from daylight to dark. I mean, they worked *all* the time."

Both Jennifer and Mandy, however, were thinking ahead to the future. They realized that, as their girls grew older, their families would need more income to care for them and pay for schooling, health care, and clothing. They thought about jobs that provided insurance benefits, which would give them a real sense of security, and they settled on the profession of nursing, because there was *always* a need for nurses. The more they talked about their plans, the more eager they became to pursue them.

And so, in 2009, when Ari was four and Mandy's girls were five and three, Jennifer and Mandy enrolled in Snead State Community College's two-year Health Sciences program, in nearby Boaz, Alabama. Mandy's goal was to one day become the head nurse in a local high school; Jennifer, who liked being around older people, saw herself running a nursing home. "She was so good with geriatric patients," says Mandy. "She would come in singing and just be so cheerful with them. She loved all her older patients. I think they just stole her heart."

The nursing program was hard and demanded a lot of reading and memorization, and, although some of the work could be done online, Jennifer was away from home for most of every weekday. She entered Ari into a lottery to get a place in the county's only pre-kindergarten program in Union Grove, and, luckily, Ari was chosen. Shane drove her to pre-K in the mornings, and in the afternoons he usually picked her up, drove her home, and kept an eye on her, all while juggling his endless farmwork. For her part, Jennifer always rushed home the instant she was free.

"Buddy, it didn't matter what time it was, Jennifer was going to get home and see her baby," says Mandy. "She didn't like being away from her and she didn't hesitate one bit when it was time to leave school. She had to go see her baby, that was the bottom line."

Jennifer's second year in the program proved even more stressful than the first. The workload was heavier and there were real-world experiences, like when the nursing students were summoned to local hospitals during busy times, or med surges. "With Jennifer, bless her heart, every time we'd go to a med surg she would always get the *C. diff* patients," says Mandy with a laugh (*C. difficile* is the bacterium that causes severe diarrhea). "And she would say in her joking way, 'Why *meeeeee*? Why do I get these patients *every time*?'"

Nursing students also took part in a series of clinicals at hospitals in the area: the medical center in Fort Payne, the Mountain View psychiatric hospital in Gadsden, and Marshall Medical Center North in Guntersville, just up State Route 69 from Arab. The clinicals helped them learn evidence-based practice and clinical research. Finally, nursing students had to fulfill a preceptorship, or a set number of hours spent with an experienced nurse, who took them under their wing.

This workload was stressful enough for Jennifer, but then she and Shane seized on a good opportunity and bought a parcel of land on Fieldcrest Drive in the Ruth community, closer to Shane's family in Arab. They sold their home in Union Grove, where they had lived for two years, and began building their true dream house from scratch in Ruth. It was a daunting and time-consuming enterprise, especially since both Shane and Jennifer already had their hands full.

Later on in her second year, something happened during one

of her clinicals that made Jennifer question her career path. She heard that a nurse made an unfortunate mistake while on duty that may have led to a patient's death. It was a shock and an eye-opener for Jennifer, and she made the sudden decision to quit nursing school. The possible accidental death "really scared her, and she was like, 'I'm done,'" says Mandy.

"She called me and told me what happened, and she was crying and upset," recalls Susan. "Someone had died and she was afraid it would happen to her, and the responsibility of other people's lives in her hands overwhelmed her, so she left. They tried to get her to stay, they wouldn't leave her alone about it, but she was too afraid."

That night, Jennifer drove home and cleaned the house and cooked supper, and when Shane came home she explained her decision.

"This is who I want to be," she declared with total clarity. "I want to be your wife and Ari's mom and I want to make sure everything gets done. That is who I want to be."

Shane heard her out and when she was done, he gently said, "No. That's not you."

Shane was heartbroken by his wife's decision, because he knew her just about as well as anyone, and he knew that getting through nursing school was important to her. "I mean, Jennifer was *so* smart, and I think Shane knew she needed to get back in school," says Mandy, who was also hoping her best friend would return. "If I didn't understand the big lingo and stuff, Jennifer would water it down to where I could understand it. Having her there was like having my own personal tutor."

Jennifer stayed away from Snead State for a day or two, but—after listening to the people who loved her and knew her best—she decided to return. "She called me and she was like, 'Okay, I'm going back, and if I ever don't want to keep going you're just gonna have to make me, and I'll do the same for you,'" says Mandy. "'We *will* get through this.'"

Yet there was one other concern that was putting extra pressure on Jennifer—even more pressure than nursing school or the new house.

There was something troubling going on with Ari.

CHAPTER FOUR

It began in the fall of 2010, just before Ari turned six. She was in kindergarten then, in Union Grove, with Laura Byars as her teacher. Laura, born and raised in Union Grove, was a loving soul who always knew she wanted to be a teacher, ever since, as a youngster, she helped take care of the congregants' children during church services. As a teacher she was kind and caring and emotionally invested in all her kids.

"I love these babies," she would tell the new parents at the start of every school year, "and if you have a hard time with me hugging on your babies, you need to tell me now."

Of course no parent had a problem with that, and neither did any of the children, who called Laura "Momma Byars" and enjoyed brushing her naturally curly hair, if she let them, which she always did.

Laura and Ari, not surprisingly, got along wonderfully. "Oh, she was the cutest little thing, very social and chatty," says Laura, who has two grown sons of her own. "The way Ari talked—when I say 'country,' the way she talked was *so* country and *so* Southern to me. She was an only child and she was around adults a lot and so she always seemed a little more mature. I just had a place in my heart for her."

One seemingly ordinary morning, Shane dropped Ari off at school on Union Grove Road. But as soon as Shane drove away, Ari began to cry. Not a tear or a sniffle, but a real cry. Laura asked her why she was upset. The night before, Ari explained, she had a terrible dream—a dream so haunting she didn't even describe it to her parents for a few more days.

In Ari's dream (that some would call a premonition), both Shane and Jennifer died at the same time.

Laura assured her it was only a bad dream and it wasn't real, but the next day Ari arrived at school crying again. She'd had the same dream, and it was just as terrifying. "It's like a voice," Ari tried to explain to her teacher. "The voice says, 'Ari, you need to prepare yourself. Soon, you're going to be alone.'"

As a result, Ari could not bear being separated from her parents for even a minute. Here was a child who began kindergarten with no separation issues at all, with a happy, energetic, outgoing personality, and suddenly she couldn't even function in class, and even became a distraction. Ari didn't just cry after Shane dropped her off, she *sobbed*, loudly and uncontrollably, all day long, a picture of grief and terror.

No matter who consoled her or what they said to her, Ari could not get past the horrible dreams, and the crying continued and lasted most of every school day, for the rest of the week, and the week after that, and for many weeks after that.

"Baby, that was just a bad dream, and I know it seems so real to you, but as real as it seems, don't let it worry you and your little heart," Laura patiently and lovingly told Ari. "Everybody has bad dreams."

Ari could not be comforted. She showed up crying, and she cried all morning, during lunch, and on into the afternoon, and she only stopped when Shane or Jennifer came to pick her up at the end of the day.

"Sometimes Ari would lean her head on my shoulder and say, 'Miss Byars, I really don't mean to worry you, and I know I'm making your job harder,'" says Laura, "but I knew she couldn't help it. I could see how scared she was and how much she believed this was going to happen. It was just so real for her that she couldn't get it out of her mind, and she worried herself to death over it."

At home, Shane and Jennifer assured Ari they weren't going anywhere, but they, too, failed to calm her fears. "Nanny," Ari told her grandmother, "when my parents leave me at school, I always look back and see them driving away, and it breaks my heart." Laura enlisted the help of the school counselor, who sat with Ari in private and offered the same assurances, to no avail. The counselor gave Ari a dream catcher, a little handmade willow hoop meant to protect her from her bad dreams.

But that didn't work, either. The counselor tried reasoning with Ari: "It is not going to happen. If your momma dies, your daddy will take care of you, and if your daddy dies, your momma will take care of you. It is going to be okay."

"But what if they *both* die?" Ari insisted. "What if I lose them *both*?"

If anything, Ari's insistence on being with her parents only grew more intense as the weeks passed. "I need to be with them," Ari cried to Laura. "I need to be with them while I still have them. I don't have much time left, you need to let me be with them before they're gone." Ari simply could not understand why, given the circumstances of her vivid dreams, she wasn't allowed to leave school and be with her parents. Couldn't people see how important time with them was? Eventually, Ari resorted to spilling milk on herself at school, just so her father would have to bring her clean clothes and she could see he was okay.

Meanwhile, all Ari's teacher, Laura, could do was continue giving her special attention. She held Ari in her lap while teaching lessons at her classroom's small kidney-shaped table, and she carried her on her hip as she moved about the room. Laura spoke with the other children about Ari's situation, and they were all kind and loving toward her, and one of her little classmates would always pat her on the back when she cried. No child ever complained about Ari's crying, but it was clear they were worried about her and didn't know how to help.

"All any of us could do was listen to her and love on her and try to be reassuring, and tell her she didn't need to worry," says Laura. "But it didn't work. Nothing worked. The crying didn't stop."

No one had an answer. Her parents told her the story of the Boy Who Cried Wolf, but that only made Ari worry people thought she was making it all up. There were brief times when Ari was busy playing or reading and temporarily calmed down, but all she had to do was stop and think about her dreams and the crying would start again. No one at the school ever thought of Ari's continuous crying as attention-grabbing: it was obvious to everyone that this was something Ari could not control. Something that was real and profoundly upsetting to her.

"We just said we're going to stick it out and get through it, so I'd tuck Ari close to me and get her through the day," Laura remembers. "But whenever things got still and quiet, the thoughts would come back to her and overwhelm her, and she would cry again."

Ari's sobbing continued through Christmas of 2010, and on

into January and February. It was now the routine reality of her life. Some days Ari was so determined to be with her parents that she threw up and got to go home. If she couldn't find a way to get out of school, she would plead for someone to call her daddy and find out if he and Jennifer were okay. Shane kept his phone with him at all times and tried to answer every call. But one day he didn't pick up, and Ari had a screaming fit in the school office.

"I just completely lost it," Ari says now. "It was really, really bad. I was a wreck, until my daddy finally called back a few minutes later."

As a result, Ari wound up missing quite a bit of school, and that became a problem. "She needed to be in school to learn," Laura says. "You can only miss so many days." In late February 2011, the school board sent Shane and Jennifer an official letter about Ari's truancy. The bottom line: Ari could not afford to miss many more days. "Jennifer told me, 'Momma, I am so worried,'" Susan recalls. "'I'm afraid the school is going to expel Ari.'" Jennifer also worried the Department of Human Resources, Alabama's child welfare agency, would get involved, and who knew what would happen then. After all, how could she explain something to the agency's officials that she couldn't even understand herself? Ari's parents felt they had no choice but to sit down with her and tell her about the truancy letter and somehow persuade her to stop her crying at school.

"Y'all are making it up about the letter," Ari responded, brushing it off. Shane and Jennifer realized that if Ari didn't even believe the letter was real, the threat of being expelled from school would probably not, on its own, stop her from crying. Having to be away from her parents while at school, after all, was what she was crying about.

There was only one other thing they thought to try.

That's when they called Ninny.

Ninny was Ari's name for her aunt Cindy, Susan's sister, someone Ari absolutely trusted and loved. It was just a feeling Ari got about Cindy—that she would never lie to her. "If Ninny told it," Ari would say, "then it must be true." Ninny worked in administration for another school system in the area, and Ari used to ride the afternoon bus to Ninny's school one day a week so they could go to Wednesday evening church together—a practice that stopped when Ari's dreams began. Shane and Jennifer knew that, if anyone could, Ninny could persuade Ari of the authenticity of the truancy letter, and explain what would happen if she kept missing school.

They arranged a family meeting at Ninny's house to address everyone's concerns. Because of Ari's crying and her insistence on being with her parents every possible moment, Ninny hadn't seen Ari in weeks. "When I saw her that night," Cindy says, "I was just in shock. I could tell she'd lost weight and she had black circles around her eyes. It absolutely broke my heart."

During their talk, "I let Ari tell me what she was worried about and I tried to console her and assure her that in my many years at the school system I had never known of *anybody* who had lost their momma and daddy both at the same time," Cindy says. But, as had been the case so far, Ari would not be so easily consoled or persuaded. Finally, remembers Cindy, "I sat her down with everyone there and told her that the truancy letter was real and that it was the law. She had to go to school and her momma and daddy would get in trouble if they didn't send her."

Ari listened to her Ninny and accepted that what she was saying was true. Now it was time to address Ari's concerns.

Because of her certainty about her dreams, Ari insisted on knowing who would raise her "when my mommy and daddy die." Shane and Jennifer openly discussed the possibilities with everyone at the meeting and thoughtfully considered every family member. Ari's choice was the same as everyone else's—her Nanny Susan. Even though Susan was still adjusting to life as a widow, there was no question she was the one for the job. Everyone also agreed that if for some reason Susan couldn't do it, Cindy and her husband, Randy, could raise Ari as well. Ari was satisfied with both decisions, and the discussion went a long way to assuaging her terrible fear of being left alone. But she did have one other condition.

She told her parents, "You need to write a will."

Shane and Jennifer agreed to do just that as soon as Jennifer graduated from nursing school in a few weeks.

Clearly, these were very serious, heavy topics for someone barely six years old to want to discuss, but Ari could not be shaken of her belief that her dreams would come true. Shane and Jennifer didn't like indulging this belief, but they also knew there was no point in trying to talk Ari out it. Instead, they agreed to Ari's terms and even sweetened the deal for her.

If Ari stopped crying at school, the three of them would all take a weeklong vacation just as soon as Jennifer graduated and go to the Great Smoky Mountains National Park in Tennessee—one of Ari's very favorite places in the world. The family had vacationed at the 520,000-acre park before, and Ari absolutely loved going there, and especially to the Dixie Stampede, where she could watch the rodeo and ride horses and then later search for arrowheads. The idea of the Smoky Mountains appealed to Ari, but she also felt the offer was a bribe, and she didn't much like being bribed to go back to school. Yet Ari, uncommonly smart for her age, or any age, also realized she had little choice.

"Okay, well, *fine*," she declared with her arms crossed firmly in front of her, and the deal was sealed.

The meeting could have ended there, but it didn't.

Sensing that Ari was still unsettled by and struggling with her dreams, Cindy called her over and let her climb up in her lap.

"Baby," Cindy told her in her warm, assuring voice, "you just can't control this. If something *is* going to happen, it's bigger than you. Momma and Daddy both are Christians, and we will know that they will be in Heaven. The only thing you can do is make the best of every moment that you have with them *right now*."

Ari stared silently at the floor. But she listened. She had never told anyone that she had come to believe she could protect her parents, and even save their lives, by being with them. It was only much later, when she was fifteen, that Ari told me, "Since my parents died in my dreams and I didn't, I thought that if I was with them, they wouldn't die, either."

In other words, on top of all the fear and dread, Ari was also shouldering an impossible, self-imposed burden for her parents' safety.

And I believe it was Cindy's very words that night—*it's bigger than you*—that allowed Ari to begin to let go of this very heavy burden.

"You know," Cindy went on, "if something is going to happen, we don't want to spend our last few days with 'em being miserable and crying. It breaks your daddy's heart to take you to school and you cry and the teachers have to peel you off him, and then you cry all day long. If something is going to happen, you need to be *happy* and you need to enjoy *every minute* you are with your momma and daddy."

Then Cindy had an idea.

"Tell you what," she said to Ari. "I want you to get up in the morning, and I'm going to call you and check on you and I want you to be up and ready, and I want you to beat Daddy to the truck. When he gets to the truck, you be sitting there waiting on him with that great big happy smile of yours, okay?"

And that's just what Ari did—beat her daddy to the truck. Ninny called three mornings in a row, and Ari was always up and ready and she always beat her daddy to the truck. That became the morning ritual, and Ari finally stopped crying at school. She was, everyone noticed, slowly going back to being her happy, cheerful self again.

The next several weeks were just like the old days, with Shane working hard and Jennifer scrambling to finish school and Ari enjoying her time with her parents and making the best of her situation. "She was having a good life again," says Susan, "and so were were her momma and daddy."

Words have power. And the words Ninny shared with Ari that night were one of the most precious gifts anyone ever gave her.

It was the third week of April 2011. The Hallmarks were nearly done with the finishing touches on their new dream home in Arab, across Fieldcrest Drive from a peaceful field where cows occasionally strayed. There was still work to be done on the house's second floor, where Ari's big playroom and future bedroom would be. But construction was far enough along for the Hallmarks to finally be able to move in—a genuinely thrilling experience for them all.

As soon as they were in, Jennifer and Susan got busy decorating the main floor and arranging furniture, while Ari and her mom put the finishing touches on Ari's giant playroom, which included a wraparound wooden kitchen play set and a special bay window that looked out over acres of green grass and trees. Ari also helped Shane lay bathroom tile and check off other small but meaningful tasks, and Shane—normally obsessive about details—didn't even mind when Ari laid her tiles slightly off-center.

Jennifer, meanwhile, had only a couple of weeks to go before she finally finished her course load and graduated as a registered nurse. One of the first rooms she finished in the new home was her office, and she crammed for her exams there, often with Ari by her side, helping her study. Ari believed she learned enough about nursing just helping her mommy study that she began practicing her new skills on her Maw Maw and Paw Paw, who obligingly stopped over and "pretended" to be sick.

"I know how to be a nurse because my momma taught me," Ari declared proudly as she checked her grandparents' hearts and lungs.

It was a very hectic time, but it was also a very happy time, and at least there was a light at the end of the tunnel, with Jennifer finishing college and Shane finishing the house and Ari finishing kindergarten. The big family trip and a sweet, leisurely summer were just ahead. For Jennifer, especially, the summer break could not come soon enough. There were just a few more difficult days of intense studying for her final exam on April 27, and then she would finally be on the other side of her long and emotionally draining ordeal.

"We were all just so ready to be done," remembers Mandy. "Jennifer was *so* excited and she was already making plans. She was like, 'When we get done with school, we're going to get our nails done and we're going to do this and that, and we are going to have ourselves a *day*!'"

THREE DAYS OUT

April 24, 2011
Birmingham, Alabama

At 7:00 a.m. on Easter Sunday, the National Weather Service (NWS) Forecast Office in Birmingham issued a Hazardous Weather Outlook for thirty-nine counties for that day and the following week. Easter Sunday would be fine. "No hazardous weather is expected at this time," the Outlook said. But there was no such optimism about the days after that.

The prediction for Tuesday, April 26, was for "severe thunderstorms across the northwestern counties," a forecast the NWS extended through Wednesday morning. The real concern, however, was what might happen *later* on Wednesday. "All modes of severe weather are possible" then, the Outlook warned, "including tornadoes."

The forecast for Wednesday was later ammended to "supercell thunderstorms capable of producing strong and long-tracked tornadoes."

And then, at 3:19 a.m. the morning of Wednesday, April 27, the Outlook included a flat-out warning:

> *Now is the time to review your severe*
> *weather plan and be prepared to take action.*

The rough weather began to form on Monday, April 25, with a wave of storms and tornado warnings in southern Tennessee and Arkansas. Around midday there were reports of funnel clouds—twisting, conical columns of water droplets—and in the evening a squall line (a row of storms) caused a good amount of wind damage.

The next day, April 26, the mid-South region saw supercell storms "explode over central Arkansas and move northeast," read one report. Storm clusters, squall lines, flash flooding, and tornadoes ravaged the area, mostly in Louisiana.

Then came Wednesday, April 27—the day that most alarmed the National Weather Service.

At 4:05 a.m., two hours before the sun rose and about an hour after the NWS issued its dire Outlook, an emergency manager in Lamar County, along Alabama's western border, called in the first report of damage.

Trees were down on State Route 96, just west of Millport.

CHAPTER FIVE

When he was a boy, James Spann could not wait for a good thunderstorm. Something about the scale and drama of a storm was exciting to him, and on hot, lazy summer afternoons in Greenville, Alabama, when the sky darkened all at once and the rains came and the temperature dropped and lightning bolts flashed, Spann would feel a familiar thrill and, rather than seek shelter inside, stay out in the open and bask in the bad weather.

"It was boneheaded being that close to a storm, but we didn't know any better back then," says Spann, now sixty-six. "The sky was blowing up all around us, but that was the thrill of it. There was something romantic about thunderstorms in the Deep South."

That youthful fascination with weather never went away and grew into a deep appreciation for the dangerous power of nature. Spann has been the chief meteorologist for the ABC affiliate in Birmingham for the past quarter century (overall, he's been a meteorologist for forty-four years), and his mission has been, and continues to be, keeping Alabamians safe when hazardous storms roll in. "Floods, hurricanes, ice storms, tornadoes—we've been through a lot together," Spann says of his loyal and trusting audience. "I feel like we're all a family."

When Spann was a senior in high school—and a ham radio

enthusiast—he would hurry down to the local emergency manage-ment office during storms and use his radio to patch in reports from people in different parts of the county, and even from people in cars. After such storms, the high school principal allowed him two or three days off from class to volunteer at whatever hospital was in the hardest-hit city.

On April 3, 1974, when Spann was seventeen, what was then the most violent tornado outbreak ever recorded, with several con-firmed EF4 and EF5 tornadoes, tore through northern Alabama. Spann grabbed his ham radio and rushed to the emergency room at Walker County Hospital, in the devastated town of Jasper, so he could set up a link between the small hospital and relief agencies in Birmingham.

What Spann witnessed there changed his life.

"For the first time I saw the serious side of weather," he remem-bers. "It was horrifying. The damage, the nature of the wounds—all these years later I still haven't spoken to anyone about the things I saw that night. Before then I loved storms and I wanted them to happen. But after that, everything was different." For a long time afterward, Spann experienced night terrors, and often woke up in a cold sweat.

That monstrous weather event, later dubbed the 1974 Super Outbreak, saw 148 tornadoes touch down in thirteen states, killing 315 people—among them, eighty-six Alabamians.

In the South, storms are as much a part of the fabric of life as any-thing else, constant and—thanks to skill, technology, and a little bit of luck—fairly predictable, especially since the advent of Doppler radar. Growing up, I learned to live with the threat of dangerous weather, simply because the threat didn't go away. I will never forget one night when I was nine years old, and my mother was sitting twisted across the living room sofa, arms folded on the back of the couch, supporting her chin. She was staring out into the nighttime darkness through our single-pane-glass window, while my younger brother and I played with our baby sister on the floor nearby. What my mother was so intently searching for, I had no idea.

Suddenly she bolted straight upright.

"*Now!*" she yelled. "*Under the kitchen table!*"

I grabbed my baby sister and we all ran into the kitchen and slid under the table and held on to its skinny metal legs. There was a huge roar outside and I heard my mother yell out, "It *does* sound like a freight train!" but I still didn't know what "it" was, or why we were under the table. After just a few minutes we got up and followed my mother outside and down our driveway and into the pitch-black street. The night was warm and the air felt heavy and the usual sound of frogs and crickets was absent, creating an odd and eerie stillness—another sensation I will never forget. Except for a few flickering lights from neighbors' flashlights, it was completely dark, and I only got fleeting glimpses of the big trees and thick tree limbs strewn all over the street, a twisty tangle of branches that seemed, to my young eyes, like they were trapping us in. I remember hearing two neighbors yelling that their pane-glass windows had shattered.

Soon enough I would learn that the quick but unnerving ordeal was simply a part of life for Southerners because of all the tornadoes.

In the last century the Deep South, and specifically Alabama, have seen some of the very worst storms ever recorded. Besides the

Super Outbreak of 1974, there were the Killer Tornadoes of April 20, 1920, which included one violent tornado that stayed on the ground for 130 miles in Alabama (ninety-two people perished in that storm). There was the harrowing Tornado Outbreak of March 21, 1932, a series of fifteen storms that claimed more than three hundred victims (one tornado alone killed forty-nine people across sixty miles). The Oak Grove Tornado on April 8, 1998, was an EF5 monster that cut through Tuscaloosa and Jefferson Counties and claimed thirty-two lives.

You will notice all these terrible disasters happened in either late March or April, the time of year in Alabama that is still considered prime tornado season (we've had some pretty terrible ones in the wintertime, too). April is when, according to James Spann, the midlatitude westerly winds bring dynamic troughs with strong wind fields and then interact with the warm, moist air lifting northward from the Gulf of Mexico, creating a prescription for violent weather.

"For those of us in operational meteorology, April is the month when you never plan a vacation," Spann writes in his recent book, *All You Can Do Is Pray.* "You don't even *think* about it."

Spann was aware that April 2011 was shaping up to be an especially bad month for storms. He had monitored and studied the deadly tornadoes of April 15, which led to thirty-eight mortalities, including four souls in Alabama. He knew exactly what to look for in terms of meteorological conditions, or signals, that suggested more hazardous weather was on the way. "You start to see signals about a week in advance," Spann says. "You need instability for tornadoes, and then you need a cold front, and strong wind fields. Upper-level divergence and lower-level convergence." In mid-April 2011, Spann was seeing just such signals.

Still, he had to be careful not to be too alarmist. "You cannot scare people," he says. "Every storm is a monster, and you can lull people to sleep if you hype each storm too much. But then there comes a day when you have to hit the warnings hard."

Working out of his office at the ABC station in the suburban Birmingham neighborhood of Riverchase, Spann issued his first warning about a potentially dangerous storm system on Wednesday, April 20, 2011. The warning, which Spann posted on his blog, was fairly mild.

"Still too early to determine the exact timing or the greatest threats," he wrote. "Stay tuned."

Two days later, on Friday, April 22, Spann's blog post was more urgent. "Still looks like a significant severe weather event coming up for the southern U.S.," he wrote. "The main event seems to be Wednesday, and the 12Z GFS hints that all modes of severe weather will be possible."

The weekend passed, and on Tuesday, April 26, Spann delivered his most alarming prediction: "Projected soundings show the classic 'loaded gun' look, meaning that a cap should keep storms at bay through the morning hours, but when that cap breaks early in the afternoon, storms will quickly become severe. This is a dangerous weather set-up."

Spann was clearly worried about the "signals" heading into Wednesday, April 27. Tornadoes are created by a dozen or so different atmospheric conditions—a recipe, in a way—that mix together in just the right way to produce the most devastating weather. And on April 26, according to Spann, all the conditions were there—vigorous wind fields, both at the surface and aloft; diffluence aloft and convergence below; a deep-surface low migrating northeast; and others.

53

Spann took these parameters, analyzed each one, added all of them together, and came up with his "loaded gun" prediction.

On the evening of Tuesday, April 26, Spann set his bedside alarm for 4:52 a.m., his usual wake-up time, and prepared for a restless night of sleep, if he could sleep at all. Whatever fitful slumber he did find was interrupted at 4:00 a.m. by an alert on his phone. A tornado warning had been issued for Pickens County, in the far western part of Alabama.

Spann took what he calls "the quickest shower of my life" and sped to the ABC studio in Riverchase. "The drive from my home is about twenty-five minutes," he says. "That day I made it in fifteen."

It had begun. The loaded gun was about to go off. But even with all the technology and skill and preparation in the world, James Spann could not have foreseen what was to come that day.

No one could have.

CHAPTER SIX

In April 2011, my two teenage sons and I were living in a small, furnished two-bedroom rental apartment in the city of Florence, about eighty-five miles northwest of Arab. We were there for only one month while we waited to move into our new house in Muscle Shoals that May. Everything we owned was in storage.

Very early on the morning of Wednesday, April 27, I got ready to drive to a school in Cullman, twenty-four miles west of Arab, where I was scheduled to work with several students. After Cullman, I had another appointment with a student in Arab that afternoon. I knew about the impending storms; I'd stayed on top of all the alerts. But by the time I got up that morning, bad thunderstorms had already hit the area, and through my window all I could see was wet pavement and a few small branches scattered around. I checked with the Cullman school district, and neither Cullman nor Arab had canceled school for the day. So I got in my car around 6:00 a.m. and headed to work. It was my birthday.

The ninety-minute drive to Cullman on Highway 157 South was uneventful. I even had the moonroof open and I enjoyed a couple of calls on the way—friends phoning to wish me a happy birthday. When I pulled into the parking lot of the school, the sky was still bright blue and calm—a gorgeous Alabama spring morning. But before I could even park my car I saw the school principal run out of the building and head toward me, waving her arms.

"You gotta go home," she yelled out. "Bad tornadoes."

The principal was by no means a frantic person. But in the parking lot that morning, she *was* frantic and, most of all, insistent.

"Turn around, go home," she said. "School's been dismissed. You need to get out of here *now*."

Only later did I discover that a serious tornado had blasted through Cullman *while* I was driving there, causing major damage to a high school and more than explaining the principal's demeanor.

At the time, however, I assumed she meant a bad tornado was forecast for the area. I pulled out of the lot and headed back to Highway 157—still bright sunshine, still no rain. I hadn't listened to the radio on the way to Cullman, but now I switched it on and tuned in the weather and heard that in parts of Alabama tornadoes had already touched down. The meteorologist sounded somber as he rattled off the names of various small towns he was monitoring, as well as Doppler radar indications, National Weather Service watches, and other familiar weather-alert lingo. For a while, nothing that was brewing sounded imminently threatening to me.

Gradually, the meteorologist's tone became more pressing. The longer I drove, the more urgent the warnings sounded. Usually there is only one big tornado that needs to be tracked. But that morning they started talking about *several* potentially dangerous tornadoes in the area. In all my life I'd never heard them talk about so many possible tornadoes touching down in so many different towns and moving in all directions. I can't say I was scared because I don't scare easily. But with about thirty miles still to drive, I *was* becoming anxious.

Keeping up with the tornado reports was difficult because I didn't know the names of all the towns and roads between Cullman and Florence. I would hear about a possible tornado touching down in a certain town, but I had no idea if I was driving straight into it or not.

Then the heavy rain began.

Suddenly, I was driving through the most hellacious downpour I'd ever experienced. The kind of rain that streams down your windshield like a little waterfall and overwhelms the wipers. I kept hearing reports of one tornado after another "on the ground" in my area. They could have been miles away from me, or right on top of me; I just didn't know. Seeking shelter wasn't an option: there weren't any stores or businesses to flee into, only trees lining the highway for miles.

I kept driving, my hazard lights on. Everyone had their hazards on, and we were all just creeping along. I peered through the fleeting gaps in the water stream on the windshield, kept my eye on the thick white right-side lane stripe, and tried to stay away from other cars. There were times when my visibility was so bad I wanted to pull over on the side of the road, but we'd always been taught that's not where you want to be during storms, stuck in a spot where other motorists might crash into you. The rain quickly puddled on the highway, and before long it was essentially flooded. Meanwhile, a big rig ripped past me and heaved great amounts of water on my car, rocking me sideways and blinding me completely. I hydroplaned several times, struggling to keep my Honda in my lane and tightly squeezing the steering wheel.

A report came over the radio: a tornado was about to cross Highway 157—the highway I was on.

Where exactly it would cross, I didn't know—the report only said it was five miles from a certain road. My best guess was that it was ahead of me. The radio was on nearly full volume so I could hear above the clapping of the wipers and the roar of the rains and winds. I could no longer afford to take my eyes off the road for even the second or two it would take to glance at the navigation system. As a result, I wasn't sure where I was and I had the awful feeling the tornado could cross over the highway, and me, at any moment.

Finally, I *did* pull over on the shoulder to wait it out, figuring that gave me the best odds of staying safe. But I didn't *feel* safe. The rain came down sideways in sheets and I felt there was no way any driver behind me could see me on the shoulder until they were just a few feet away. All I could do was *hope* I wouldn't get hit, either by a car or the tornado.

For those several minutes, I truly *was* scared. You bet I was.

A few minutes later, I heard a report saying that the tornado was now north of the highway. I crawled back into the right lane and drove the rest of the way home, the final thirty minutes turning into sixty. They were by far the hardest sixty minutes of driving I've ever had to do.

But, somehow, I made it to our temporary little apartment in Florence. By then, I knew my two sons were okay: Michael, fifteen, was at the apartment, while Tyler, seventeen, was safe with his grandparents. The city of Florence had been largely spared, although we did have flash flooding (all our items in storage were a soggy mess) and we lost power. I heard that the town of Phil Campbell, several miles south of Florence and Muscle Shoals, had been hit badly, and its school had sustained significant damage. But beyond that, I didn't know much that day about any other tornado damage in northern Alabama. I was one of the lucky ones. My family and I, and my city, were okay.

I didn't hear about the reality of April 27 until the following day when the power came back on.

CHAPTER SEVEN

Finally, it was here, April 27—the day of Jennifer Hallmark's final nursing school exam.

This was literally the last difficult thing Jennifer needed to do to graduate the program and be done with all the classes and the clinicals and the preceptorship (similar to an apprenticeship), and all the tests and lectures, and everything else that had nearly driven her to drop out, after five long semesters and nearly two years.

"I mean, we were really doing well just to survive," says Mandy Garmany, who was also taking the final exam that morning, and who, like Jennifer, had neglected chores for days on end and had bags of laundry piled up in her home. "All those times when we'd just throw up our hair and throw on some old shorts and a raggedy T-shirt and make it back and forth to school, not caring how we looked—we were just so focused on school."

Jennifer and Mandy had developed a kind of ritual: driving separately to the unincorporated community of Scant City, between Arab and Guntersville, parking outside the Barry Latham pharmacy, and hopping into one of their cars to drive together the rest of the way to the school or a clinical. Those drives were bonding moments, and they talked about all kinds of life matters, including their Christian faith. Toward the end of school, says Mandy, Jennifer was preoccupied with the part of the Bible that talks about Jesus returning to earth. "She would say things like 'Any day, any second, Jesus can just be here!'" Mandy recalls. "And then one of us would say, 'If people could hear our conversations they'd think we were insane.' But that's what was pressing on her mind at the time."

Remarkably, Jennifer—who wrestled so hard with the demands of the nursing program—did so well in school that she was named her class valedictorian, something that absolutely thrilled her mother. After all, as Susan would say, Jennifer was so much smarter than she often let on. Jennifer finished the school year so strongly that she surprised Mandy by expressing an interest in continuing her schooling, even though they were both so desperate to finally be done with it.

"She was like, 'Okay, I'm about to sign up for my bachelor's degree, you want to do it with me?'" says Mandy (who instantly replied, "Nope!"). Jennifer's plan was to manage a nursing home one day, and she was already thinking about the next steps needed to get her there.

The morning of their final exam, Jennifer awoke in her new, nearly finished home on Fieldcrest Drive in Arab—the house Shane built from scratch. Set back some thirty yards from the road on a gentle upslope, and next to a dry creek bed now populated by trees, it was a dark brick, two-story, four-bedroom home with a spacious kitchen and large living room and a fireplace, along with two generous porches and a roomy play area for Ari upstairs. It sat on twelve quiet, grassy acres.

Shane was not quite finished with the house. He'd just completed the outside garage he built specifically to house his treasured 1967 red Silverado truck, the first truck he ever owned and the truck he lovingly restored alongside his dad (Ari helped whenever she could, standing up on the bumper and peering down at the engine). The exterior of the home wasn't finished, either; Shane had yet to pour the driveway, put in the black iron rails around the porches, and pave a walkway to the front door (as it was, visitors had to cross the front lawn to enter, which, if it rained, might lead to muddy footprints—and Shane could *not* have that). He was getting ready to build a sturdy farm fence around the entire property so that he and Ari could raise goats together. And Jennifer was bugging him to hurry up and pour the concrete basketball court he'd promised her.

But overall, the house was in great shape and it was wonderful, and the Hallmarks were thrilled to move in ten days before the final exam. One of the reasons Jennifer couldn't wait to be done with school was so, during her long and blissful summer break with Ari, she would have more time to help with all the finishing touches— curtains in the living room, setting up the kitchen, hanging pictures on the walls. The little personal details that turn a house into a home. And she'd have time to beat anyone she could entice to play a little pickup basketball with her.

The morning of April 27, however, Jennifer had no time to help. She woke up early, hopped in her car, and drove to meet Mandy in the pharmacy parking lot in Scant City. It was normally a short and easy drive, but that morning it was slow and stressful. A first wave of storms had crashed through northern Alabama, downing trees and causing havoc on the roads. One windstorm hit Guntersville and left a good amount of damage. "We had to literally drive around fallen limbs and other debris on the roads," says Mandy. "I think the only reason we made it to school that morning was because we drove into Guntersville just before the emergency services and pickup crews got there. Otherwise they would have closed the roads."

Jennifer and Mandy made it to Snead State on time—just barely—and were relieved to see the school hadn't closed and the final exam was still on. Certainly the weather didn't look bad—the skies were clear and the sun was out. They sat in a classroom to take the exam and, not surprisingly, or at least not to Mandy, Jennifer finished first. "She was a really fast test taker," says Mandy. "She *always* finished first."

When Mandy was done she found Jennifer lying on a bench in the hallway, exhausted. The two called in their lunch orders to Granny's Corner along State Route 69 in Guntersville, their usual lunch spot, and at Granny's they watched a TV report about a new band of threatening weather heading toward them. They took their food to go and began the drive home, but the roads were even worse than earlier, with tree crews and power trucks clogging the way, and it took them forever to make it home.

"We had just enough time to get to Snead, take the test, get home, and get settled in with our families before the next storm hit," Mandy says.

Earlier that morning, after Jennifer and Mandy left to take their tests, Shane and Josh drove their children to Susan's home and dropped them off with her. The men were eager to get their farmwork done before the big storms came through. Susan's school in Arab had closed early and she was home and able to care for the kids, which was lucky. But just a short while later, Susan got a call from the principal. They'd decided to open up again and they needed her to come in. Reluctantly, Susan called Shane and Josh and told them they had to come and pick up their girls.

When Susan arrived at the school, a fellow teacher told her how a tornado destroyed her father's chicken houses that morning. "She was so upset by what happened to all these little chickens and it was so awful, and she said, 'I don't know how things could get any worse than that,'" Susan recalls. But Susan knew things could get worse—*much* worse. Susan was just sixteen years old when the great 1974 tornado swept through Huntsville, and she remembered the shock of seeing the damage it caused.

"Houses picked up and torn apart," she says. "That really scared me." She remembers, too, hearing haunting stories—a man being decapitated, a child found alive in a dresser drawer. And now, thirty-seven years later, these memories came streaming back. The forecast called for another round of dangerous storms to pass near Arab that afternoon. In her gut, Susan felt a gnawing sense of dread.

When her school closed early a second time, Susan called Jennifer, who had just made it back home after taking her exam.

"Momma, come on over to the new house," Jennifer said. "You can see everything we've done and you'll be safe here with us."

At the new house Jennifer showed Susan where her bedroom would be for when she slept over, and she showed her Ari's big new bedroom, where Ari kept a jewelry box Susan gave her. Susan helped Jennifer hang pictures, including a slightly warped metal wall-art piece with a quote stamped into it. "We were fussing with it, trying to get it to hang straight, and we just couldn't do it," Susan recalls. "Shane comes by and takes the picture and straightens it out with his hands, and we hang it on the wall and it's perfect." The quote stamped into the metal was *Trust in the Lord.*

"It's surreal," Susan says now, looking back, "that the three of us were all together that morning in front of that message. *Trust in the Lord.*"

CHAPTER EIGHT

James Spann was alarmed. The storms that hit northern Alabama on the morning of April 27 were more powerful and impactful than he'd expected, not by a little, but by a lot. Spann spent the early morning on the air, broadcasting forecasts as quickly as they came in, and what he saw in the reports surprised him. What is known as a quasi-linear convective system (a QLCS, or a family of storms moving in a row) had passed through and, as it often can, produced a series of tornadoes.

But normally, Spann saw weak EF0 or EF1 tornadoes in the wake of a QLCS. That morning, he saw something else:

Three tornadoes rated EF3, and five others rated EF2.

The damage was severe. At 4:16 a.m., an EF2 roared across Mississippi and downed trees and wrecked an outbuilding in Dancy. The same tornado, its winds up to 120 mph, snapped thousands of trees in the forestland near the tiny town of Reform. An EF3 touched down outside Coaling in Alabama's Tuscaloosa County and damaged the roof of the Mercedes plant there, keeping 155 mph winds on the ground for more than eighteen miles. A truck blown into a ditch on Interstate 22; an eighteen-wheeler rolled over in Odenville; downed phone lines blocking four lanes in Calhoun. The morning storms eventually swept out of Alabama at around 8:30, with a final flurry of hail in Hackleburg.

There were dozens of reported injuries, and some 250,000 people were left without power. In the ABC station building in Birmingham, engineers rushed into Spann's office with news of damaged infrastructure. Some of the station's Skycams were down. Several microwave paths—lines of information signals traveling across a relay of transmission points—were not operational. The newsroom was severely crippled, with very little time to make fixes. Spann's primary worry was that, with so much damage to the station, and the power out in so many cities, receiving reports about the impending second wave of storms would be extremely difficult—and for many residents, impossible.

There was another problem. As Spann checked social media feeds, he saw comments about how forecasters had got it all wrong. The storms arrived earlier than predicted, and now, in midmorning, the sun was out and it looked like it might be a beautiful day. Many suggested there was no longer any reason to be concerned.

One of the worst scenarios of all was now possible—a turn toward complacency.

Spann knew better. The sunshine was in fact a bad sign, since warmer surface temperatures were destabilizing and a necessary component of hazardous tornadoes. Spann and the engineers hustled to fix what they could, and redeploy other resources, and get as ready as possible for the afternoon wave of storms.

The worst, Spann feared, was yet to come.

Gary Beam, the mayor of Arab, had done all he could to prepare his city for the storms of April 27. The sad truth, however, was that there wasn't much he could do. He'd activated all the emergency personnel available to him, made sure all the shelters were open and ready, and checked on the local hospitals. What he couldn't do, what was beyond his or anyone else's power, was to stop the storms from coming.

"Sometimes when the big one hits," Beam says, "all you can do is clean up afterward."

Raised in Arab ("And I'll die here, far as I know," he says), Beam has a degree in civil engineering from Auburn University, and two grown sons with Olethia, his wife of nearly half a century. He'd never actually seen a tornado, but he had lived through a few, including one that snuck up on him when he was newly married to Olethia and watching his younger twin brothers play baseball in a ball field in Arab. "We got word the tornado was three miles away, and we were told to evacuate the field," remembers Beam. "My brothers were scared and I was scared, too. I got everyone into my car and took off. So I've always been very aware of tornadoes."

Early on April 27, Beam, then sixty-two, was in his office at city hall on Arab's North Main Street. Most of his staff was there, including Tony, a city clerk, and two administrative assistants. Right around noon, Beam watched reports that said the bad weather was heading his way and would be there in about two hours. Sometime around 3:15 p.m., the town's tornado alarms began to wail. The city hall building had a walk-in safe, and Beam's staff huddled there while Beam and Tony stepped out the back door of the building, which looked out over the community of Ruth. They wanted to see what they could see.

Then they saw it.

In the distance, maybe two miles away, the iconic swirling black funnel, topped by an unthinkably massive dark mass. "I'd never seen anything that huge in my *life*," says Beam. "It was so vivid. It looked like one of those cooling towers at a nuclear plant. Thousands of feet high and so, so wide at the top. We just watched this thing and in the middle of it I could see something flying around the funnel."

"What is that?" he asked Tony.

Tony squinted. "It's a boat," he said.

The men watched as the enormous tornado stayed on the ground and ripped through Ruth, not heading toward them, but heading somewhere. They watched until it disappeared from view.

"It all happened so fast," Beam says. "The whole thing was two minutes, maybe three. Maybe even just one. I was scared to death it had hit my mom's house, and one of my assistants, whose kids were home alone, was scared it might have hit them. I knew right away it was going to be one of the biggest tornadoes to ever hit Alabama."

Eleven years later, Beam says, "I can see it now as clearly as I did back then. It was the most monstrous thing I have ever seen."

Charles Whisenant saw it, too.

He remembered the ritual from when he was a boy growing up in Arab in the 1970s. "No Doppler radar, no forecasting, nothing back then," says Whisenant. "And there's my dad standing out on the front porch, watching the skies, and if it wasn't looking good, he'd say, 'Okay, let's go see your grandmother,' because she had a basement across the pasture."

The signs his father looked for were always the same. "Dark clouds," Whisenant says. "Fast-moving dark clouds, any sign of a funnel. We had one of those old party-line telephone systems where all these families shared the line, and all our neighbors would check in with us to see if my dad thought a bad cloud was coming."

Years later, when he was grown and had a young son of his own, Whisenant survived an EF4 tornado blasting through Huntsville, where he lived, in 1989. "My wife and I ran next door to our neighbors, who had a basement," he says, "and it was only twenty yards or so away, but I remember having to hold on extra tight to my son, Drew, because the wind felt like it could rip him right out of my arms." (That tornado destroyed eighty businesses and more than a thousand cars, and killed twenty-one people right before Thanksgiving.)

In 2011, Whisenant was the editor of Arab's newspaper, the Arab *Tribune* (a job he still holds) and was working at the paper's office on South Brindlee Mountain Parkway the morning of April 27.

The TV forecasters had spent the past week talking about big storms on the way, and Whisenant had a scanner that kept him apprised of activity at the Arab fire station. That morning the scanner went off every few minutes. At around nine o'clock, Whisenant grabbed his camera and headed for the south end of town, where the storms had hit hard. He took a picture of a collapsed barn and several shots of other damaged structures in Morgan City and Hopewell. He was back in the office by noon.

All around him, Whisenant felt a strong sense of apprehension, hanging as heavy as the uncommonly muggy air. "On TV they were saying, 'Don't be fooled by what happened this morning, more storms are coming,'" Whisenant says. Not much later, Tennessee Valley Authority power lines at the Guntersville dam, which was damaged in the morning storms, gave out altogether, and the *Tribune*'s office on South Brindlee Mountain Parkway lost power. The paper's publisher made a decision—since the worst weather was still to come, and the office was essentially unusable, all twelve staffers were told to go home and make sure their families were safe, and then return after the storms, if they were needed.

Whisenant went out to his trusty red 1990 Chevy pickup truck and headed home to Allens Crossroads, ten miles north of downtown Arab. But because journalism is in his blood, he didn't just drive home: he had his Canon 35-millimeter camera and a video recorder on the passenger seat, and he looked around for damage he could document. Waiting for him at home were his wife, their three children, and the niece and nephew they took in. But first, he had a job to do.

He drove onto US 231 and headed north. It was bright sunshine overhead, but about two miles to the west he noticed some very dark clouds. He drove another mile, past the Gilliam Springs Baptist Church, and as soon as he wheeled around the building, he looked west again. This time, he saw it—the unmistakable outline of a tornado.

"First one I ever saw up close," he says.

Whisenant pulled over, hooked up his long lens, and started snapping photos. After a minute or so he got back on US 231 and headed south. He looped around buildings and streets, trying to get a good shot of the tornado. When he stopped in front of the John Deere dealership, there it was again. It was closer now, and it looked like it had grown.

"I mean, it was *massive*," Whisenant says. "Tremendously bigger. I just stopped in the middle of the four-lane and sat there, looking at this thing." Whisenant put the truck in gear and followed the tornado, driving with his knees while recording video with one hand and taking pictures with the other. His cell phone was pinging, and he knew his wife and mother were calling him to make sure he was okay, but he did not stop to answer it.

Finally, Whisenant saw the tornado in front of him. He stopped in the middle of the highway, stepped out onto the asphalt, and took a picture of the powerful tornado—a photo that would later appear everywhere.

"I was stunned by the size of it," he recalls. "I could not get over the width of it. Even the picture doesn't do it justice. I don't know why I wasn't afraid, but I wasn't. I guess I was just in the moment."

Whisenant heard sirens and saw police cars and fire engines racing up behind him on the highway. He jumped back in his truck and instinctively followed the emergency workers, and in just a few seconds they all stopped and watched the tornado cross US 231, a mile in front of them, and stood there helplessly as it pulverized a gas station. When the tornado was gone they drove to the gas station and saw people clawing their way out of the rubble, and other people trying to pull them out.

Whisenant pitched in to help and snapped more photos before a police officer came over to him. The officer had heard a community two miles north had suffered major damage. Whisenant got back in his truck and headed to the community. He knew it well.

"It was Ruth," he says.

Jordin Putnam stepped out of his apartment building at 4:30 a.m. on April 27 and the first thing he noticed was the air.

The air was *different.*

"There was this orange haze and it looked weird, and when I stepped outside it was like, 'Oh man, is it hot,'" he says. "I mean, especially hot. There was something weird in the air, like something was going on. You could feel the *pressure*."

A native of Arab, Jordin, then twenty-two, was on his way to his job in the registration department of Marshall Medical Center North. His truck was in the shop, so his aunt Sheila kindly gave him an early-morning lift. They both knew storms were forecast for that day, and Sheila told him to call her if he needed a lift back home. "She didn't want me to be in my apartment by myself," says Jordin, who lived in a one-bedroom apartment above the Pass Realty agency in Arab. "She wanted to pick me up and make sure I was with other people."

Jordin had been through the usual tornado drills in school, hunkering down in hallways with a book over his head and giggling his way through an imaginary storm. Still, he knew to be properly respectful of tornadoes, and he knew his aunt was right—he would be safer in a shelter somewhere, with other people. So when hospital administrators let the registration staff out early, Jordin called his aunt to pick him up, and they drove to a place they believed they would be safe.

Just after 3:00 p.m., Sheila dropped Jordin off at the home of Shane Hallmark's parents, Phillip and Ann—Jordin's uncle and aunt—off Frontier Road in Ruth. Phillip arrived just before they did and he was happy to see them both there. There was a storm shelter on their property just a few dozen yards from their house, and that would be as safe a place as any if the tornado came through. Sheila was going to stay there, too, but she got called back to work, and Jordin stayed behind with the Hallmarks.

Harold Buchanan, a cousin, had also just arrived and joined the Hallmarks and one-year-old twins, Jayden and Julie, the children of Ann and Phillip's other son, Ricky, and his wife, Regina. Ann frequently watched the twins while Ricky and Regina were at work.

Regina worked for an insurance company, and that day they were already swamped with claims from the morning storms.

That meant there were six people, two of them babies, in the Hallmarks' two-bedroom, ranch-style home—a number the storm shelter could easily accommodate. It was around 3:15 p.m., about an hour later than meteorologists had first predicted the storms would hit, and all Jordin and the others could do was wait on the first sign of rough weather, then scramble into the shelter and ride it out. For the time being Ann stayed inside the house with the twins, while Phillip, Harold, and Jordin stood outside, under the carport, searching the still-clear skies.

It was a strange time in Jordin's life. He'd recently broken up with his girlfriend of nine years, for reasons he'd rather not get into, other than to say, "My lifestyle was not the best in Arab." Still, he had his circle of friends at the hospital, including one female colleague who called him Bubba and had become his best friend. In high school Putnam played all the sports—football, basketball, track—and he was still fit and athletic. He just needed to figure out his place in the world, and lay out a plan for his future, and there was plenty of time for that.

Standing outside the Hallmarks' home, waiting for the storm, Putnam saw two things happen in quick succession.

First, he watched a pickup truck turn off Frontier Road and speed toward the house.

At almost the same time, over the tree line two or three miles in the distance, Putnam saw precisely what he'd been waiting to see.

The funnel. The tornado.

"It wasn't coming at us at first, but then we watched it turn," Jordin says. "Clear as anything, we saw it turn our way."

CHAPTER NINE

Ari Hallmark was not happy that her mother was leaving their house early on April 27. Ari knew bad weather was coming, and she hated the idea of her mom driving herself to school to take her final exam, or, really, being away from her at all. She wanted both her parents with her. Ari wasn't scared because she thought the storms might hurt *her*; that wasn't her fear and it had never been. Her deepest fear, the one that had caused all those months of crying, was that both her parents were going to die at the same time and she would be left on her own.

But at least her father was at home with her, and that helped lessen her anxiety, and so Ari hid her bad feelings and waited patiently for her mother to return. When Jennifer did make it back, and the family was together again, Ari breathed a little easier.

"It will not get that bad," Shane assured his daughter. "It's not going to hit us. It may hit Arab, but not us. So we're not worried."

But Ari *was* worried. She worried that the storm could be what killed both her parents. She just couldn't help it.

"What are we going to do if it *does* get bad here?" she asked.

"Ari, it's most likely not going to happen," Shane said.

And anyway, her parents told Ari, the new house was very strong and made of bricks, and if things did get bad they could all go down to the basement, where they would be safe.

Ari's grandmother Susan was also feeling uneasy that morning. They were all together in the new house, Jennifer had made it safely back from school, and Shane and Jennifer felt they would all be fine in the new house, so on the face of it there really wasn't anything for Susan to be anxious about. "Jennifer told me, 'I put some pillows and blankets in the inside bathroom, and we can always go to the basement,'" Susan recalls. That made Susan feel better.

But then the sun came out.

A bright, brilliant sun—the kind Susan dreaded most of all on a day like this day. "I was telling Shane, 'They're saying it's gonna be really bad, and if the sun comes out, it will be *horribly* bad,'" says Susan. "When the sun comes out and things are calm, *that's* when you worry."

Shane and Jennifer kept assuring Susan they'd all be safe in the house. But the longer the sun stayed out, the more anxious Susan became. Shortly before 2:00 p.m., Susan decided she should leave Jennifer's new home and ride out the storm in her own house on the chicken farm.

"I don't know why I decided to leave, I really don't," she says now. "I didn't have to, I could have stayed. But then I thought, they're doing all this stuff in their new house and maybe I'm just getting in the way, and so I decided to drive home. It was the weirdest thing."

Susan took the short drive in bright sunshine. Once she was home she turned on the radio to hear the weather, scooped up several pillows and put them in her hallway, and called her son Josh to find out where he was. He told her he was at a neighbor's house near the Brashiers Chapel church in Arab, chainsawing trees damaged by the morning storms. As they were talking, Susan listened with one ear to an updated weather report.

They were now saying a tornado was headed straight for Arab.

"There's one coming this way," Susan told Josh. "Get home now."

"Okay, Momma," he said.

Susan then called Shane and told him about the tornado. Shane thanked her and told her again they were safe at home. He cleared the line just in time for Shane's mother, Ann, to call him. Ann told Shane that his father, Phillip, was still at work and she was home alone on Frontier Road with the young twins, and she was afraid she might not be able to handle the babies by herself if she had to rush them across the yard to the storm shelter. That was enough to make Shane get worried.

As for Jennifer's mother, Susan, as far as she knew everyone she loved and cared about was indoors somewhere, out—hopefully—of harm's way. Susan sat with her pillows in the hallway and waited for whatever came next.

About thirty minutes later, she heard an awful noise. An explosion, like thunder, but not quite—deeper, louder, stranger. The noise stopped, and Susan got up and stepped out her back door to have a look. And there it was, less than a mile away—the tornado. "I saw it," Susan remembers. "I could see the tornado right there! I didn't even see the funnel, just this big black monster cloud on the ground. And I knew where it was. It was in Pea Ridge, where my sister, Cindy, lived."

Susan frantically called her sister on her cell phone. To her great relief, Cindy picked up.

"There's a tornado right there!" Susan screamed into the phone. "It's at your house!"

Cindy already knew. She'd just finished squeezing into a little closet under the stairs with her adult son, Cad. Cad was standing and bent over in the tiny, angled space, while Cindy was scrunched up on the floor. The tornado was roaring monstrously now and Cindy did her best to scream over it into her cell phone.

"Susan, we're under the stairs, I'm holding on to Cad's leg because *all the air is being sucked right out of the house*!"

Just as she finished this sentence, the line went dead.

After Shane Hallmark got off the phone with his mother, Ann, he made a decision. If the storms in Arab were going to be as bad as they were saying, he could not leave his mother alone with the babies. He wanted—*needed*—to know that they were all safe, too. The sun was still out, and there wasn't the slightest visual hint of a storm. Shane figured there was enough time for him to drive the three miles to his parents' home off Frontier Road and bring his mother and the twins back with him. Fifteen minutes, that's all it would take. He announced his plans to Jennifer and Ari and said he would be right back.

Ari's reaction was instant.

"That's a *bad* idea," she said as her tears began to fall and her voice choked up. "We need to stay here together and be safe."

"They're my family, too, Ari, and I want all my family to be safe," Shane gently explained. He called his mother back to say he was on his way, but got no answer.

"We are *not* going!" Ari insisted.

Jennifer came close to agreeing with Ari and asking Shane to stay, but she realized that, after Shane's mother didn't answer the phone, Shane was not going to change his mind. Ari realized this, too, and she and Jennifer decided that if Shane was going to go, they were going to go with him. Wherever the Hallmarks went, they would go together.

So Shane, Jennifer, and Ari scrambled up into Shane's work truck and started the short ride to Frontier Road.

On the way, Jennifer had a change of heart. Now she began to cry and she begged Shane to turn the truck around. Ari joined in. Shane stayed calm.

"Everything's going to be fine," he assured them, looking at his two favorite girls and smiling. "Y'all are just being too dramatic. This will only take a few more minutes. It'll be fine."

There was nothing else to say, and the truck raced ahead to Frontier Road.

In the quietness of the truck, Ari had a thought.

A thought she knew was actually a realization.

This is it, she said to herself. *This is what I was dreaming about. I know it is. It's happening now.*

Shane's truck barreled up the driveway moments after Jordin, Harold, and Phillip ran into the house at the sight of the tornado turning. In the truck, Shane and Jennifer and Ari saw the tornado, too. At first glance, it didn't seem to be heading their way. "It didn't even seem to be *moving*," Ari recalls. Still, there was no time to waste—and certainly no time to drive back to their new home. With the tornado in sight, they had to get to safety immediately.

Shane quickly considered their options. "We could go straight to the shelter," he said out loud, referring to the storm shelter burrowed into the side of a hill several yards away. But in that moment, he decided against it. If his mother and niece and nephew were in the main house, Shane simply could not leave them there alone. He had to help them. He had to be with his *whole* family when the tornado hit.

In the distance, tornado sirens blared and speakers blasted an alert in a clear, male voice: *"This is a tornado warning. Seek shelter now."*

Shane and Jennifer jumped out of the truck and Jennifer reached back in to get Ari. Suddenly, Jennifer paused and looked directly into her young daughter's eyes.

"How did you know?" she asked Ari. "How did you know?"

"Jesus told me," Ari said simply. "He put it into my dreams."

Jennifer took hold of Ari and ran toward the main house. She held Ari as tightly as she'd ever held anyone or anything before. On the way she dropped her cell phone and instinctively turned back for it, but the winds intensified and swept the phone away just as hail rained down from the nearly black sky.

"No, come on, we have to go!" Ari screamed.

Jennifer gave up on the phone and ran into the house, clutching Ari, Shane by their side. The power was out and the house appeared empty.

"Is anybody here?" Shane yelled out.

"We're in the bathroom," came the reply.

They ran to the small bathroom in the center of the home and found more people than they expected—Jordin, Harold, Phillip, Ann, and the twins. Now there were nine people in all.

"Shane, I'm so sorry," Ann Hallmark cried to her son. "I tried to call you back and tell you Dad got home, but the phones wouldn't work. I called you over and over, but there was no ring. I'm so sorry."

In the bathroom there was a vanity and sink to the right and a toilet and bathtub across from the empty left wall, and the room was packed with people and pillows and cushions. Jordin and Harold sat together by the bathtub. Next to them were Shane's parents, Phillip and Ann, each holding one of the twins. Jennifer put Ari down and took her baby nephew from Phillip, who ran with Shane to grab a flashlight. Jennifer sat down in the tub with the baby. Pepper, the twins' little dog, was barking just outside the bathroom.

"Pepper, come on!" Ari pleaded with him. *"Come on, Pepper!"*

But Pepper just wouldn't come in.

Shane and Phillip hurried back from the kitchen with flashlights. Shane slammed and latched the bathroom door behind him. Phillip took his baby granddaughter from Maw Maw and held her, while Shane grabbed Ari and pulled her to his chest and sat with her, his back pressed against the door. Everyone could hear the rumbling outside, deepening, getting closer, second by second, faster than seemed possible. Jordin took out his Android phone and switched the video camera to record. Everyone quietly prayed.

Lord, be with us now and help us get through the storm . . .

The rumbling became a roar. The crashing sounds of items falling off walls and shelves and glass shattering and spraying. "There goes one of the windows!" Ann yelled out. Shane pushed hard against the bathroom door, willing it to stay shut, but a great pressure filled the house and it began to violently vibrate before the entire structure was picked up off its foundation and rattled side to side like a shaker and finally turned over, and the bathroom sink fell out and crashed to the floor.

The house is moving, Ari thought. *The house is moving fast!*

Jennifer let out an awful scream. Ann yelled a final message.

"This is it, we love y'all!"

The bathroom door exploded off its hinges. Dirt and debris rained into the crumbling room. "It was like a bomb going off," says Jordin. The house was spinning round and round and the roof peeled away and sailed into the darkness. There were no walls and windows now, no house, even. There was only the tornado.

Ari—squeezed so tightly by her father that her lungs were damaged and her ribs were bruised—was suddenly up inside the tornado with several cows spinning through the air and mooing frantically, and also the little dog, Pepper, airborne as well, barking hysterically. "Why aren't any of my family members with me?" she remembers thinking.

These were Ari's last earthly memories of the storm.

CHAPTER TEN

ARI'S TESTIMONY

We drove to Maw Maw's house to get her and my baby cousins. We wanted to take them back to our house, but the tornado got there too fast. As soon as we got there we saw the tornado almost in the backyard. There was nothing we could do at that point. It was like, if you've seen pictures of the tornado, it was a mile wide. There was no outrunning it, there was nowhere to go, so we ran into the house and everyone was there and we were all in the bathroom, this one tiny bathroom. No windows or anything. I know we were all scared and frantic, but no one said much of anything.

About a minute went by and we could hear the tornado outside getting louder. Just rattling the house. I remember my Maw Maw saying, "This is it, we love y'all." And my dad, I was holding on to my dad, and you could hear the windows breaking, things hitting the house, *trucks* hitting the house, and then the door came off the hinges and the roof came right off, and then I was up in the tornado, with cows, mooing *so* loud, all around me, and poor little Pepper barking, too. I remember being aware that none of my family was with me in the tornado and I remember wondering why at least my dad wasn't there, because he was squeezing me so tight just a few seconds before.

Then something knocked me out and I don't remember anything about the tornado after that.

I must have passed out. Actually, I don't really know what to call it. It was by far the weirdest experience I will ever have. It was almost like an out-of-body experience. It didn't feel like I was there. It was like I was getting to watch what was happening, but that was all—just watch. It was kind of like what I do sometimes when I go to the mall. I just sit in the food court and I watch people. I'm a people watcher. So it's like I am there, watching everything going on around me, but I'm not a part of it. And that's how I felt after the tornado— I couldn't be part of what was happening, all I could do was watch.

So this is what happened:

I got to walk with my whole family up to Heaven.

People always ask me how long it took me to travel to Heaven. I never know how to answer it. They ask, "Did you move through space? Did you see a light at the end of a tunnel?" No, I did not. It was like—here is the sky all around me, and then here is Heaven. That was it, no more, no less. It wasn't like I was traveling through space. I wasn't seeing stars everywhere. It was just, the sky opened up and there I was, in Heaven.

So just after the tornado hit my grandparents' house, I saw my Maw Maw pointing at something. She said, "Oh, look at that. What's that? Let's go see." I looked over and it was a staircase. That was the first thing I saw, a really long staircase. From what I could tell it had over a thousand steps. I mean, it looked like it went on forever. But even so, as we were walking up, you could see that at the top of the steps was a gate. The gate was huge and I think it was rounded at the top. People have asked me what the gate was made of and exactly how big it was, and it's very hard to say. The best way I would describe it is to say that the gates were iridescent. You know how pearls are iridescent? Like that. They weren't white, but they were a color, except I wouldn't know what to call that color because there is no color like it on earth. So I say iridescent, like a pearl. But they were beautiful, I know that.

Before we all went up the stairs I saw an angel fly down to be with my family. And I say he flew, but it looked like he was standing up, he wasn't on his belly or anything, but he was just . . . flying. I hadn't ever seen anything like that before in my life. The angel had wings, but he wasn't flying as we know it. He moved very lightly and gracefully. And I had my own angel, too. She was with me before we all started up the stairs and she held my hand as we watched everything happen. She walked with me the whole way. It wasn't really walking, it was more like she . . . I wouldn't call it gliding, but she was *really* light on her feet.

I call my angel a "she" because she had long, wavy blond hair and it was curly at the bottom. She looked so young and beautiful and healthy. I'm saying "he" and "she," but actually it was really hard to tell. I mean, the angels were very tall, taller than Shaquille O'Neal, so I kind of thought of the angel who walked up the stairs with my family as masculine in a way that signified protection—like the angel was there to protect us. But with my angel, there was also this strong feminine side. I knew that my angel was very caring and nurturing, and so there was both the caring and the strength, and those were the two stereotypes I had in my head whenever I sat down afterward and thought about my angel and the other angels.

And, as odd as it sounds now, it seemed very normal to me that my angel and I were there together. Somehow it made sense.

I also understood that my family didn't know where they were, and their angel *knew* this, and so he was there to guide them. Like the angel was saying, "Let me go help them, 'cause they don't know where they are." He didn't talk because he didn't have to. No one communicated with words like we do on earth; I just knew what they were expressing to each other, and everybody just followed the angel because they knew, too. I don't remember a lot of sounds in Heaven, so with my angel it was more like, when she would communicate something, I could feel what she was saying without her actually saying it. Almost nothing in Heaven is like it is here—sights, sounds, walking, talking, even time. I can't even say things happened in any particular order. It was like everything just sort of happened at once. That's the way Heaven is.

So there was my family, and I even saw my Paw Paw Mike [Susan's husband, Mike Garmany] with them. Paw Paw Mike died a few years before the tornado and I'd only known him when I was very young, about eighteen months old, I think, so I didn't really get the chance to know him. But when I saw him in Heaven I instantly knew he was my Paw Paw Mike. He did not look like how he looked when he was older. He had no wrinkles, no sunspots, nothing—just a beautiful, graceful face. Not like a baby face, but just younger than he was at the end. But it wasn't like he was twenty-one or twenty-two when I saw him, or any particular age. He was an indescribable age, I would say. He was just who he is. And even though I knew he had died, I wasn't surprised to see him again. I had the sense that he was part of my family and he belonged there with us. And I also had this feeling of great peace, because my momma was also there, and my

Paw Paw came down the stairs to hug her and my dad, and I knew my momma was getting to see her own daddy again, and that was very beautiful.

So my mother was there, and so was my dad, but with my dad . . . he had alopecia, which is this autoimmune disorder that attacks your hair follicles, and so his hair had fallen out when he was thirteen and you can't ever grow it back, so my whole life my dad was completely bald. I mean, no hair on his head or his arms and no eyebrows, nothing. But then, going up the stairs in Heaven—and this was amazing—my dad had hair! Which was weird. So weird. Because I'd never seen him with hair, ever, and we always used to joke about how slick his head was, and we all used to rub it all the time, so suddenly seeing him with hair, it was . . . different. He had this straight hair like a boy's hair. And my dad always wore these thick glasses, but in Heaven he didn't have glasses, either, and he didn't even have the marks on the top of his nose from his heavy glasses.

And what that showed me was that whatever pain people had endured on earth, they don't feel it anymore in Heaven. It was like, all the bad stuff, all the insecurities, are just gone. And that just made me feel so . . . thankful. Even as a six-year-old. To be able to know that my whole family was there, and everyone was beautiful and free of all their pain and suffering, that was just so special to me. I mean, we'd just gone through a tornado, and you don't look all that great after you go through a tornado. But in Heaven, everyone was so beautiful. And that brought me peace.

Okay, so that is who I saw in Heaven—my Maw Maw and Paw Paw Hallmark, who went through the tornado with me, and also my Paw Paw Mike, who passed before the tornado, and also my mom and dad. And me and my angel, except that, even though my family was there, I wasn't really *with* my family. It was like me and my angel were just behind them. No one in my family acknowledged me in Heaven. It was like they didn't even know I was there.

There was also this feeling that I could hear my family talking to each other in Heaven, but it wasn't like how we talk down here. I could hear it, but it was muffled, sort of like listening in on a conversation you're not supposed to be hearing. So, yeah, I could hear them, but it wasn't like a lot of words were being said, and no one was saying anything to me except my angel. Like I said, even talking and conversation are different in Heaven, and it's not easy to describe.

There was one other person there with us, and that was my little baby cousin Jayden, and my mom was carrying him on her hip all the way up the stairs. So there were seven of us, plus the angels.

And then everyone just started walking up this huge staircase. My family was all in a line going up, and I was behind them. My angel was holding my hand, and we were just watching them walk up. No one talked. I remember that my Paw Paw Mike went up the stairs really *fast*. I don't know why, maybe because he'd been in Heaven longer than everyone else. But the rest of us were just going up together, and it seemed like it took forever, but at the same time it didn't feel like forever, it even felt a little quick, because you weren't feeling tired or anything, and, again, in Heaven there was no concept of time. Whatsoever. Things just happen.

At some point I realized that everyone in my family had their own angel as they walked up the stairs to the gate. Each of their angels was like my angel, just with them as we all went up. And that made me feel very peaceful. Everything in Heaven is *soooo* peaceful.

We all got to the top of the staircase and we were right at the big, iridescent gates. I was allowed to go through the gates, but there were also two really, really big doors, fancy doors, the kind that you pull open in the middle. I remember the doors had what looked like diamond handles, and there were two more "male" angels, one on each side of the doors. I felt like they were there to guard the doors, to control who went through them. When they pulled the doors open, I saw what looked like humongous bright white clouds in the sky, and then this incredible light just streamed in from the right and then the left and just brightened up everything, like some kind of massive sunshine. I have never seen anything like that light before, and I can't really even describe it now, except to say that it was incredible and it just filled everything with such beautiful brightness.

Past the open doors, I understood, was Heaven. And at the very same time I also understood that I wouldn't be going in. No one said that to me, I just understood it. The doors weren't opened for me, they were opened for my family, and I could tell that what I was experiencing was different from what they were experiencing. As if it was meant for them, but it wasn't really meant for me. Like I didn't actually belong there, which I didn't. I mean, I didn't know what was going to happen, but I did know that I would not be staying there with my family. I just knew that inside.

But I *was* allowed to watch, and I watched my family pass through the doors and go right in. I didn't get to see very much of what was behind the doors, but I did see some things that I will never forget. I could see what looked like other people, but they were very far in the distance. They were all dressed in beautiful, creamy-white clothes. I remember that babies had on cream-white dresses, and the women had on the same color dresses or maybe white skirts with a shirt. I even remember the dresses were long, but still above their ankles. Of course, none of them had wings, because they were people, not angels. Going up the stairs my family just all had their normal clothes on, but once they got to the doors, closer to Heaven, their clothes changed to the gorgeous creamy-white clothes I could see people wearing inside.

And it wasn't like the people in Heaven were coming forward to greet me and my family; they weren't. I don't remember anyone greeting us at the door, and anyway, Paw Paw Mike had already greeted us at the bottom of the staircase.

Well, there *was* someone there to greet us, and that was Jesus.

I never really saw God, but I did see Jesus. He was just beyond the doors and He was sitting on His throne, but He didn't just sit there, He also moved around. In my memory He wore a long robe down to the floor, but I can't remember or describe the color. He had medium long hair. It was the same kind of thing where I knew right away that He was Jesus. It was just instantly obvious to me. He was just so perfect to look at.

I saw other things. I saw these beautiful orchards with all these trees—I can't even explain how many trees—and I remember seeing apples and oranges and plums and grapes. For some reason I also specifically remember there were no bugs, because there are always bugs around fruit down here. I saw flowers that looked similar to flowers on earth: yellow buttercups and blue irises and some other orange flowers. But the colors were different in Heaven. The blues were *so* blue that they weren't blue. And the purples were *so* purple they weren't purple.

And I saw houses, but they weren't really like the houses we know. They weren't really big, but they weren't really small, either. The houses were in a type of row and they had windows and there was some type of light inside them that I clearly saw through the windows. They all had beautiful backyards with flowers that I can't explain and a different architecture that I can't describe. I've tried to draw them, but I can't even draw them. When I try they just come out as little stick drawings of a house, which doesn't at all capture what I saw. It's funny that I can remember seeing these amazing houses but I can't draw what they looked like, or even start to describe what they were like.

Two other things I saw that I can remember very well is that there was a long shining road that looked kind of like it was made of gold, sparkling like it had mirrored lights on it. I *did* draw this street when I was little, only I needed glue and glitter to really depict what I saw. And also, on the side of the road I saw these beautiful streams. To me, they looked a little like the streams I saw when my family took me to the Smoky Mountains. A little like those streams, but not exactly like them; that's the best way I can describe them.

Sometimes people ask me if I saw specific things like grass in Heaven. And I always say that it wasn't like I saw the trees and I walked up to them and said, "Oh, wow, look at these trees!" For one thing, I wasn't allowed to go through the doors, so I couldn't see anything up close. And for another, I wasn't allowed to see past the doors for very long, so it wasn't like I got the chance to see everything. And anyway, I was in Heaven! So something like grass is not really what I was focused on. I mean, you don't go to Heaven and say, "Oh, look, there's some grass."

So I'm sure there was grass, because I did see trees and orchards, but I just don't remember seeing the grass. I did see animals just like we have here. I saw some deer, and I saw a robin, and some other ordinary animals, but that's all I can remember.

And then I saw Jesus do two amazing things.

At one point, I watched Jesus gently take my little cousin Jayden out of my mom's arms and hold him in His own arms. That was incredible. I think Jesus gave Jayden back to my mom before she went all the way in, but I can't exactly remember.

I also remember that my dad asked Jesus a question. It's one of my most vivid memories of all.

My dad said, "I am here. Is there anything I can do to serve you?"

Jesus said, "You can build houses. The kingdom's not done yet."

Now, my dad *loved* building things on earth. He built houses all the time, that was just something he loved doing. So when Jesus told him that, my dad was so, so happy. They weren't communicating with words, I just knew what they were expressing to each other. And I knew without a doubt that my dad was just so happy to be able to serve Jesus by building in Heaven. And so it was really just so beautiful to see that, to see my dad so happy.

And I think it was right around then that I felt my angel speaking to me, and what she said was "Okay, Ari, your time here is over. It's time for you to go back because you have some things to do."

The angels closed the two big doors back together, and so now my family was in Heaven. I did not get to talk to them or interact with them, I just got to see them all go to Heaven together, so I knew that they were there. And then it was time for me to go and my angel was still with me and we went down the stairs together just like we went up, only I remember thinking that going up was a lot more fun.

Maybe it was knowing that it was time for me to go, but it definitely felt different walking down than walking up, more *normal*, I think. I also wondered if these were the same stairs we walked up, or if they were different stairs, or even if every family had their own set of stairs leading up to Heaven.

It took us what seemed to be a very long time to get back to earth. I would see the grass below and I would think we were almost there, but then we had to keep going because we weren't there yet. So it felt like it took a while to come back. Looking back at it now, I think I was feeling impatient as we walked back to earth. I guess that would be understandable because I was just six years old, but I also think I was starting to get those earthly emotions back . . . the ones that were totally absent in Heaven.

And the next thing I can remember after that is waking up in the field, and not being able to open my eyes. I couldn't open my eyes on earth, even though I could in Heaven. And I remember lying there for about thirty seconds and hearing an ambulance siren, but I don't remember being in an ambulance. The next thing I remember is waking up in the hospital in Huntsville. That's all I can remember about coming back.

People always ask me how it felt to be in Heaven. All I can say is that it felt normal. It seemed kind of like an ordinary thing. I understood what was going on—somehow, I just knew—and it all made perfect sense, and so I wasn't scared and I wasn't really excited, either. I guess I was somewhere in the middle. When I was six years old and I drew a picture of me in Heaven, I captioned it "I am not sad or happy, I was in between." That's what it felt like, just an ordinary thing. I was supposed to see my family go to Heaven and I got to see it, and I knew that they were okay.

People also always ask me about specific things, like "Did I hear music?" or "Did I smell the fruit?" or "Is there music in Heaven?" Someone wanted to know if I heard a chorus of angels singing. Well, I did hear something that might have been a chorus of angels, but it wasn't like listening to a choir at church. Honestly, I can't explain the sound, just like I can't explain what colors are like in Heaven. There are no words that we have that even come close to describing what I saw and what I heard. It's just very different. I wish I could explain it better, but I just can't. The sound I heard is just not something I can explain to anyone.

Really, the only way I could attempt to explain Heaven was to describe it through pictures, which I did, beginning right after the tornado happened and I was still in the hospital. I drew everything I saw. I drew my angel and the other angels, and I drew my family walking up the steps and in front of the doors in Heaven, and the streets of gold and all the fruit trees, and I even drew Jesus. I remember I had these crayons and I couldn't get the colors right, so I told my Ninny, who was with me in the hospital for a little while, to go down and get me more crayons, and she came back with a twenty-four-pack of these Crayola Twistables, and I was mad and I said, "Is that all they have?" Because there simply weren't any colors that even came close to what I saw in Heaven. And I was just so frustrated, and I pitched a fit and I said, "These are not all the colors there are. There are so many more." And my Ninny said, "Ari, I just don't know what you mean," and I said, "Ninny, *there is more than this in Heaven!*"

For me, what I will never, ever forget is getting to see my family *all together* going into Heaven and seeing that they were all so beautiful and peaceful and happy. I mean, to see them all go into Heaven was just so, so beautiful and meaningful. It was just the greatest gift I could ever receive.

It's like I first described when I was six years old. I wrote:

"Everybody's happy in Heaven. Nobody looks old and nobody's puny or anything in Heaven. My dad didn't need his glasses anymore, and he wasn't even bald anymore! Everybody looks so healthy. Heaven is a really pretty place."

But there was another message that I took from my time in Heaven, and that is what I think the angel meant when she said I had to go back because I had things to do. I believe I am supposed to share this message with other people. And the message is simple:

You are going to see your loved ones again. Your time on earth with them is not your last time with them.

Your time on earth is temporary. You won't have to hurt forever. It's okay to miss people who have passed, but you should be at peace with where your loved ones are. And remember that they aren't hurting or sad at all. Even if something *horrible* happened to them when they passed away, like dying in a tornado. As far as I could tell, my family didn't even remember it. Or maybe they just didn't care.

"If someone you love ever passes away," I wrote when I was seven years old, "you can remember what happened to me and know they are at peace. They're just in a different place, and you will see them again."

There is one other thing I wrote down when I was seven that I think captures how I felt when I came back from Heaven. What I wrote is this:

"You don't ever have to be afraid. There is nowhere that you can go that God will not be with you. God is always with you."

I don't know why I got to see Heaven. Like I said, I think it was an incredible gift to receive, to be able to be at peace with where my parents are. I don't have all the answers, just like I can't explain everything that happened in my short time in Heaven. But I don't think that all the details are the most important thing. To me, the message is most important. This is what God wants us to know down here on earth.

God is always with us and we will see our loved ones again.

CHAPTER ELEVEN

Susan Garmany squeezed the phone in her hand and screamed into it, calling out her sister's name, imploring her to answer.

"Cindy! Cindy are you there?!"

There was no response. Cindy had been on the line just seconds earlier, but now—while Susan watched with horror from her back door as, a mile away, the monstrous black cloud swept through Pea Ridge, where Cindy lived—there was only silence. Susan put down the phone and ran outside to her car. She watched and waited until the tornado finally swept out of Pea Ridge, and then she started the car and headed straight to her sister's house, fueled by adrenaline and instinct.

Susan didn't make it into the town of Pea Ridge. "The police wouldn't let me through," she recalls. "There was a gas leak somewhere and they were blocking the roads. I pleaded with them. I said, '*I have a sister in there!*' They just said they couldn't let me pass."

Susan drove back home and called her son Josh, trying not to sound too frantic.

"I know Cindy's house was hit," she told him. "I just know it. We have to get to her."

Josh Garmany climbed into his red-and-silver 1990 Chevy Z71 truck and picked up Susan, and together they tried to get into Pea

Ridge, but Josh fared no better in persuading the policemen, some of whom were friends of his, to let them through the barricades. Meanwhile, the storms were not yet over, and reports of other possible tornadoes in the area blared over Josh's truck radio. The danger was still present.

"Momma, come with me to our house," Josh said.

When Josh built his house in Arab, his wife, Mandy, insisted they build a storm shelter. Josh had no special fear of tornadoes, but Mandy was terrified of them, so Josh built a modern shelter beneath the back porch. Thankfully they'd never had occasion to use it, and in fact it had become a bit cluttered with storage. So instead of going there, Josh took his mother and his family to Mandy's father's house right behind their own. "My father-in-law built a storm pit, too, and he's a very neat fellow," says Josh. "I knew he kept it pretty clean down there."

In all, seven people were in the pit, and Josh went outside every few minutes so he could get reception on the radio and listen to the weather reports. Susan followed right behind him, desperate for any news about Cindy and Cindy's husband, Randy, a telephone lineman who'd been up on a pole repairing the morning's damage when the afternoon storms began. Susan also tried calling Shane and Jennifer, but she couldn't reach them, either. No one had any idea where the big tornado went after it hit Pea Ridge, and Susan worried it might have passed near Ruth. She kept calling Jennifer, but no one picked up.

Susan was already very scared. Now what she felt was panic.

Susan and Josh both stepped outside again for a moment to listen to the radio, and they saw Mandy's stepmother driving up to the house.

"Right away," Susan says, "I could tell from the look on her face that she was very worried. She knew something."

In fact, Mandy's stepmother did bring news. Terrible news. She'd heard reports out of the Ruth community.

Reports of fatalities.

"When she said that," Susan remembers, "I knew. I just knew."

The last thing Jordin Putnam remembered was feeling dirt and debris splashing his body and face as the tornado picked up the house.

In his next conscious moment, he was on the ground with his arms around a tree, and he was hugging it as tightly as he could.

One of the neighbors in the area, he can't remember who, was the person who found him. Jordin was in the field some forty yards from where the house had been. A shorn tree was lying on the ground and Jordin was clinging to it as if for dear life. He was lying on his right leg, which had been dislocated. His right hip was broken, too, and so was his back. He had a collapsed lung and bleeding on his brain, and a large stick was jutting out of his right arm. The neighbor who found him knew enough not to remove the stick, and possibly cause Jordin to bleed out.

There was no way an ambulance could get through all the fallen trees, so the neighbor and another man made a stretcher out of some stray two-by-fours and carried Jordin over to a Gator ATV and then drove him to an ambulance on the main road. Jordin had already bled so much that his blond hair was matted red, and though people in town knew who he was, the blood fooled them all, including family members, and Jordin went into Marshall Medical Center North in Guntersville (where he worked), as a John Doe.

"Nobody could tell who I was for days," he says.

At Marshall Medical, doctors stabilized Jordin before moving him to Huntsville Hospital. There, doctors immediately put Jordin on a respirator and induced a coma so they could manage the swelling on his brain.

He remained in the coma for six days.

When he finally came out of it, Jordin remembered everything that had happened. He remembered the tornado, and he remembered Pepper the dog, who never made it into the bathroom. He remembered waking up and clutching the tree. His aunt Sheila was at the hospital when he came out of the coma, and the first thing she said to him was "I'm so sorry I took you to that house. I shouldn't have taken you there."

"Stop apologizing," Jordin told her. "It's not your fault."

Then his friend from work came to see him, the one who affectionately called him Bubba, and when she saw him awake and alert she smiled with relief, and said, "Hey, Bubba, how you doing?"

Jordin stared blankly at her face.

"I didn't know who she was," he says. "I couldn't remember her. And then I got really freaked out, and my vital signs shot up."

Jordin could remember all his old friends and relatives, but, because of his brain injury, he did not recognize anyone he'd known for fewer than two years. Those memories, those friends, were now gone.

What never went away was his memory of the storm, and the question that began to haunt him as soon as he awoke from his coma.

"Why me?" he says. "Why did I survive? There were other people who should have survived other than me, so why me? I kept searching and searching for an answer to that question, and the best I could ever come up with was 'It just wasn't my time.'"

But even that answer "didn't make the guilt go away," he says. "Coming to terms with why I survived has been the toughest battle of my life."

Kenny Casey was saying his prayers in the storm shelter when, after just a few seconds, the horrible overhead roar lessened and then stopped. He knew it was over—that's how tornadoes worked. They moved fast and didn't stay anywhere long. From the tornado's trajectory, he could tell it headed straight for his home in the Ruth community.

"I knew there was no way around it, my house was gonna get totaled," he says. "Now I had to go find out."

Kenny drove toward the hollow where he lived, but trees blocked the way. He was wearing his back brace, which he always wore to work, but even so his back hurt. His bad hip, too, felt like it was out of place. Still, Kenny got down from his truck and headed to his house.

"I walked under some trees, rolled over others, went around some," he says. "Finally, I came across the double lot where I had my house. This eighty-year-old tree had been picked up by the storm and dropped right on the house and squashed it. You could see the pilings coming straight up through the floor. It was totally wrecked."

Kenny kept walking in the footprint of the tornado. The silence and stillness were eerie. No one crying out for help, no one crawling through debris. Just absolute quiet. Kenny headed to where he knew Shane's parents had their home. Only a few minutes earlier, before the tornado hit and when Kenny was hustling his family into the shelter, he had to step out of the road to let a truck speed past, and he recognized it as his friend Shane's truck. He'd watched Shane turn the truck onto his parents' road, so he knew he had been there during the storm.

But now, when he looked for the Hallmarks' house, he could not see it. "All that was there were eight foundational blocks and the two-hundred-fifty-gallon propane tank," he says. "Nothing else. Just the foundation."

Kenny called out into the silence.

"Shane? Shane!"

A little over a hundred yards away, he found what remained of the Hallmark home scattered around in pieces.

By then, Kenny's brother-in-law had joined him in the field. Together, about eighty yards past the wreckage of the house, they came upon what they recognized as their worst fears come true. There, on the ground, were Shane and Jennifer, and Shane's parents, Phillip and Ann, all lying there motionless, in a circle no greater than ten feet across.

"They were all gone," Kenny says.

In his arms, Phillip Hallmark still held tight to his seventeen-month-old granddaughter, Julie, the most fragile of them all.

By some miracle, little Julie was still alive.

And then, some distance away, Kenny saw movement.

His brother-in-law stayed with the baby while Kenny went toward the figure in the grass. There, on the ground, was Ari Hallmark. She was fully clothed, and had some blood on her face, but not much.

"Her eyes were closed and she wasn't alert, but she was trying to wake up," Kenny says. "I said, 'Okay, I'm gonna take her.' There was propane spewing out of these tanks and I had to get her to safety."

Just a few seconds earlier the pain in Kenny's back and legs had felt nearly crippling, but now he was full of adrenaline and felt no pain at all. He heard sirens in the distance, and he carried Ari through the field of debris toward the sound. On the way, he heard someone call out:

"Kenny! Kenny, over here!"

It was his neighbor Wayne Cooper, lying in a ditch along a road. Wayne's house, if it was even still there, was at least a hundred yards from the ditch, and Kenny supposed Wayne had been thrown that far.

"He was banged up, worse even than Ari," says Kenny. "But I couldn't stop. I promised him I'd come back for him, and later on I did, and another man and I put him on a piece of door we found and carried him to an ambulance." Leaving his friend behind, even for a short period of time, was excruciating for Kenny.

But he knew he had to quickly get Ari to the main road, over a mile away, and he did, and there he handed Ari over to a fireman and wrapped his red sweatshirt around her head to support it.

Then Kenny sat down on the edge of the road in the rain for a moment to catch his breath, and he watched the fire truck screech away, its horn blaring. Within seconds another fire truck pulled up, and a fireman came over to Kenny, and Kenny pointed him in the direction of where his brother-in-law and little Julie would be. When the fireman got to that spot, he saw Kenny's brother-in-law holding a piece of plywood over Julie's head to shield her from the rain. The baby was unconscious and very badly wounded. Just beyond them were the four bodies, which Kenny's brother-in-law had covered with blankets and any other strips of clothing he could find.

Kenny had no idea how badly Ari was hurt. "All I knew was that she was moving, and that was good," he says. Later on, people would say that he saved Ari's life, but Kenny would not agree.

"No, I can't say that," he says. "I don't look at it that way. I carried her to the rescue people, and that's all I did. Nothing more."

Kenny and his family had been spared by the tornado, but only physically. For the next year of his life, Kenny had serious trouble sleeping, so much trouble that some nights he couldn't sleep at all.

"And if I slept, I'd wake up every night thinking about it," he says. "I would see them. I would see them all on the ground. I could never get that image out of my head."

Hearing from Mandy's mother-in-law that there were fatalities in Ruth startled Susan into action. She grabbed her phone and called the local police. She told them about not being able to reach her daughter or son-in-law, and she begged them to please tell her who the fatalities were in Ruth, or at least, *where* in Ruth they were.

"Mrs. Garmany, we can't help you," an officer kept repeating. "You're going to have to call the hospital."

"But everyone's saying the hospital's been hit, too," Susan pleaded. "I've got to find my family. You've got to help me!"

The police simply would not release information.

Susan then called Marshall Medical Center North. She got through to a staffer and asked if Shane and Jennifer were there, but the staffer would not say, either. "If you think they might be here," Susan was told, "you just have to come down and see."

Susan knew what she had to do. She told Josh to drive her to the hospital. Josh thought they should wait. So did his wife, Mandy. "There's still tornadoes out there," Mandy said, "and we don't know anything yet." Just a few days earlier, Mandy and Jennifer had finished their preceptorships at Marshall Medical, and Mandy knew that just showing up at a hospital during a crisis could add to the chaos and make things worse. Besides, Josh told Susan, the roads would most likely be impassable. It was better to wait.

But Susan could not wait. She could not wait a minute longer.

"I can't reach my daughter and I'm fixing to go find her," Susan said. "I don't care if it's ten miles away, if I have to I'll start walking."

That was that. "She just kept going on and on and on, saying, '*We have to go, we have to go now, come on, let's go, LET'S GO!*'" Mandy says. "It was her motherly instinct kicking in. Finally, I said, 'Okay, fine, let's go.'" Josh, Mandy, and Susan piled into Josh's truck and headed out for Marshall Medical. Meanwhile, Susan sent her other son, Jason, to the Hallmarks' new house to look for Shane, Jennifer, and Ari.

Alabama State Route 69 North to Guntersville was clear, and Josh pulled right up to Marshall Medical's emergency room entrance. Before Josh could even think to look for a parking spot, Susan jumped out of the truck and ran to the hospital. The scene was chaotic. Triage stations were set up in various spots and corners. Susan went inside and found a nurse and asked about Shane and Jennifer.

"Follow me," is all the nurse said.

Back in Ruth, Josh's brother didn't find anyone at Shane and Jennifer's new house and decided to drive to the Arab Police Department on North Main Street. Jason knew an officer there and hoped the man could tell him about the fatalities. But that officer wasn't forthcoming, either.

"Look," a frustrated Jason finally said, "if you don't tell me what's happening I'm going to start flipping over tables until you do."

The officer told Jason what he knew.

What would later be classified as an EF4 tornado had ripped through Ruth. There were four fatalities, all from the same family. Phillip and Ann Hallmark, Shane's parents, were among the dead.

So were Shane and Jennifer Hallmark.

As for the twins, Julie had survived, but Jayden was still missing.

Jason Garmany, a picture of physical strength, listened to the news and sagged helplessly into a chair, his head in his hands, weeping.

Then there was Ari.

At Marshall Medical Center North, the nurse guided Susan through a busy hallway until they reached a small cubicle cordoned off by a pale curtain. The nurse pulled the curtain aside, and Susan saw a small patient lying on a stretcher. It was a child, and the child was wearing a huge neck brace and she had tubes sticking out of her arms and other wires coming out from all parts of her body. There was blood on her head. Susan looked at the child and could not tell who it was.

"Is this Ari?" she asked the nurse. "Is *this* my Ari?"

"Yes," the nurse said as gently as she could, "this is Ari."

CHAPTER TWELVE

Josh and Mandy Garmany found a parking spot in the lot outside the hospital and walked through the emergency room entrance a few minutes after Susan. Mandy saw a nurse walk by and flagged her down.

"Do you have Jennifer or Shane Hallmark, or Ari?" she asked.

"You need to come with me," the nurse said.

The nurse brought them to the little cubicle where Ari was lying on a stretcher and Susan was standing by the curtain.

"Where's Shane and Jennifer?" Mandy said more urgently. *"Where are Shane and Jennifer?"*

The nurse did not answer and left to help another patient. No one was telling anyone anything. The area was filled with people, and more kept coming in, waves of people, most of them crying, all visibly shaken, while nurses, EMTs, and doctors hustled past them, focused intently on their tasks, too busy to stop. Susan—still without any news of her daughter and son-in-law or her sister, Cindy—lost her composure. She was angry and she was fed up with not getting answers. She thought, *If Ari's momma and daddy aren't with her, something has to be really wrong.*

"We were all going ballistic," Mandy says. "It was a mess."

Finally, a young male nurse in white walked up to Susan, who was slumped against a wall for support. He put his arm around her shoulders and a hand on her arm and helped her stand free of the wall.

"Come with me," he said, leading Susan to the nurses' station, where a nurse pulled out a chair for her.

"Okay," the male nurse said, kneeling in front of Susan, "you're going to have to calm down. Ari is in bad condition and we need to transport her to Huntsville Children. She has major glass abrasions on her back and she's losing blood. We don't know what her other injuries are. We need you to ride with her to the hospital, but you're going to have to calm down."

Susan took a deep breath and asked, "What about her mother, Jennifer?"

The young nurse didn't answer.

Susan buried her face in her hands and wept. Her son Josh came over. "Mother," he said firmly, lifting Susan from her chair, "if you don't stop crying, they can't let you go with Ari. Ari needs you now."

Susan gathered herself and moved toward the flashing red lights of the ambulance parked right outside. In this moment she pushed aside her own fears and feelings so she could focus on Ari—an act of strength and grace that would become the template for the next several years of her life. Quietly, she climbed into the passenger seat of the ambulance.

In the back, Susan thought Ari was conscious, but in shock.

"She was just lying there and her eyes were big and wide, but she wasn't talking or crying," Susan says. "She had this big neck brace, which was pushing up against her little face."

The ambulance sped onto the highway, lights flashing and siren wailing until, after a few miles, the driver turned off the siren because there weren't many cars on the road.

"Do you know anything about the people who died in Ruth?" Susan asked the driver. "Anything about Shane and Jennifer Hallmark?"

The driver didn't respond. He was busy with some switches on the dashboard. A few minutes later, Susan asked again, and again—more times than she can remember. Susan was sure he was acting busy to avoid having to answer her.

Finally, though, the driver did answer her.

"I don't know about that," he said in a kind voice. "But I do know that God is with us during stressful and bad times. You can count on Him. *I do know that.*"

The ambulance sped straight up US 231 North, lights flashing, for thirty-seven miles, until it reached Huntsville Hospital for Women and Children, a not-for-profit facility known for its pediatric emergency services and intensive care units. Susan followed as two EMTs raced Ari's gurney into the hospital and finally into a small room. There, several doctors, nurses, and technicians swarmed the bed and stood around Ari, each doing something to stabilize her. "There were three at her head and three at her side," Susan says. "I wasn't allowed to stay there, so I went outside and just slumped down on the floor next to the door."

Susan felt her heart racing and dug through her purse for her blood pressure pills. She realized she had not brought them. She called to a nurse walking by and said, "My blood pressure is shooting up and I don't have my medicine." The nurse returned with a cuff and took her blood pressure, then rushed back with a plastic cup of water and a single pill, which Susan swallowed without even asking what it was. Not much later, another nurse came by and asked if she was Mrs. Susan Garmany.

"I am," Susan answered.

"There is a Miss Hallmark outside the ER wanting to speak to you."

Susan's heart leapt in her chest. *Miss Hallmark? Could that be Jennifer? Could she be alive?* She sprang up from the floor and hurried over to the automatic doors, hoping—*praying*—that her daughter might be standing there. But when the doors opened, it wasn't Jennifer. It was Regina Hallmark, the wife of Shane's brother, Ricky.

"Jennifer and Shane are gone," Regina told Susan. "Jayden is missing, and Julie is here at the hospital somewhere, but we haven't found her yet."

Susan said nothing. She realized she was still holding the plastic cup of water the nurse had given her, and, afraid she might be shaking so much she would spill it, she set it carefully down on the floor.

"Are you sure?" Susan asked, looking up pleadingly at Regina. "Did you see them?"

"I'm sure," Regina said. "I saw them."

No words came to Susan. None seemed at all capable of conveying what she was feeling. But she felt she should say something, so she did.

"At least we know where they are now," she said.

Susan walked back to the room where the doctors were tending to Ari. She watched, completely numb now, as the team worked methodically and intently, sewing wounds, applying sutures, fixing the little child. Lost in her nothingness, Susan heard a voice behind her.

"Hey, sis."

It was Cindy. From behind, Cindy wrapped her arms around

Susan and pressed her head against Susan's head, and they held the embrace and swayed slightly, staring blankly into Ari's room.

"Cindy, our babies are gone," Susan said. "But at least they're safe. They aren't hurting or cold. I don't have to worry anymore."

"You're right, sis," Cindy said. "They are safe now."

Later, Cindy told her sister what happened after their call cut off.

The tornado, she explained, seemed to suck all the air out of her house. "It felt like the house took a deep breath and then exhaled," said Cindy, who had clung to her son's legs in their tiny hiding space. "I felt him being pulled by the vacuum, but he wasn't going anywhere without me."

The tornado, which Cindy described as having "several fingers," passed over them in just a few seconds. Cindy and Cad emerged unharmed. The house was damaged, but not torn apart. When they went outside, what they saw made them cry out in shock. Every one of their nine tall, centuries-old pecan and oak trees had been felled, though none, miraculously, had landed on the home. Later, Cindy could barely look at the sad sight of torn-up roots and trees encircling the house. It felt like the grand old trees had sacrificed themselves to protect Cindy and her home.

The tornado also leveled Cindy's much-loved old family barn out back, as well as Randy's garage and workshop. The sweet antique 1956 car that Randy had been lovingly restoring was destroyed.

Some neighbors arrived to check on Cindy and Cad. One couple from town told Cindy they had heard on the radio about five fatalities in the Ruth community.

"When I learned that, I knew," Cindy says. "I knew in my heart that it was Jennifer and Shane. I called Jennifer and got no answer, so I called Shane, who *always* answered, usually by the second ring. When Shane didn't answer, I felt sick. I knew they were gone. I just felt it."

Cindy felt something else, just as strongly: "I knew Ari was alive. How I knew, I don't know. But I knew we had to somehow get to Ari."

By then, her husband, Randy, had returned from helping clean up after the morning storms with his crew. When he saw the damage to his property, he was staggered. In his shock, Randy rushed to salvage what he could from the wreckage, throwing tarps over whatever needed protection from the heavy rains and from more predicted tornadoes. "I understood what he was doing, but I told him he had to quit and we had to go find Ari," Cindy says. "But when I told him I knew that Shane and Jennifer were gone, he said, 'You don't know that for sure.'"

And yet, Cindy *did* know. She knew it as well as she knew anything. She kept pushing Randy to help her find Ari, and finally he relented. Randy drove Cindy and Cad to the new house. It was undisturbed, but no one was home. They headed toward Shane's parents' house, and to their horror saw only a leveled field. Randy parked the truck, got out, and ultimately spoke with Kenneth Putnam, who was wandering the field in search of his son, Jordin. It was Kenneth who confirmed to Randy that Shane and Jennifer Hallmark were dead.

Randy walked slowly back to his truck, leaned heavily against the door, and through the open window forced himself to look at Cad and Cindy and tell them what Cindy already knew.

∞

At the Huntsville Hospital for Women and Children, Susan held tight to her sister, Cindy, as she watched the doctors work on Ari. Susan did not think back to Ari's dreams of her parents' fate. She didn't think about anything, really, other than what was happening around her, and what would happen next. "All I felt was shock and grief and sorrow," she says, "and whether or not Ari was even going to be okay. And the question that kept coming was 'What on earth are we gonna do with this baby? *Her parents are dead.*'"

Later that night, Susan's son Josh and his wife, Mandy, arrived at the hospital. They found Susan in the chapel. They sat there with her, while, one by one, the relatives who were present went in to see Ari, who was recovering in her room in the pediatric intensive care unit. So far, doctors had told Susan that Ari broke her wrist and collarbone, and that they had stitched and stapled up her head wound with somewhere between thirty and forty staples. They were still tending to the deep wound on Ari's lower back, as well as running more tests. Ari was on her second pint of blood.

When Mandy went in to see her, Ari was somewhere between consciousness and sleep. Her eyes were open, but she wasn't responsive. The blood on her head had not been fully cleaned. Mandy touched her hand and spoke to her.

"When we get out of here we're going to take you to Chuck E. Cheese," Mandy told her. "It's all going to be okay."

That evening, emergency workers recovered the bodies of Shane and Jennifer Hallmark, and of Shane's parents, Ann and Phillip, and the body of little Jayden, who eventually was found surrounded by trees in an area far from where the rest of the bodies were discovered. There was no power in the Arab area, so the bodies of the Hallmarks were temporarily taken to the Blount County Medical

Examiner & Coroner's office in Oneonta, halfway between Huntsville and Birmingham. They would stay there until memorial services for them could be planned and scheduled, and with all the
ongoing turmoil and horror in northern Alabama, no one had any
idea of when that might be.

The very last field weather report of April 27 came in at
9:48 p.m., from a National Weather Service storm surveyor in Chil-
ton County.

He reported a tornado touching down at the intersection of
Highway 31 and County Road 24, northeast of Verbena. The tornado uprooted a few oak trees and swept northeast, damaging a
metal carport and lifting the roof off a single-wide mobile home
near County Road 59. It downed a few more trees before dissipat-
ing just past the road. Later, it would be classified as an EF0 on the
Enhanced Fujita Scale, meaning its winds never topped 85 mph—
fierce enough to clear all the trees out of a fifty-foot-wide swath, but
still the weakest possible tornado.

It was the relatively harmless end to what had been a historically
devastating day in Alabama.

At Huntsville Hospital, the end of the storms made no difference to the exhausted doctors and nurses and staffers, nor to the
wounded victims or the waiting families. Their ordeal was only
just beginning and would not be tallied in terms of hours or even
days. Time had stopped, and now there was only a slow and somber
march through grief and anguish, toward a future that could not
be known.

Around 2:00 a.m., Mandy and Josh went home. Cindy stayed in
the hospital with her sister, Susan, and they spent the night in Ari's
room in the ICU, Susan in a chair, and Cindy lying on a coat on the

floor. The doctors had sedated Ari, and for most of the night she was quiet. But not all of the night.

"Now and then you could hear this muffled little moaning noise coming from her," Susan says. "Soft moaning. It was so, so sad. All night long we heard a lot of kids crying. Some of the nurses had lost their own homes in Huntsville, so they were crying, too. I didn't sleep at all and I don't think Cindy slept much, either. And if she did, it wasn't a very good sleep."

CHAPTER THIRTEEN

The earliest news reports of casualties were sketchy and far from complete. The day after the storms there were estimates that the April 27 tornadoes killed thirty people. Then fifty. Then a hundred. The length and breadth of the three-day event was so vast and so nearly unfathomable that it would take *years* before all the estimates caught up with the reality.

In the end, what became known as the 2011 Super Outbreak impacted more than half the states in the US—and of those twenty-six states, by far the hardest hit was Alabama.

On the third day of the outbreak, April 27, there were three distinct rounds of extremely severe weather activity—early in the morning, late in the morning, and finally middle of the afternoon into evening. The storms ran through northern Alabama and then ran through it again, and again, and again. A record-shattering total of *sixty-two verified tornadoes* touched down in the state on that one day. Dozens of counties were affected, and one of the least fortunate was Marshall County—home to Arab and Ruth—which, incredibly, had to absorb *fifteen violent tornadoes* in a single day.

All but six of those sixty-two tornadoes had winds that measured above 100 mph. Nine of them were EF2s (111 to 135 mph winds), seven were EF3s (136 to 165 mph), eight were monstrous EF4 tornadoes (up to 200 mph winds), and three were EF5s, the most fearsome possible tornado, with winds of more than 200 mph. One of these EF5s touched down in Marion County, a hundred miles west of Arab, at 3:05 in the afternoon, and laid waste to the towns of Hackleburg and Phil Campbell. That tornado traveled 132 miles on the ground, all while spewing winds strong enough to lift any human being off the earth and into the sky and turn small planes and trucks into airborne missiles.

The final death toll of the 2011 Super Outbreak, arrived at only years later, is staggering. There were 348 fatalities across several states, with a horrifying 253 of them occurring in Alabama. Additionally, more than two thousand Alabamians were injured, many quite seriously. About 70 percent of the deaths happened in rural parts of the state, and some 60 percent of the fatalities were women. Thirteen victims were over eighty-five years old; the oldest, Tennie Mozelle Lancaster of Tuscaloosa, was ninety-five when she perished. Five of the deaths were children under the age of five; the youngest, Ta'Christianna Dixon, also of Tuscaloosa, was only eleven months old.

A total of 214 people died on the scene where the tornado struck; twenty-seven others died in a hospital, and at least three died in ambulances. Ninety percent of fatalities happened indoors, including one in a church, one in a factory, and one in a hospice facility. Eleven people died in their vehicles. Most victims had sought safety in their home's bathroom, but four victims were found in the ruins of their garages, and three others in what remained of their kitchens. The vast majority of deaths—95 percent—were the result of being directly in a tornado's path. Some 112 people were struck by debris, 81 were picked up and thrown, and 44 others were crushed beneath rubble. Two people suffered fatal heart attacks. More than half the victims received warning that the storms were coming and sought shelter. Even so, two people were killed in their storm shelters.

The full extent of all the pain and suffering and heartbreak that followed the storms is, of course, incalculable. Ashley Mims, the mother of University of Alabama student Loryn Brown, recalled her daughter's last words over the phone before the tornado took Loryn's life: "Momma, I'm scared." Buddy and Martha Michaels, a carpenter and his wife and the parents of four grown children, died in their home in DeKalb County precisely two months shy of what would have been their fiftieth wedding anniversary, leaving their son Perry to say, "You wonder if they suffered." Joseph Wayne Haney was asleep in his living room recliner in Pisgah when a tornado ravaged his home and heaved a piano on top of his wife, Kathy, who said to Joseph as he wrapped his arms around her, "Honey, I love you, but I'm hurting." Kathy Haney passed away.

Ronnie McGaha, a navy veteran, threw himself on top of his fifteen-year-old daughter, Denae, just as the chimney collapsed on top of them when the tornado struck their home in Harvest. Firefighters used a carjack to raise the remains of the chimney and only then realized that the father had shielded his daughter and saved her life. Denae escaped with cuts and bruises; her father, Ronnie, passed on. The defining moment of Ronnie's life, one reporter later wrote, "occurred as it ended."

Along with the many stories of loss were stories of survival. In Tuscaloosa, a terrifying EF4 tornado directly hit the home of Wesley and Katie Britt, where the couple had scrambled into a small space between two closets with their new baby boy, two-year-old daughter,

Katie's two sisters, and a friend. Wesley, a former Alabama football player, shoved two bureaus to block them in, then grabbed a king-size mattress, curled it over the group, and threw his six-foot-eight, 330-pound body on top of it. Someone in the pile below held on to the baby, while others reached out and held on to Wesley's legs as the tornado tried to rip him away. The Britts' two-year-old daughter sang "Jesus Loves Me" until the tornado finally passed. When the Britts looked up they saw the entire second floor of their house was gone. The rest of the house was all but destroyed. But everyone was alive. A few days later, the Britts' daughter told them that Jesus had played with her and her baby brother during the tornado, and comforted them while their parents fought to survive.

These stories, and many hundreds like them, are mere attempts to capture the horror and drama of April 27. Another way to begin to understand the extent of the damage is to look at the photographs taken that day. Some of them look like war photos; others like they were shot on some alien, postapocalyptic planet. Cars crumpled like soda cans in a ditch in Pleasant Grove; a half-missing house in Pratt City, its roof and second story gone, exposing a bed and dresser and unbroken mirror; a shaken first responder cradling an injured child in the flatbed of a pickup truck rolling down a devastated street in the town of Phil Campbell; neighbors helping neighbors emerge from the rubble of their former homes, their clothes muddied and bloodied. Whole neighborhoods reduced to pile after pile after pile of debris, the odd coatrack or refrigerator still standing, but the rest completely leveled, as if the sky itself had collapsed and crashed to the ground, which, in a way, it had.

Technically, thousands of people faced the very real possibility of being in the path of a killer tornado that day. How many of them huddled together and joined hands and prayed to God in what they feared might be their final moments on earth? In the months that followed, Pastor Tim Haney of the First Baptist Church in Phil Campbell, ninety-five miles west of Arab, welcomed an unusually large number of storm survivors who asked to be baptized. "You were able to see people's lives change because of the storm," he said at the time. "When something like this happens, it brings you face-to-face with your own mortality."

James Spann, the ABC meteorologist, spent nearly the entirety of April 27 live on the air (as so many meteorologists did that day), sorting through endless National Weather Service updates, scanning online chat sessions and social media feeds, and watching live streams from ABC's Skycams in the field, all while talking directly to viewers and trying desperately to help as many people as he could survive the storms. There was no regular programming that day; there was only wall-to-wall storm coverage. Through it all, Spann remained calm, coherent, and focused, even as adrenaline coursed wildly through his body. *These are my people*, he thought as reports of one massive tornado after another reached his desk. *I've gone to Rotary Club meetings and school trips and luncheons with them. I cannot let them down.*

But it was clear the day's events would be beyond anyone's imagining, beyond all projections. Spann's heart sank as, on a Skycam feed, he watched a tornado pull down a freestanding communications tower and rip off chunks of the Cullman County Courthouse. It sank even further when the tornado wrecked the Skycam and caused the feed to go dead. Standing there, in front of a blank monitor, Spann knew that just this one EF5 tornado was traveling in a direction that would put at least fifteen thousand Alabamians directly in its path. He tried not to imagine the probable structural damage or think about the potential loss of life. Those thoughts would not help him, or anyone else, on the air.

But on the following day, and for years afterward, when Spann had time to assess the full impact of the storms of April 27, one thought persisted above all others:

All these people died on my watch. That is inexcusable.

"I took it really, really personally," Spann says now. "These people were my family, and every one of them was precious, and all two hundred fifty-three of them should be getting ready to go to an Alabama football game on Saturday afternoons. I expected that we might lose thirty people that day. But two hundred fifty-three? Even people who did everything right, it was just their time."

In fact, all the improvements to the system over the previous years had no doubt saved many, many lives on April 27. (In the many post-storm analyses that followed, several further precautions and changes were recommended.) Nor could anyone say that a lack of preparation was what led to so many deaths. Instead, it was the sheer number and unprecedented ferocity of the tornadoes that seems to have been the decisive factor. "The truth is, all it takes is one tornado," Spann says. "And if it comes down your street, that is your April 27."

Spann spent the months after the tornado meeting with survivors, sitting down and talking with them, crying with them, comforting them, everyone helping each other process the unthinkable losses they endured. Driven perhaps by his sense of guilt, Spann felt the need to immerse himself in the aftermath of the tragedy. As an exercise in remembering, he even set himself the task of memorizing the names of every single fatality, "including the name of an unborn child who died at six months gestation," he says. These talks he had, and the stories he heard, were the saddest conversations he'd ever had in his life.

But one tragedy he heard about, and one victim he talked to, stood out. It was, believes Spann, "the saddest story of the entire event."

The story of Ari Hallmark.

The sun finally rose in the sky at 5:59 a.m. on April 28, 2011, one day after the tornadoes, though the dark horror of the previous day remained. In her room in the ICU at the Huntsville Children's Hospital, Ari was still sedated and largely unresponsive. Doctors had scheduled a series of early-morning tests for her—X-rays, an MRI—and when they came to her room to take her, her grandmother Susan used the opportunity to have her brother drive her home so she could pack some clothes and pick up her blood pressure pills.

At the hospital, the day unfolded with a surreal mixture of dazed disbelief, crippling sorrow, and continuing chaos. For the staff, there was no time to stop or rest or take stock—victims kept streaming in from across northern Alabama. At one point in the aftermath of the tornadoes, nearly five hundred people were reported missing and unaccounted for. Relief and rescue efforts would go on for days. In the rooms and hallways of the hospital, life and death still hung in the balance for many patients, including Ari's young cousin Julie, who had been found alive in her grandfather's arms and was now in an induced coma in the ICU, just a few doors down from Ari.

As for Ari, the injuries that were apparent early on were a fractured skull, major damage to her mouth and teeth, a broken collarbone, a broken left wrist, and several severe cuts and lacerations.

The broken wrist alone would require her to wear a cast for six weeks. Still, in the context of the tragic storms, her injuries were not considered grave, at least not medically. There was confidence she would survive.

It wasn't until late in the afternoon of April 29, Ari's second full day in the hospital, that she finally spoke.

That morning, she woke up with more awareness of where she was and what had happened. She remembered huddling in the bathroom with her family. She remembered not being able to open her eyes in the field for a few moments. But she did not remember her time in the local hospital or being transferred to Huntsville. So much of what had happened was still a horrible, undefinable blur.

In that moment of awakening, Ari thought about her parents.

"I guess I was still in denial," Ari says now. "I felt like I already knew what had happened to them, but I was hoping that maybe at least one of them had survived. And I also knew everyone was waiting for me to ask the question, so I finally did."

In her hospital room, Ari looked up and saw her grandmother sitting in the chair by her bed.

"Nanny, why are Momma and Daddy not here?" Ari asked.

Susan got up and sat next to Ari on the bed.

"Well, honey," she said softly, "they didn't make it through the tornado."

Ari said nothing. She did not ask any questions. She did not cry. She just lay back on her bed in silence.

"I wasn't too shocked," she remembers now. "It wasn't too overwhelming. I'd already cried about it so much before it even happened."

But Ari was only six years old, and now she'd heard the words that confirmed her mother and her father were gone, and thoughts ran inescapably through her head—that her mommy would never get to be a nurse or enjoy their beautiful new home, that they wouldn't get to go on the vacation they had waited so long to go on, or have their long summer together, that it was only going to be *a few more days* until all these good things happened, that they had been so, *so* close.

And so she screamed, and she screamed more and screamed louder, and her screaming did not stop. There was talk of sedating Ari again. This did not sound right to Susan, since Ari had just come around, but in all the commotion she wasn't sure what to do. Hearing Ari screaming, seeing her in such pain and distress, was nearly unbearable. But was knocking her out again the answer?

Susan asked if the nurses could sit and wait with Ari for just a few minutes while she went out into the hallway and called me.

Early in the morning the day after the storms, the power in Florence was restored and I was able to watch TV reports about what had happened. I heard about the nearby town of Phil Campbell, which, tragically, fell directly in the path of the single deadliest tornado of the 2011 Super Outbreak. It would come to be known as the Hackleburg–Phil Campbell tornado, and it was an extremely powerful EF5 monster that carved a 132-mile path of destruction through Alabama and Tennessee. The tornado was so strong that it swept away large brick homes as if they were made of straw. It destroyed three schools, a grocery store, a shopping center, and the Wrangler jeans plant, where parked cars were hurled hundreds of yards and one pair of blue jeans was sent swirling in the air until it landed *forty miles away* in Courtland. The tornado even yanked set concrete out of the ground and pitched it like cardboard.

The Red Cross estimated that the tornado destroyed 75 percent of Hackleburg and killed eighteen people there. Another twenty-seven people died in the town of Phil Campbell.

I didn't have any classes to teach at the university on April 28, so I took the day off and drove into Phil Campbell at dawn to see if there was anything I could do to help. Seeing all the devastation up close filled me with sadness and summoned the awful memory of the destruction I had witnessed on the Gulf Coast in the wake of Hurricane Katrina in 2005.

But as I walked into what had been, just a day before, a typically quiet small town, I also saw the people. A lot of people, coming from all directions, coming to make things better. A small army of volunteers. Someone steered me to the fire station, and within thirty minutes I was assigned a partner, given a grid map, a clipboard, pen and paper, a bottle of water, and a brief training session. Then we set out to do house-to-house wellness checks in our assigned areas the entire day.

I went back to help again the next day, April 29, and it was while I was in my car driving back home late that afternoon that I answered the phone call from Susan Garmany. Susan knew I had experience helping children through grief and other challenging experiences. On the phone, Susan spoke so quickly that I couldn't make sense of what she was saying.

"I've got Ari and she's in the ICU and she's hurt really bad and she's screaming and she won't stop and I need your help," she said.

I had no idea who Ari was.

"Susan, you need to go back and start at the beginning," I said as I pulled to the side of the road. "What's going on?"

Susan slowed down and gave me more of the story: she was with her injured six-year-old granddaughter in the ICU, and Ari was regaining consciousness, and she'd just learned her parents had died in the tornado, and now she was screaming inconsolably and wouldn't stop.

"They want to sedate her and I'm not sure what to do," Susan said.

I asked her if Ari was hurting herself in any way. Susan said no.

I asked Susan if anyone there was helping her with the decision.

"I need to know what you think," Susan said.

I paused for a moment, trying to take it all in. Then I gave Susan my best advice.

"I think you should let Ari scream," I said. "If you need to close the door, fine, but just let her scream. If she does start to hurt herself, just see if you can hold her in some loving way so that she doesn't get hurt and then call for the nurses to help. But if she's just screaming, I'd let her do it. Just sit on the bed and be there with her. Don't say anything, don't ask her any questions. Just be there. If she asks you anything, answer her question very simply and directly. But I would not sedate her. I think screaming is what she needs to do right now."

I also suggested that Susan get some paper and crayons or pencils and put them somewhere near Ari's bed so that, once she calmed down, Ari could start working through her feelings by drawing, if she wanted to.

"Don't ask her to draw anything," I said. "You can start drawing a little bit, if it feels right, and maybe she will join in. She might just scribble or punch holes in the paper, but that's okay."

In the end, the doctors did not sedate Ari. Instead, the nurses brought her some pink-colored computer paper, crayons, and markers from their station, and Susan began doodling something on her own. Before too long, Ari stopped screaming and picked up a red crayon. She drew shapes on her paper—the same shape over and over.

"It was a heart," Susan says. "Hearts with three little dots in them, for her and her parents. Hearts with smaller hearts in them. A big heart with two smaller hearts on each side." There was also a drawing of a small circle with a large heart coming out of it. The circle, Ari later explained, represented her parents, while the heart was her big love for them.

Then Susan watched Ari draw a shape that was different from all the others.

"It was only half of a heart," Susan says. "This was Ari's own heart, and she was saying her little heart was broken."

CHAPTER FOURTEEN

Ari spent five days in the hospital, three of those in the ICU. Her cousin Julie's recovery was slower. She spent two weeks in the hospital before being transferred to Children's Healthcare of Atlanta for eleven days of rehab before being released. The final, official list of Ari's injuries was frightening. She suffered a frontal skull fracture, acute dental trauma, two compressed vertebrae, and spinal subluxation, which means parts of her spine were misaligned. Ari's right clavicle was broken, and so was her left wrist, and she'd been diagnosed with bilateral lung contusions, which made it harder for her lungs to absorb oxygen. Doctors had used nearly seventy stitches to close the deep triangle laceration in Ari's lower back, and nearly forty surgical staples to seal up her head wound.

Her primary doctor at Huntsville Children's Hospital discharged Ari on Sunday, May 1, 2011. He gave her a prescription for a painkiller, to handle her nighttime pain, and recommended she use an incentive spirometer—a device that measures and improves lung strength. Her uncle Jason brought Ari some clothes to wear to leave the hospital: a sweatshirt and some pants with fur in them. ("Isn't that silly?" Ari would later tell me about the furry pants. "It was May!") Ari's blond hair had been cut into a little bob, though the right side of her head was shaved and her surgical staples were visible, as were purple bruises on various parts of her body. Ari's broken wrist was in a cast and sling.

She looked like a very banged-up little girl.

By May 1, Susan had arranged for an extra room in her house on the family farm to be turned into a bedroom for Ari. Cindy and Randy retrieved Ari's mattress from the new home Shane had built, as well as some of her clothes, while family members cleared out the meat that had spoiled in Susan's refrigerator after the power went out and scrubbed down the walls to get rid of the smell.

That Sunday morning, Cindy and Randy picked up Ari and Susan at the hospital and drove them to Cindy's house in Pea Ridge for a quick visit. The area around Pea Ridge was still in a state of devastation, all of it caused by the same tornado that hit the home where Ari and her family had sought shelter. It was Ari's first look at any of the terrible physical destruction the tornado had wrought, and Susan worried what her reaction might be.

But as they pulled up to Cindy's home, Ari also saw that some of the local children and parents had made colorful chalk drawings of hearts and rainbows and other happy scenes on the front pavement, just for her to see.

It was a small but hugely meaningful gesture, and one of many such gestures to come.

Some members of the local church were at Cindy's home to greet Ari and welcome her back. After a while there, Cindy drove Ari and Susan to Susan's home in Union Grove. That evening, Laura Byars—the teacher who had comforted Ari at school while she was having her ongoing dreams—came to the house to see her. Laura survived the tornadoes in the Union Grove communal shelter, a big, metal cylinder with space for one hundred people. She was in the shelter when her father, the manager of a local electric company, rushed in with news that a tornado had torn through Ruth, and that several members of a single family had been killed.

"When I heard that, I got physically sick," says Laura. "I thought, 'Ari and her parents have been killed. My God, this really happened. Ari knew it was going to happen, and now it has.'"

At Susan's house, Laura sat on the floor with Ari, and Ari slipped familiarly into her lap. "I just held her and didn't try to talk to her too much about anything," says Laura, who felt that Ari understood why she was there—to comfort her, just as she'd done for many months at school.

"It was almost like, 'Okay, I spent so much time in your lap, so I'll just sit there again,'" Laura recalls. "I painted her fingernails and toenails a bright shade of pink."

Laura remembers that during her visit, Ari did not cry, not even once. She was quiet, and somber, but she did not cry.

"It was like she knew beforehand that it would happen, and then it was over and there was nothing she could do about it now," Laura says. "I am a Christian, and I believe the Lord showed her what would happen so He could prepare her for it. Some of us tried to suggest her dreams were just bad nightmares, but that's not what they were. They were the Lord getting her ready for what lay ahead."

After speaking with Susan about Ari's screaming, I immediately called Dr. Tom Phillips, a friend of mine who is a pastor and counselor and holds two PhDs, one in theology and one in psychology and counseling. He was the first person I thought to ask about the advice I'd given Susan, and he assured me that my recommendations were sound.

I also contacted Kay Parker, who ran The Healing Place, an incredible support center for grieving children and families in Muscle Shoals. I had taken two brothers who lost their father to one of Kay's summer grief camps for children, and I valued her advice. I wanted to be as prepared as possible to help Ari if Susan called me again.

What I did not know when I first spoke to Susan was the full extent of Ari's loss. I knew she had lost her parents, which on its own was unthinkable, but I only found out later that she'd lost five members of her family in the blink of an eye. *Five family members.* I couldn't even begin to fathom the depths of such a loss.

The next day, Susan called me again and told me Ari had calmed down and drawn some pictures. She also asked if I could come to Arab and help with Ari on the day of her parents' visitation, an informal gathering of friends and family generally held the day before the funeral. Susan said she'd let me know the date of the visitation once it was set.

I'd received specialized training in helping young children during their parents' visitation, and I understood my job would be to figure out what Ari did or did not comprehend about what was happening and help her with any misunderstandings, questions, or concerns. I wanted to allow her to participate in her parents' visitation in her own way. I began assembling things I thought I would need—construction paper, Lincoln Logs, Tinker Toys, crayons, stickers, magic markers, glue. Everything I could think of. I knew Ari was an only child, but I was hoping there'd be enough other children there to be with Ari and play and chat with her.

Children don't always understand the vocabulary used during

a visitation—*funeral, caskets, death, passing away*—and they might also be confused by certain events. For instance, why would people at the visitation laugh and tell funny stories? Didn't they know the child was sad about the death of their parent? Why were they *happy* about it?

"People come to a visitation to remember their friends who passed away, and they are very sad, too," you might respond. "But if you see them laughing and joking, it's because they're remembering all the happy and funny moments they shared. They're remembering just how important your parent was to them, and how much they loved them."

Sometimes, adults can forget how different a child's perspective is from our own. Sometimes, we can forget about the children altogether.

Before the visitation, Susan asked her daughter-in-law Mandy to do Jennifer's hair and makeup for the viewing. She knew Mandy styled hair and applied makeup for her friends and other nursing students, and she didn't want to leave it up to someone who didn't know Jennifer. She wanted to be sure her daughter looked her best.

Mandy went to the funeral home in Guntersville, steeling herself to see the body of her sister-in-law and best friend. A staffer there wasn't sure about allowing Mandy to do Jennifer's makeup. "Any other time, you would be more than welcome to do it," he said. "But hair and makeup with the kind of trauma she suffered is a very hard thing to do." Mandy said that was fine, but asked to see Jennifer's body anyway.

"You could see all her injuries," Mandy says. "A lot of trauma."

In the end, the funeral home allowed her to at least do Jennifer's hair. By the end of the process, Mandy says, "I thought Jennifer looked *so* beautiful. In nursing school we were always in scrubs and T-shirts and we never cared how we looked, so this was the first time in a long time I got to see her all dressed up, and she was gorgeous."

On May 4, 2011, I drove the ninety-two miles from Florence to Arab. Just past County Road 1815 and next to a rolling horse farm, I found the Union Hill First Congregational Methodist Church. It's an old church—it opened as a one-room redbrick building in 1942, before an expansion created a second, much larger space for the people of Arab to pray. And, just like they did in the old days, worshippers there still hosted a hearty meal after every Sunday service, setting out two huge churns of lemonade and tea and heaping plates of hot food. Like a lot of things in Arab, Union Hill is an old-fashioned kind of place.

I pulled into the church parking lot in the early afternoon. I had a lot to get ready for, so I got there about two hours early.

The first thing I saw confused me.

There, in the parking lot of the church, were five shiny black hearses, parked side by side, perfectly spaced apart, as if they were for sale at a big dealership. I'd never seen that many hearses all together anywhere, and my first thought was that the church had allotted a part of their parking lot for hearses from other local funeral homes.

I walked into the seemingly empty church and looked around, but couldn't see anyone anywhere. Then I searched for a place where I could sit with Ari. I came to the sanctuary and stepped inside. Something there made no sense to me, so I walked down the aisle to get a closer look at it. Just in front of the altar, stretching from one side of the sanctuary to the other, were five open caskets—four made of dark cherry wood, and, in the middle, one that was completely white. The white casket was smaller than the others, and I could see a baby boy lying in it. The boy reminded me of my two sons when they were little.

Oh no, this sweet little baby, I thought.

I saw the other people in their caskets. An older man and a woman, and also a man in a baseball cap and a beautiful woman who seemed to glow. I was confused—was I in the wrong place? I didn't yet understand that these poor people were *all* part of Ari's family. That this visitation wasn't just for her parents.

An attendant came up to me and told me who everyone was, and then took me to a room I could use with Ari. The room was small, but it had a long window that looked out at the sanctuary. Understanding now that the visitation was not just for Ari's parents, I realized there would be a lot more people there than I had anticipated. And when I laid out all my paper and crayons and safety scissors and art project kits, I could immediately tell I hadn't brought enough supplies. I ran to the parking lot and got in my car and made a quick dash to the nearby primary school and explained my situation to the school administrative assistant.

"I'm going to need *buckets* of crayons," I said.

The assistant sent out an intercom request for help, and in no time I had all the supplies I needed.

Even so, I felt anxious. More anxious than I thought I would be. I didn't really know anything about Ari Hallmark, other than her age and the sad facts of her circumstances. Would I be able to connect with her? Would I be able to help her? I took some deep breaths and made myself calm down. The last thing Ari needed was for me to be in a panic, or to break down in tears. I vowed to myself that I would not let that happen.

Family members began to arrive. The only person I knew was Susan, and I was glad to see her when she walked into the church with her sister, Cindy, as well as a strapping young man holding a little girl.

The strapping man was Susan's son Josh, and the child, I knew right away, was Ari.

She was the tiniest thing. Her left wrist was in a cast, and with her right arm she held tightly to Josh's strong neck. Her short blond hair, cut so it cupped around her face, was shaved down to stubble on one side. She wore a pretty white bow on the side that wasn't shaved. She had on a black-and-white chiffon dress and little shiny black shoes, and she was just so precious. Even with all the evidence of trauma she looked like a perfect little angel.

"Be careful how you touch her," Susan whispered to me. "She's got like seventy stiches running up her back."

When I looked over at Ari, she was already looking at me. Our eyes met. She didn't look away, and neither did I. Neither of us said a word, either, but in that moment, I felt like we both understood what our relationship would be, at least on that evening, but possibly for a lot longer than that. I know that sounds strange, and if I think back on that moment today I can easily start to cry, but I truly felt like something passed between us, as if Ari were letting me know:

This is going to be okay. We'll get through this together.

I think you can tell a lot about a person in the moment you first meet, and what I could tell was that this was an uncommonly mature and resolute child. As soon as I saw her, my anxiety melted away.

I brought the little group to our special room in front of the sanctuary and showed them around. I needed Ari to feel comfortable there.

"Ari, do you think it'll be okay for us to be in here?" I asked her. "You can go into the big room anytime, and your family can come in here anytime you want them to. Do you think that will be okay?"

Ari slid down out of Josh's arms, walked straight over to me, and took my hand. That was her way of telling me she was okay.

Soon, Susan, Cindy, and Josh all left the room and went to the sanctuary to say their goodbyes to the loved ones they lost before all the other visitors were allowed in. Ari and I sat at one of the two little tables and Ari looked over the supplies.

"You brought a lot of things," she said softly, and with the slightest little smile.

"Yeah, I sure did," I said.

Ari pulled a basket of crayons and a sheet of paper toward her. I let her draw for a while before asking her a few questions—nothing too heavy, just conversation.

"Ari, do you understand what's going on out there?"

"Yes," she said.

"Okay. It's just people who know your mom and dad coming here to visit with the family and to talk about how much they loved your parents. And to tell your parents goodbye. They are here to visit. That's why it's called a visitation."

Ari nodded and kept on drawing and coloring flowers.

"It's kind of like having people who visit you in your home when something special is going on."

Then Ari said, "I'm not staying at my house right now. My parents can't be with me right now, so I'm staying with Nanny."

I took note of her unique way of describing her situation. *My parents can't be with me right now.* Since Ari seemed fine with talking, I told her about some words she might hear over the next few days, and what they meant. *Funeral. Cemetery. Caskets.*

"They are *not* caskets," Ari said firmly.

"Oh. Okay. Well, that's a word a lot of people use for them."

"They're not caskets," she repeated. "They are *treasure boxes.*"

I sat there in silence. I'd never heard anyone refer to caskets that way, and I thought it was the most beautiful thing in the world. Treasure boxes. Of *course* they are treasure boxes. That's exactly what they are.

"Ari, if you want to go see the treasure boxes at any time, I'll go with you or your Nanny can take you. Or you don't have to see them at all if you don't want to."

"I don't want to see them," she said in the same firm way.

"That's fine, then you don't have to. But if you decide later that you want to—"

"I won't change my mind," Ari interrupted, bending a little closer to the paper to concentrate on her flowers.

Two young girls scampered into the room. As soon as Ari saw them, she shut down. She held her crayons motionless over the page and didn't utter a word. The little girls ran around and giggled, and Ari's discomfort became more evident. The children were around Ari's age and they were a little loud and acting a bit silly.

"You're going to be someone else's daughter now," the older little girl casually said to Ari.

She was too young to realize the cruelty of what she was saying.

Nor could she interpret Ari's nonverbal but clearly unhappy reaction. Ari sat there in frozen stillness, staring the girls down.

"Okay, let's stop talking about that," I jumped in and told the girls. "We're not going to talk about that now."

It was the first time I acted to protect Ari.

Soon enough, Susan and Cindy came back in and spent some time with us. Other children arrived. Some sat with Ari and worked on art projects with her, and they all chatted in their normal, carefree way. Other children came in and sat close by and busily built things on their own or in other groups on the floor. The room had a happy buzz.

Another woman walked in—Ari's kindergarten teacher, Laura Byars, I soon learned. She gently hugged Ari, gave her a little kiss on the cheek, and sat at the table with us, slipping easily into the cramped, undersized child's seat as if she'd sat in a thousand tiny chairs, which I'm sure she had (and which I had, too). She didn't speak loudly or try to take over, she just joined in what we were doing. I liked her immediately, and I could tell Ari did, too. Laura told me she'd be willing to spend the whole night with us in that room if we wanted her to. We both did. I'd brought along the separate parts of a little stuffed animal that the children could all assemble for Ari together, one or two stitches each, and Laura took that on as her primary task.

With Laura there, Ari let down her guard again, and though she didn't move from her chair beside me or talk a whole lot, I could see she was doing okay. We were getting through it.

Then more adults came in.

Friends, relatives, acquaintances. One by one they came up to Ari and told her how sorry they were, and broke into tears, and talked about Ari's parents, and wore their pain on their faces and in their gestures, and all the grief was simply too much for Ari, or any child, to have to absorb. Ari did not cry, but she did freeze up and shut down again.

I understood they were all clearly heartbroken, and they all undoubtedly meant well, but to me, I knew it was not the best thing for Ari to have to be exposed to so many deep, raw emotions. I didn't say anything at first, but sitting there watching it happen was upsetting, and when that first group of people left, I turned straight to Laura.

"We have to keep the adults out," I whispered. "It's too much for Ari. Just kids and you and me and Cindy and Susan. No other adults."

"I agree," Laura said.

Maybe it wasn't the right thing to do. I don't know. But it's what my heart told me to do, so I did it. After that, all the children settled in or came and went and we all continued with our little creative projects, while in the sanctuary people paid their respects and mourned.

So many people, I would soon learn, that they formed a line that wrapped around the church aisles, through the reception area, out the front door, through the parking lot, and all the way down the street to some distant, unseen ending point. There were so many people waiting to pay respects that hundreds of them never even made it to the church door.

One of those who needed time to mourn, of course, was Susan Garmany. For five days at the hospital, Susan had focused entirely on

Ari and her needs, even though her own daughter and son-in-law had perished in the tornado. My helping with Ari gave Susan a tiny bit of time to at least begin grieving her own losses, to address her own wounds and sorrow, and she began that process at the visitation, and continued it at a memorial service for the five victims the following day.

"I had blocked out a lot of stuff," Susan recalls. "Then at the memorial they played this song about making it through the storm, and my friend was doing sign language to the song, and right there in the front pew I suddenly felt this amazing peace come right down over me."

Susan felt "an overwhelming gratitude to God for having put Jennifer and Shane in my life, and for allowing me to spend time with them. I felt appreciative for all the lives Shane and Jennifer touched. Now, I've never been a hand raiser in church, I'm normally very reserved. But that day, when they finished singing that song, it was almost like I felt an electric shock go through me, and I stood up, and I had a songbook in my lap and it fell to the floor, and I raised my hands in appreciation and praise and thankfulness to God.

"I don't know," Susan says. "On that day, at that moment, God just felt very praise-worthy to me."

The visitation stretched into its second hour. Ari handled everything better than I could have hoped. She still hadn't moved from the chair where she first sat down—I later learned she was good at locking herself in place if she was uncomfortable with a situation. But she focused on the tasks, listened attentively to the children around her, and made cards for her parents and family, though she was upset that her handwriting wasn't great because of her broken collarbone.

Ari also made a beautiful little white and blue beaded bracelet for her mother that said "MOM." Ari told me she wanted the cards she made for her mother to be put in her mother's treasure box with her, and she wanted her mother to wear the beaded bracelet when she was buried. I told her I would find the right person and make sure her mother got them. Later on, I arranged with one of the morticians to have Jennifer buried with Ari's bracelet on her wrist, and Ari's cards by her side.

Around the two-hour mark of Ari's three hours at the church, Cindy stopped in to see Ari again.

"Ari, Kenny Casey is here," Cindy said. "Kenny is the man who found you and saved your life. Would you like to meet him?"

Ari thought about it for a moment and said, "Yes."

Cindy picked her up and I watched from a distance as they went into the sanctuary. Ari had yet to set foot in the room where mourners were filing past the five caskets. Cindy carried Ari down the aisle until they arrived at a pew near the middle of the sanctuary. I watched as Cindy put Ari down and pointed out Kenny Casey. Ari went over and climbed up in the pew and gave Kenny a hug with her one good arm. He hugged her back. I only later learned that Ari did not remember their first meeting, in the flat remnants of the tornado just one week earlier. But I could tell she understood the gravity of their reunion. I was already in awe of this little girl. Her hug with the man who saved her was a beautiful moment of healing for them both.

What happened next was even more astonishing.

Ari came down from the pew and began walking up the center aisle back to Susan, who was waiting for her by the sanctuary doors. To Ari's left, a young man was bent forward in his pew, holding his head in his hands and quietly sobbing. It was Cindy's son, Cad, who was almost like a big brother to Ari.

When she saw him crying, she walked over to his pew, climbed up next to him, put her arm on his back, and held him as he wept.

She did not say a word; she just patted him on the back and stayed with him as he grieved—the same way one of Ari's classmates had tried to comfort her when she was crying at school. As she held on to Cad, Ari did not cry herself; I didn't see her cry even one time that evening. Yet she had gone to this man's side all on her own, and she was determined to comfort him and ease his pain.

I had told myself not to cry in front of Ari, but as I watched what she was doing, I couldn't hold back the tears.

"We were used to comforting Ari," Susan later said to me. "But now she was comforting us."

There was one more thing I was determined to do for Ari before the night was over. I'd never been to a visitation attended by so many people. The sanctuary itself was full, but there were more people outside—*many* more people—standing in the longest line I'd ever seen for anything anywhere. Even two hours into the visitation the line went on forever. I wanted Ari to have a sense of how much she and her family were loved, so when I noticed an outside balcony near our little playroom that overlooked the parking lot, I asked Ari if she wanted to go there and see all the people who were waiting for a long time just because they loved her family so much. Ari said she did.

I took Ari's hand and together we walked alone to the overlook.

From there, we could see the sprawling parking lot, filled beyond capacity and busy with people coming and going and gathering in small clusters. A line to enter the church snaked back *nearly half a mile*. It was like the entire town of Arab had turned out to lend their love and support to the survivors, and to say goodbye to the good people they had lost.

"The town was so grieved by what happened," says Laura Byars. "Everyone pitched in to help clean up or provide food or have people in their homes to shower. Everyone pulled together, and it showed the best of people, and the town became one big family. It was like everyone had a place in their heart for Ari."

The sun was beginning to set. I held Ari's tiny hand in mine as she looked out at the parking lot and took it all in. We stood there in silence for a minute or two.

"There's a lot of people here," Ari said softly.

"Yes, there sure are," I replied.

That was all that needed to be said. I looked at Ari's face and thought I saw the slightest smile come over it. It's odd to say, but Ari seemed relaxed and, in that special moment, possibly even at peace.

We went back to the playroom, and a little while later Ari said she was tired and wanted to go home. I remember thinking: *Where is Ari's home now?* Susan and Cindy took her back to Susan's house, and Ari and I said a quick goodbye before she left, both of us knowing, I believe, that we would see each other again. Once all the children were gone, I excused myself to the restroom, where tears just exploded from my eyes. Ari's silent strength hit me in a very profound way.

Laura Byars stayed behind and helped me scoop up the crayons and paper on the tables and put the toys back in their oversized tubs. When we were done we both just sat there for a moment, and Laura asked me if I could help her figure out what to say to all of Ari's kindergarten classmates returning to school the next day— their first day back since the tornadoes.

"How do you explain what happened to them?" she asked. "How do you explain it to anyone?"

I started to offer a suggestion, but before too long Laura stopped me. She looked at me as if I were missing something.

"You *do* know about Ari's dreams, don't you?" she asked.

"No, I don't know about any dreams."

Laura took a deep breath and sighed.

"Well, you're not going to believe this," she said, "but it's true."

CHAPTER FIFTEEN

The story Laura shared with me was astonishing. A story about a sweet, happy, energetic little girl who suddenly, six months before the tornadoes, began to weep uncontrollably at school every day. A girl who told everyone, *My mommy and daddy are both gonna die and I need to be with them while I still have them with me.* A girl whose horrible dreams then came true. I sat in silence trying to comprehend what Laura was telling me. How could she possibly explain this to Ari's young classmates? They had heard Ari say her parents would die, and then they *did* die. How in the world would children be able to process that?

When Laura finished the story I had no idea what to say or what advice to give.

"Sometimes," I finally said, "we just don't know everything there is to know."

I had spoken briefly with Susan before she left the visitation and we agreed to stay in close touch so I could get updates about Ari. We all knew this was going to be a really hard time for her. For one thing, she was in a lot of pain. For another, all her wounds had to be carefully cleaned and dressed two or three times a day. Fortunately, Ari's aunt Mandy—who was due to formally graduate nursing school as an RN in just a few days—and two other nurses came over often and helped care for Ari.

Then there were the doctor visits. *Dozens* of doctor visits. Susan had to drive Ari to an appointment at a physical therapy facility, dental clinic, or doctor's office several times a week. Ari had stitches and staples that had to be dealt with, and two broken bones, and back pain stemming from her spinal misalignment and deep wound. Some of her front baby teeth had been badly damaged and needed to be pulled. Ari's physical recovery alone would consume the whole summer of 2011 and go on, to some extent, for years afterward. Like hundreds of others who were injured by the tornadoes, Ari had to endure many months of pain and treatment and setbacks and new hurdles. I can only imagine how grueling it was for her, and for all of them.

But that was only the physical part of her recovery.

After Ari got out of the hospital and went to live with Susan, she remained in something like a state of shock for weeks. She didn't cry often, if at all—she was, as she explained, all cried out. But the emotional anguish of missing her parents, and the challenge of trying to make sense of what happened, must have been staggering, and she often seemed like she was in a daze. I figured out how strong Ari was within a few minutes of meeting her, but strong or not, she was still a child forced to confront an unthinkable reality: the loss of her parents, her only immediate family, the two people in the world she most feared losing, lest her very worst fear be realized: being left alone.

There was one lucky thing that happened that helped bring Ari some small measure of comfort.

During the tornado Ari had witnessed her cousins' dog, Pepper, being swept away by the tornado that hit Maw Maw's house. But back at her family's newly built home, Ari had three dogs of her own, who were, in the days after the storm, unaccounted for. There was Quigley, a sweet-natured Australian shepherd mix who was originally Nanny's dog until Ari fell in love with her, and there was little Foxy, who had reddish-brown hair and looked like a corgi, and then there was Goober, a small black-and-white mixed breed who had been Jennifer's favorite. On top of that, there was Foxy's new litter of puppies, who showed up just a day or two before the storms. It seemed unlikely that such small, fragile creatures could have survived such a ferocious assault.

Quigley, Foxy, and Goober did survive—though Foxy's little babies did not. Quigley and Goober were pretty banged up, and Foxy had part of one ear cut off and suffered other lacerations that had to be sutured. (Eleven years later, she still runs into the bathroom and cowers in the shower at the first hint of a thunderstorm, and *no one* can coax her out.) All three dogs were rescued after the storm and brought to Dr. J. Michael Brown, a vet at the Arab Veterinary Hospital, and Dr. Brown stitched them up and helped to heal them. He knew who they belonged to and he gave them loving care. Once they were better, Susan's son Josh purchased an outdoor pen for them and brought them back to Susan's house, and Ari was just so delighted to have them around with her.

As if Quigley, Goober, and Foxy weren't enough, Ari soon added a fourth furry friend—an adorable miniature schnauzer puppy. A generous benefactor from Tennessee, who remained anonymous, arranged to send Ari the new puppy, which had been born on April 27, the day of the storm. Sadly, the dog's mother died giving birth to her that day. When the benefactor read about Ari losing her own mother on the same day, she wanted the little orphan dog to be her gift to Ari (after she bottle-fed it for a few weeks). Ari fell in love with the tiny animal and named her Chloe, and she delighted in dressing Chloe up in scarves and bows and doggy shirts, putting her in a little baby stroller and taking her wherever she went. Chloe was Ari's constant companion for years and years.

Ari's beloved little army of dogs were one of the few things that brought her any kind of genuine happiness and comfort that summer.

Ari decided she did not want to attend the memorial and funeral for her parents the day after the visitation. So on May 7, Ari's teacher, Laura Byars, drove to Susan's house and stayed with Ari and other young cousins who also wouldn't be attending the memorial service. Mandy's cousin Hanna Shirley Millwood also helped watch the kids. Beforehand, Laura went to a farmers market and bought spring flowers and little clay pots so the children could replant the flowers. She also showed up with ice cream and sprinkles and cherries so the kids could have an ice cream party.

"That was the day they were burying her mommy and daddy," Laura says. "I just wanted to keep things light."

That afternoon, the funeral service was held at the Union Hill First Congregational Methodist Church. Brother Jeff Rowan officiated the service. Susan's sons, Jason and Josh, and Cindy's husband, Randy, were among the pallbearers. Shane and Jennifer were buried in the Arab Memorial Cemetery on South Main Street, right next to Shane's parents, Phillip and Ann, and near to where little Jayden Hallmark was laid to rest. An extra-wide black marble stone marks the graves of Ari's parents, and a photo of the couple is embedded in the stone.

Meanwhile, when the time was right for her, Ari conducted memorial activities of her own. She painted and decorated a little treasure box for each of her parents and placed special items in the boxes to remember them by—a photo, a note, a piece of jewelry. With the help of two neighbors she also planted three red birch trees in the front yard of the home her father, Shane, built for her. The trees, Ari understood, were a symbol of the unbreakable bond she shared with her parents.

Two days later, Susan took Ari to the graduation ceremony for her kindergarten class at Brindlee Mountain Primary School in Union Grove. More than a week of classes had been canceled after the storms, but the children were now reassembled so they could properly graduate.

Ari told me later that she had *not* wanted to attend because she knew she would be the only child in attendance with no parents there.

"She didn't voice to me that she didn't want to go," Susan says, "but she just sat there with her arms crossed in front of her the whole time, and you could tell she was uncomfortable."

Susan is a teacher at heart, and she had compassion for all the children in Ari's class, and she believed it was important for them to see that Ari had survived, that she was doing okay. "They were all so sweet and attentive to her," Susan recalls. "I don't think they knew exactly what had happened, but they knew *something* big had happened, and they also knew about Ari's dreams that her parents would die. They all lived through Ari's difficult months together. But they didn't ask her any questions, they were just happy to see her again."

In the days that followed, Ari attended two more graduation ceremonies. Both were for her mother, Jennifer.

Before the tornado, Jennifer learned she would be named the valedictorian of her nursing class. The school held an honors ceremony to acknowledge the achievements of top students like her, and Jennifer asked Susan to join her and Shane there. "She just wanted it to be the three of us at the ceremony," Susan recalls. "She didn't tell anyone else about it. She wanted it to be quiet and personal."

The dean of the nursing school handed Jennifer her valedictorian certificate, and afterward Susan went with Shane and Jennifer to pick up Ari from school. "I remember watching Jennifer walk into the school to get Ari, and in that moment I was just *so* proud of her," Susan says. "It was the last day I ever got to go out anywhere with Jennifer, and it was such a wonderful day."

Jennifer did not make it to the two ceremonies that followed.

Before the tornado struck, Jennifer completed every last bit of work required to become a full-fledged nurse, her longtime goal. She had been all set to graduate from Snead State Community College's nursing program and receive a Florence Nightingale pin in a traditional pinning ceremony. She just did not make it there.

Instead, Ari told Susan that she wanted to go to the ceremonies in her mother's place.

On May 11, more than fifty new nurses, dressed in bright white scrubs, gathered at the Bevill Conference Center on the campus of the University of Alabama in Huntsville. Ari wore a beautiful ruffled white dress with a yellow carnation pinned near the top and a white ribbon bow in her hair. Jennifer's classmate and sister-in-law, Mandy, took Ari with her onstage, where a chair, empty except for a large bouquet of white roses and other flowers, marked Jennifer's place in the class—the first seat in the front row, the valedictorian's chair. The dean of nursing had to kneel to properly affix the Florence Nightingale pin on Ari, who proudly and stoically accepted it on her mother's behalf.

"You are all very deserving of this great honor," school president Robert Exley told the graduates. "This is such a joyous occasion."

At the same time, Exley said, they were all there "with heavy hearts because of the absence of Jennifer. Tonight, we pay tribute to her and honor the courage, tenacity, and love you have all shown each other during this trying time. Through you all, Jennifer's legacy will continue to live on. She will forever be a member of the SSCC Class of 2011."

Another speaker, Carrie Brothers, a certified RN at Huntsville Hospital, remembered Jennifer as "a great mom and friend, and a wonderful Christian lady. She had a giggle that everyone remembered."

Then Mandy took the stage to read a poem Jennifer had written, and to speak from the heart about her best friend.

"Jennifer lived her life with excellence and with purpose," Mandy told the crowd. "Tonight would have been a great reward for her, but she has gained an even greater reward in Heaven."

Ari showed great poise and strength throughout the ceremony, and yet, up there onstage with Mandy and the other nurses—this tiny, adorable girl surrounded by adults—she almost seemed lost, even a little shell-shocked, as if everything that was happening around her was simply too complex and too tragic for her to comprehend, which, of course, it was.

"She was the saddest, most courageous girl I've ever seen," says Cindy of that moment. "Just thinking about it, my heart breaks and swells with pride at the same time. Ari was determined to finish what her mother started. The only dry eyes in the whole place were hers."

The next night, Ari returned to accept her mother's college degree at the formal graduation ceremony. A nurse in Jennifer's class—who'd heard that Ari wanted to be there in place of her mom—cut down Jennifer's graduation gown to Ari's size and also made Ari a miniature graduation cap, and everything fit Ari perfectly and made her look like the school's smallest graduate. Ari even participated in all the formal proceedings—filing into the room with all the graduates, taking her assigned seat, and walking single-file to the stage when it was time to receive the degrees.

When her mother's name was called, Ari, in her little cap and gown, strode gracefully across the stage like all the other graduates and took Jennifer's hard-earned degree in her tiny hands.

And in a soft but clear voice, she said, "I wanted to accept my mom's degree for her since she couldn't be here."

After the ceremonies, Ari faced the long and lonely summer months without her parents. Susan and others tried to keep her busy, and some friends in the community, led by the editor of the local paper, Charles Whisenant, raised funds for Ari and Susan to go to Ari's favorite vacation spot—the Great Smoky Mountains National Park (Cindy and Cindy's husband, Randy, went along, too). Charles and the others wanted Ari to be able to ride the rides and play games and swim in the lake and just forget about life for a while. But they were also fulfilling the promise that Shane and Jennifer had made to Ari to get her to stop crying at school—the promise that they would all go away to her favorite place as soon as Jennifer graduated.

It was not the vacation with her parents that Ari had expected and been so excited about. But it was the best anyone could do for her.

Yet while everyone around Ari tried to give her some sense of normalcy and routine in her life, her days remained filled with medications and new bandages and visits to different doctors. Ari was not a crier or a complainer—though not a soul could have possibly faulted her if she had been—but even so it was clear the enormous physical and emotional burdens on her were taking their toll.

A grief counselor spoke with Ari and recommended that whenever she felt really angry, she should just punch something. Find a pillow and punch it. Let the anger out. Ari tried it and found that it helped.

"I remember one time when I had Ari in the car, and we had just seen a therapist or doctor, and she just started punching the daylights out of my car seats," says Mandy. "I mean, she just kept punching and punching! I said, 'Baby, you've got to stop, I'm not sure this is really a good thing. We've got to find a way to channel this in a different manner.'"

That's when Susan bought a punching bag and hooked it up in the garage for Ari to pummel.

There were also times when Ari took out her frustrations with fussiness and hurtful comments directed at Mandy's young daughters, Ari's cousins AnnaClaire and Addi. "That was a really hard time, and really hard on the girls," Mandy says. "Ari had so much frustration and so much hurt and so much anger built up, and who do you take it out on sometimes? Sometimes it's the people closest to you, the ones you love the most. Ari probably felt more comfortable releasing some of those feelings around the girls than she did around adults."

Mandy explained to her daughters that Ari was acting the way she was because "she is devastated that the one thing she wants in the world is to have her mommy and daddy, and she can't have them, and you *do* have yours," Mandy says. "I don't think they understood exactly what had happened, but they did know there had been a tragedy and it was a very hard time for Ari. It was a frustrating and sad time for them, too." Addi was particularly close to Jennifer and missed her terribly. After learning Jennifer wouldn't be able to visit her anymore, Addi began crawling into her parents' bed in the middle of the night and taking refuge in their arms, a habit that proved hard for her to outgrow.

Only in hindsight could Ari process some of what she was feeling that first summer after losing her parents. "I remember I didn't cry a lot, but I did sometimes have these crying fits," she says now. "I would go through these phases where I was really angry. A little bit of being angry at God, of this not being very fair to me. And some time of being a little mad at my mom and dad for not turning around during the storm. Mad at my dad, mostly. But then I got over it. I found ways to cope with it. Like having something to do, keeping busy, keeping my mind off it."

Susan was so good about finding positive ways for Ari to deal with her feelings. "I thought it would be good for her to help other people who were also fighting battles in their lives," she says. Susan knew about an organization called Thursday's Child, which took over the care of children with disabilities for a day to give their usual caretakers a little time off. The group met twice a week in a church in Guntersville, a few miles east of Arab, and both Susan and Ari signed up as volunteers. "She really wanted to do it," says Susan. "She liked the idea of caring for someone, just like her momma had done."

Jennifer's sister-in-law, Mandy, now a registered nurse, was also a volunteer with the group, and Ari helped Mandy care for a ten-year-old girl who used a wheelchair and was fed through a tube.

"Ari would hold up the tube and talk with the little girl, just do whatever she could," says Susan. "Helping someone else get through their own hardships really helped her, too."

Ari did not stop there. She saved up the gift money she received on her seventh birthday and donated it toward buying a mobility scooter for a child with no legs. She visited the Alabama Baptist Children's Home in Decatur and spent time with foster children and orphans who were living there. Ari and her cousin took sign language classes together so they could sign some songs in church.

But that fall and winter, just a few months after the tornado, were especially painful for Ari. It was the time of year she usually associated with fun and family and celebration: Halloween, Thanksgiving, and Christmas, as well as her birthday and those of Shane and Jennifer. But in 2011, she had to face all those special, formerly happy days without her parents. "Ari got very sad around that time," Susan recalls. "She didn't cry, she just sort of got closed off, the way she can. It was totally understandable." Ari even came down with recurring ear infections and other nagging ailments, physical manifestations of her emotional distress.

That winter I connected Ari to a friend and colleague of mine, a remarkable Kenyan-born woman named Grace Jepkemboi, who was then an associate professor teaching education studies at the University of Alabama at Birmingham. Dr. Grace, as she was fondly known to her students, created a foundation that helped orphaned children in Kenya, and through her foundation we were able to sponsor the education of a group of sixteen orphans being raised by their grandmother—a situation similar to Ari's. Ari jumped enthusiastically into the project and worked with Dr. Grace to help gather donations and raise money for a huge amount of school supplies we sent to the orphans and other children in Kenya.

Ari also decided it would be fun to make a Christmas box for each of the sixteen orphans. She helped prepare the unique boxes and fill them with wrapped Christmas presents, and we sent them to the sixteen children, who, we learned, had never received any kind of Christmas presents before. (Susan and I also slipped in a new colorful shawl for the grandmother.) Ari was so taken with Dr. Grace and the orphans that she vowed to one day travel to Kenya with Dr. Grace so she could meet all the children in person—children half a world away who, just like her, had to learn to live without their parents.

There was one other charitable endeavor Ari undertook.

In December 2011, she signed on to be in a little Christmas pageant held at the local church where Susan's son Josh was a new pastor. The pageant was staged to help children in need in the community. Ari played the part of a Christmas angel, dressed in white and wearing heavenly wings.

"She did a really good job," says Susan. "She was a perfect little angel."

CHAPTER SIXTEEN

Since I lived nearly two hours away from Ari I didn't see her all that often during those first few months. But in early June, Susan called to catch me up on how Ari was doing. I heard about how she was constantly dealing with one injury or another, and how, emotionally, it was a daily struggle to keep Ari occupied and keep her thoughts off the tragedy of April 27. Overall, the thinking among her doctors and her family was that Ari was doing about as well as any six-year-old in her shoes could possibly do—which, having met her only once, didn't surprise me. I already knew she was one of the most determined humans I had ever encountered.

Susan brought up something else on our call. She said that Ari had begun talking a lot about watching her family go to Heaven.

I didn't know about Ari's experience in Heaven until then.

Susan told me Ari first tried expressing what she saw while she was still in the Huntsville Children's Hospital.

"I always felt like I wanted to talk about it right away at the hospital," Ari says now. "But I think the nurses and everyone there were told not to talk about anything like that with me."

At first, Ari tried to capture her experience primarily through drawings. She began by drawing hearts, but before long she was drawing angels and swirling lights and then houses, and then herself and her family, all in the simple stick-figure kind of way that young children draw. And from there, she moved on to illustrating what she saw when her angel took her up to Heaven. "As a six-year-old, it was really hard for me to describe what I saw to Nanny," Ari recalls. "It was really, *really* hard. So I tried to describe it through pictures."

These were the beginnings of Ari sharing her story, with crayons, markers, and pencils and whatever words she could find.

I was raised in the Methodist Church and made my own decision to be a Christian when I was twelve years old, and I have always believed in Heaven. But still, when Susan shared the first few details about Ari's experience in Heaven, I have to admit that my first reaction was, well, a little skeptical. *You know,* I thought, *she's such a young child and she was raised in the church and she knows her parents went to Heaven, and this is probably just her natural way of coping, to have a sweet dream about seeing them all walk up the steps to Heaven and go in. What a beautiful image for her to hold on to.*

In her first few weeks in Susan's home, Ari did not talk about her time in Heaven, at least not as far as Susan understood. But then, one evening in early June, when Ari and Susan were sitting on a bed together and chatting, Ari perceived that her Nanny felt extra sad, and in an effort to cheer her up she brought up her trip to Heaven.

"You know, Nanny, I saw Paw Paw Mike come down the stairs from Heaven and give Momma and Daddy a really big hug," Ari told her. "Momma was so happy to see him again."

Susan responded by bursting out in tears.

Ari was genuinely perplexed. "Why are you crying, Nanny?" she asked. "They're all so happy, and we will see them all again!"

It was the first time Ari had directly communicated, with words, a significant part of her Heaven experience. "It's not the kind of story you'd expect to hear from a six-year-old," Susan later told me.

Once she regained her composure, Susan gently asked Ari to do something for her.

"Write it all down," she said. "Write down everything you saw as best you can. Just write it all down, every bit of it."

Susan's thinking was that she wanted Ari's story to be in her own words from the very beginning, rather than having her, or any adult, interpret what Ari was trying to say. And so Ari sat at the kitchen table with a pen and some paper and wrote down everything that had happened to her, or at least tried to.

"I was pretty minimalistic with the words," Ari recalls. "I was six years old and I couldn't spell all that well."

Susan didn't mention Ari's Heaven talk to me because she needed advice on how to handle it. She told me because she thought I should know about Ari's interest in sharing her story. We both agreed that talking about her experience was good for Ari. And we were both intrigued by how, as she spoke more and more about it, she was always a lot less impressed by the story than we were.

"I didn't think it was anything too extraordinary," Ari explains. "I wasn't overwhelmed by it or anything like that. It's just what I saw."

Nevertheless, it was clear that Ari wanted to share her story with others. That interest never went away. It only got stronger.

This is where a remarkable little girl named Julia comes in.

I met Julia Fleming a few years before the tornado, when I was working as a professor at the University of Alabama at Birmingham, directing a postgraduate-level professional program for teachers who worked with people who were blind and/or visually impaired.

Despite being a full-time assistant research professor, I still wanted to be involved in working directly with children who were blind and with their schoolteachers. I contracted for one day of work a week and split those days between Cullman County schools and Arab's primary school. I was brought into Arab when their first blind student enrolled in the school as a three-year-old.

That student was Julia.

At the time, Susan Garmany was the paraprofessional at Arab Primary who was assigned to Julia, and we began working together.

Julia, I discovered, was a wonderfully gifted, articulate, and strong-willed little girl, and Susan was the perfect person to help her. Susan was so creative and so good at adapting materials for Julia and finding unique ways for her to participate in class (she paid for many of the extra supplies herself). I could see that Julia was really thriving under Susan's watch—and I could see how Julia was helping Susan walk through the grief of losing her husband, Mike.

One of my first responsibilities was teaching Julia how to read braille. As one of my methods, I created short, simple books about Julia, or about an experience we had together, and then brailled the words and let Julia help me illustrate the pages using craft foam and other items she could feel. These books helped me teach Julia how to read using her fingers. Our first book together was about a rather unfortunate granddaddy longlegs spider who, without going into the gory details, provided a good lesson about exactly how many legs a spider *should* have.

After a few years of creating these books, Julia had quite the collection. When she was in kindergarten, Julia decided she wanted to write her own book. I encouraged her, but did not help her—she wanted to do it alone. And, in fact, she created a truly inspirational little book about a blind snake, Seymore ("pun intended," she later joked with me), who accidentally crawled inside an abandoned Coke bottle and realized he could see better. What a beautiful story she came up with! I'd helped children tell their stories in different ways, and I knew it was a healthy, cathartic thing to do, so I was happy to watch as Julia told her story in her own way. Julia's parents loved her book so much they hired an illustrator to make it even more amazing, and Julia even held a Christmastime book signing in an event venue on Main Street in Arab, where she brailled her name on her books for her customers.

When Ari heard Susan talking about Julia's special book, Ari said she wanted to make a book, too, and she asked Susan to call me about helping her.

In early August, Ari was set to return to school. Susan, too, had to go back to work full-time at Arab Primary. Susan could not afford to quit her school job, so the decision was made to have Ari attend Arab Primary, where Susan taught, rather than return to her previous school in Union Grove. That way Susan could take Ari to and from school and be near her all day long.

Even so, having to attend a new school and meet all new class-mates would have been challenging for any child, let alone a child who'd endured what Ari had. During the summer it became clear that Ari clung desperately to Susan. The tornado had destroyed any sense of safety and security Ari had, and no amount of reassurance could erase the fear that still haunted her—that she would be left all alone in the world, with no one to care for her.

Ari's counselor diagnosed her with separation anxiety, which, given the circumstances, seemed almost inevitable. There was no choice but to have her attend Arab Primary with Susan. Ari needed consistency—getting up with Susan, going to school together, having lunch, leaving together—because *that was all she had.* Ari had to be able to depend on that consistency while she healed, and Susan made sure she could.

Ari was assigned to the classroom next to Susan's, so she always knew Susan was nearby. And whenever Ari felt upset or panicked or unsure of Susan's whereabouts—which happened more than occasionally—the school graciously allowed her to go next door and sit in her grandmother's lap or just be close to her for a few minutes while Susan went about working with her students.

One day, as Ari's class was entering the lunchroom, Ari did not see Susan standing in her usual spot and frantically searched the room for her. When she couldn't find her, Ari fell to the floor sobbing and screaming. Another teacher spotted Susan down the hall, returning from a quick errand, and told her what was happening. Together they ran back to the lunchroom. Susan scooped up Ari and Ari wrapped her arms and legs around her Nanny and sobbed. Ari had always kept up such a brave face, and this was a rare glimpse into her hurting soul.

That fall, I was driving from my home in Birmingham to work with Julia and her teachers at Arab Primary once a week, so it was easy for me to set time aside to be with Ari after school and help her write her story.

I arranged for us to work together once a week in a sectioned-off teacher's workroom in the cafeteria. The room was built to look like a happy barn. Our time together usually began with us meeting in the office and me asking Susan if it was okay for Ari to have a soda and a snack from the teachers-only vending machine, and Susan pretending to deliberate over the issue before saying, "Well, maybe just this time," and then Ari giggling as she dropped the coins into the machine herself because she liked the tinkling sound they made.

Then Ari and I would walk to the workroom and sit at the large six-person wood school table surrounded by well-organized supplies—scissors, hole punchers, glue and tape, crayons and markers. There were also several large rolls of craft paper in different colors on a big rack, so that you could tear off a sheet, like a butcher tears off brown butcher paper. I'd pull off a large sheet of white paper and set it on the table for Ari to draw on with a pencil. I sat beside her and listened as she drew and talked, occasionally asking a question and taking notes so that eventually I could write her own words beneath her drawings in her book. Ari usually started by walking around before settling in a chair, and then sitting up on her knees, and then finally winding up on top of the table, drawing intently as she talked.

My thinking was to allow Ari to tell her story at her pace and in her words, rather than me steering her through questions toward some narrative. Basically, I wanted Ari to think of me as a safe person to talk to who was just a little removed from her family. I had helped other children tell stories about themselves, and I had seen how emotionally healing it could be, and I wanted Ari to have that same opportunity to simply unspool her thoughts and feelings.

So I mostly allowed Ari to talk about whatever was on her mind—

school, friends, family, her dogs, her teachers. What was interesting to me was that Ari never sat down and started her story from the beginning—not even once. She would start in different places and jump from one part to another, letting the images just tumble out. Which was fine with me, because I never wanted our sessions to feel like I was drawing out a linear story. I just wanted Ari to talk about her life.

In the beginning, I imagined that Ari's little book would mainly be about her family, and her life before the tornado, so that she could have a record of what her family had been like—loving mommy, hardworking daddy, three yappy little dogs, lots of family nearby. That way, she would always be able to look at her book and remember her life before the storm.

But that wasn't what Ari had in mind.

From our first meeting, it was clear that all Ari wanted her book to be about was the day of the tornado and her time in Heaven.

Ari often began her Heaven recollections by describing how weird it was for her to see her father, Shane, with all his hair. She just thought it was the funniest thing and she was always animated when talking about that one experience in Heaven. It made me happy to see her get so excited about anything, and I wasn't surprised she reacted that way to a memory of her father.

Over time, Ari shared the other remarkable moments she experienced, and the full story of her time in Heaven began to emerge. Susan had described the story to me, but not in much detail, so this was the first I was hearing about many facets of Ari's journey.

My reaction was *amazement*—and a feeling of privilege and responsibility for having been given the chance, the honor, of being part of Ari sharing her story.

What was striking to me was that Ari always described the events the same way, and without any manufactured drama or emphasis. Instead, she talked about Heaven the way she might talk about an interesting class field trip. Her storytelling was simple and plain, even when she was talking about her angel and the big staircase and the roads that seemed paved with gold. Ari *would* occasionally get wide-eyed when she talked about the "humongous clouds of light" or just how big the doors of Heaven are. But I had never spoken with anyone who'd said they'd been to Heaven, and maybe I expected Ari to get more excited when describing it. For the most part, she simply told her story without ever making it seem fantastical or far-fetched or shocking.

For Ari, it was a normal and ordinary event.

That is one of the reasons why, from the very start of our conversations together, I believed her. I believed her *completely*. Any skepticism I'd had simply disappeared. This was not a little girl describing a vision or a dream.

This was a child talking about something that had *happened* to her.

And if I ever got a detail wrong, Ari was always quick to correct me. During one of our later meetings, I made the mistake of referring to Ari's parents as dead.

"That's not right," Ari said.

"What's not right?"

"They're not *dead*. They're just someplace else."

Ari wasn't angry or confrontational, she was just stating something that to her seemed obvious. Simply correcting my mistake. Her parents were not *dead*. They were not *gone*. They were in a place where she couldn't be with them right now.

"They are just not *here*," Ari would say.

I learned quickly not to use that word with Ari. I recently heard someone say, "Can you lose someone if you know where they are?" Maybe this was just what Ari was thinking.

It took about two months of Ari talking and drawing, and me taking notes, for us to feel like we had her full story laid out. Now we could begin assembling her book. In all that time, I never asked Ari why she wanted to write a book about her time in Heaven, and she never volunteered a reason—with one exception.

I can't quite remember the context in which she said it, but I will never forget the remarkable reason she gave me.

I want people who've lost someone they love to know where their families are.

CHAPTER SEVENTEEN

It did not seem possible that Ari's life could get any harder or more unfair than it was. She'd already experienced the very worst thing that, in her mind, she could experience. How could things get worse?

But they did.

Among the many tragedies of April 27 was that Shane and Jennifer Hallmark died without completing a will. They'd planned to draw one up—in fact, it had been part of the contract they'd made with Ari the night of the family meeting. But, as can happen, they didn't get to it. Overall, only about 40 percent of all American adults have a will, and I'm sure the percentage is far lower for people in their thirties. But because Ari asked them to, they promised her they would do it—just as soon as Jennifer finished the grind of nursing school and graduated.

Neither of them could have possibly fathomed how quickly they would run out of time.

According to the Alabama Code, Title 43, Chapter 8, Article 3, if you die without a will in the state of Alabama, your assets automatically go to your closest relatives, as outlined in several "intestate succession" laws. One of the many possible scenarios described is being survived by a child but no spouse, as was the case with Shane and Jennifer. The law clearly states that, in that case, the child inherits everything.

However, that still leaves room for interpretation. Which assets are included? What about assets that were co-owned? And who supervises the estate while the child is still, well, a child?

Shane and Jennifer weren't rich, but they were exceptionally hard workers and they'd accumulated significant assets, chief among them their share of the chicken farm, their property, and their new house. Certainly they left enough behind to insure Ari could live comfortably in their absence. Beyond financial issues, though, there is the matter of appointing a guardian for any child under the age of nineteen. Since there could be several different close relatives who could conceivably assume the care of a child, naming a specific guardian in a will eliminates potential conflicts and difficult decisions.

Without a will, Ari was left with no official guardian.

Ari was still in the hospital recovering from the tornado when a court named her grandmother Susan as Ari's temporary guardian. Susan was the obvious choice. She was closer to Ari than any other relative, and she'd formed a tight bond with her in the several weeks that Jennifer was hospitalized right after Ari's birth. Ari and her parents had also lived with Susan for nearly a year while Shane was building their first house in the Union Grove area. Susan was more than capable of caring for Ari; in fact, caring for children was largely the focus of her life. It was the best solution to the problem.

Yet there was a complication.

There was another couple who believed they should be Ari's guardians. Because they have their own story to tell, and I am only telling Ari's story, I hope you understand that I'd prefer not to name or otherwise identify them. Nor do I wish to depict them in any negative way. I don't personally know them well enough to make any public judgment. Like I said, I see my role with this book as helping Ari tell *her* story. Life is complicated, and people are complicated, and there are always two sides, or more, to any story. I can only convey Ari's and Susan's perspectives of what happened, as well as what I observed.

From what I understood, it was not inconceivable that Shane and Jennifer could have named this couple as Ari's guardians. But in the family meeting Ari convened specifically to address the issue of who would care for her if her parents died, Shane and Jennifer and Ari discussed every possible choice before selecting Susan as their first choice, and Susan's sister, Cindy, and her husband, Randy, as their second choice.

Shane and Jennifer's core religious beliefs aligned much more closely to those of Susan and Cindy, and those beliefs played a prominent role in the Hallmarks' stated wishes for how they wanted their daughter to be raised and who they wanted to raise her. All these matters were discussed openly with Ari at the family meeting, and her parents fully explained their reasons for making their decisions. In the end, Ari was very satisfied with the choice of her grandmother Susan, as well as Cindy and Randy.

So it's fair to say that while others may have had some legal standing to ask the court for guardianship, Shane and Jennifer's clear choice to raise their daughter in their absence was Susan, and Ari herself was also very clear about wanting to live with her Nanny. Indeed, Susan was named the temporary guardian very quickly after the tornado. She would need to go through a lot of paperwork to be appointed Ari's permanent guardian, but there was time for that.

After all, Susan was not only caring for Ari, but grieving her own losses, and the bureaucracy of guardianship just wasn't something she had time to zone in on in those terrible first few days.

Fortunately, her son Jason, who majored in political science in college and studied to be a lawyer, researched the matter and figured out what documents Susan needed in order to claim custody of Ari and be entrusted to take her home from the hospital. Those documents, including Ari's birth certificate, were in the Hallmarks' new home, which hadn't been damaged by the tornado. Jason drove to the house and found it locked, so he broke a window and went inside and gathered the documents.

Jason also had a friend and former classmate who was a lawyer, and he asked him to help Susan gain permanent custody of Ari. But the weeks after the tragedy were all but consumed by Ari's physical problems, and even with the lawyer's help it was slow going.

One month after the tornado, the court-appointed official tasked with representing Ari's legal interests in court, the guardian ad litem, or GAL (as a minor, Ari was required to have one), pulled Susan aside after a hearing. "You have to hurry up and get the legal guardianship finished in court," the GAL told her. Meanwhile, Susan thought she *was* hurrying.

"I was pushed into having to deal with it very quickly," Susan recalls. "I wanted to make sure I did everything by the letter."

What made the process even more complicated was that the other couple officially petitioned the court for guardianship and custodianship of Ari, and one of them filed for conservatorship. Had there been no other claims, Susan would have been able to assume permanent guardianship with far less stress and pressure. As it was, she found herself in a real battle over Ari's future. Susan is, at heart, a very trusting person, and she was blindsided by the extent of the couple's legal efforts to win custodianship and guardianship. She hadn't seen it coming and she wasn't prepared to deal with it. She'd never needed lawyers for much of anything in her life, and she'd only once set foot in a courtroom, after her brother died.

Now, I am someone whose blood boils when I'm backed into a corner, and who tends to wholeheartedly jump into a fight, but Susan simply isn't that kind of a person. She is someone who always tries to do what is decent and right and she gives *everybody* the benefit of the doubt. She reminds me of my own grandmother, Grandmother Darby, who always thought the very best of everyone, even when, in my mind at least, they didn't deserve it. So I knew that Susan would have a difficult time fighting for Ari in court by herself, with so many issues being thrown at her at the same time. As Susan told me, "It feels like I'm being attacked."

And I believe she *was* being attacked. It may have been unintentional, but I saw and heard it happen. To me, it felt like there was an overwhelming number of court filings, hearings, and legal meetings that first year, more than seemed necessary, and that further complicated Susan's life. Also, rumors about Susan began to circulate around Arab. That she was mishandling Ari's finances. That she was only interested in Ari's money or in getting her house. That she had sponged off Shane and Jennifer when they were alive. I ran into someone I respected in a town thirty miles away from Arab who leaned in and told me, "I've heard that Ari is having a lot of trouble with *that grandmother*."

Susan mainly chose to deal with the accusations by not responding to them, except in court. She simply wanted to protect Ari from any more negativity. "She has already lost so much," Susan told me.

"She just doesn't need this, too." Susan's attempt to hide as much of the turmoil as possible from Ari, even at her own expense, now strikes me as one of the most selfless things I've ever seen anyone do. I know that I could *not* have shown such restraint in the face of such an assault. But Susan's *only* concern was not making things any harder for Ari.

The first thing I did after learning about the court complications was to call a friend of mine named Jimmy Sandlin. Jimmy grew up in the same neighborhood I did, in Florence, and his father owned the only toy store anywhere around, and we all *loved* Mr. Sandlin, as we respectfully called him. I knew his son Jimmy to be a real sweet-heart of a person. He became a lawyer and eventually a family court judge, and we volunteered together on the local Children's Policy Council for several years. I asked Jimmy if he could help Susan with Ari's case and I told him there wouldn't be much money in it, but I offered to pay part of his fee. Jimmy agreed to come on board regardless of how much, or even if, he would be paid.

Jimmy was incredible. With his help, in the summer of 2011, the court named Susan as Ari's sole and permanent guardian and, a year later, as her conservator. Thanks to Jimmy the court also established a $20,000 discretionary spending account (out of Ari's inheritance) for any expenses incurred caring for Ari. Susan was put in charge of that account. Ari also began receiving a monthly survivor's check from social security, another regular check based on proceeds from the chicken farm, and an orphan's check from a policy Shane had taken out for her.

This is where Susan really came through for Ari. Though she had discretion over how to use all these funds, in her first year caring for Ari, aside from paying for Ari's lawyers, accountants, and taxes,

Susan decided not to touch the discretionary spending account. She saved *all* the orphan money and the farm income for Ari, and she invested all the insurance money left by Ari's parents, as well as any donated funds, in a secure long-term investment. Susan only used the monthly survivor's money—and her own money—for all of Ari's living expenses.

Now, Susan had a full-time job as a school aide, but she'd only taken the job to secure health insurance for her and her husband, Mike. Her monthly income from the school (after paying for medical insurance) wasn't very much at all. She had a second full-time summer job and a part-time fall job as part of the school's extended-hours program, but she had given those up after April 27 in order to care for Ari. All of which didn't leave her much money to pay her own mortgage and expenses. And still, Susan found a way to make it all work.

Without even touching the discretionary account, Susan made sure Ari didn't want for or need anything in those first two difficult years.

One year after becoming Ari's official conservator, Susan attended her first annual court-ordered review of Ari's finances. Jimmy Sandlin assured her it was a routine matter. In any case, Susan was *more* than prepared. She'd been meticulous in preparing a 164-page report about Ari's income and expenses. Every expenditure was listed and every receipt attached. Susan's husband, Mike, handled their finances when he was alive, but Susan made up for her lack of accounting experience by working extra hard and being extra thorough (and she hired an accountant to review all her work before submitting it to the court). Susan said she thought Mike would be very proud of the job she'd done, and she was proud of it, too.

Yet while Susan was getting ready for the routine review, another drama was unfolding.

Susan learned there were plans in the works for the court to put Ari's new house up for sale. Up to that point, the arrangement had been that Ari lived with Susan at Susan's house, but could go to the house Shane built for her whenever she wanted to get a toy or some clothes or anything, as long as it was her idea to go.

Ari could also decide which house she and Susan would live in, but there was no timetable for her to decide: Shane and Jennifer had left Ari a house that was completely paid for. Over time, Ari came to enjoy visiting the house, particularly after the first night she and Susan stayed there as a trial run, after Ari's counselor approved an overnight visit.

"We'd held an Easter egg hunt there, and we had lunch there with all the grandchildren, but when Ari spent the night she was just *so* excited," Susan says. "She opened the drawers and pulled out her momma's clothes and put them to her face and breathed them in, and she sat in her daddy's chair, and she loved how that made her feel closer to them. She couldn't believe she got to take a bath in her own tub. I mean, she was jumping up and down and doing flips all over the house."

"Nanny," Ari told Susan that night, "it feels like home to me."

At that moment, Susan made a big decision: she would move out of her own home so that she and Ari could live in Ari's new house, if that's what Ari wanted to do. "I didn't care how it affected me," she says. "If it would help Ari, I was going to do it."

Not much later, Susan and Ari returned to the new house to

pick up one of Ari's toys. Susan put her key in the front door, but it wouldn't turn in the cylinder. She took it out, made sure it was the right key, and tried again. Still no luck. Finally, she figured it out.

The locks had been changed.

———✜———

Not being able to get into the house truly frightened Ari.

"What's wrong?" she asked Susan frantically. "Why can't we get into my house? Are we going to be able to keep it?"

We eventually learned more about the plan to sell not only Ari's house but also everything in it except for Ari's personal things— including *all* of her parents' belongings. Apparently, the plan had been approved by Ari's out-of-town guardian ad litem. No one from the court ever mentioned it to Susan. When I heard about it, I was worried. Actually I felt sick. The possibility of Ari losing the house and everything that belonged to her parents struck me as unconscionable. Ari didn't need the money from the sale to get by, so why sell everything? That anyone would even consider taking away Ari's house—which Ari herself had helped to build and decorate, and in which she had a playroom built especially for her—was shocking.

And when I finally saw a photo of the big red-and-white For Sale sign hanging from a six-foot wooden post plunged into the dirt in Ari's front yard, I knew I had to do *something*, and I came up with a plan.

I drafted a "Dear Editor" letter, titled "Stand Up for Ari," that described the injustice I felt was about to happen to Ari and expressed my personal views about it.

"Another catastrophe is unfolding," I wrote. "As a community, and in the absence of her parents, we all have to stand up for this orphan child. We couldn't stop the first disaster, but we *can* stop this one."

Before I mailed the letter, I sent a copy to Jimmy Sandlin and told him he could pass it along to the GAL to alert her of my intention to share Ari's story with the newspapers in and around Arab. I'd already looked up the newspapers and had their addresses, so the letters were ready to go.

Was the letter a threat? Well, I guess it could have been perceived that way. I saw it as an opportunity for the court to at least *consider* Ari's thoughts and fears about losing her family's house. And I firmly believed the community of Arab would never let such a thing happen, should people learn about the proposed sale and how detrimental it would be to Ari.

The letter, apparently, succeeded, and the GAL promised to drop any plans to sell the house when they went to court. Still, Jimmy Sandlin advised Susan to immediately move into the house with Ari, because that would make it harder to sell should something go wrong in court. Susan hired a locksmith to change the locks again and I went with her to the new house. When we got there, I saw the big For Sale sign in the front yard, and something came over me. The moment Susan went inside the house to get something for Ari, I went up to the sign and kicked it with my black leather pumps and rocked the post back and forth until I finally knocked it out of the ground. Then I dragged it across the street and dumped it in a shallow ditch.

I have to admit it felt pretty good.

The following day, Susan and Ari finally moved into the home that Shane and Jennifer had envisioned for their little girl.

That left only the formal court accounting review to get through.

Before the review, Susan had already sent the court her carefully prepared accounting report, covering two full years, secure in the knowledge that she'd saved every receipt (over six hundred of them) and never once dipped into Ari's discretionary account. There was a positive balance in Ari's survivor social security account, and her farm and orphan checks hadn't been touched, either. I can't say for sure, but it's possible this was the first time the court ever saw "Yard Sale Money" and "Clothes Sold Money" listed as line items under an income column.

Susan had been incredibly resourceful, and also spent a fair amount of her own money, to raise and care for Ari. (In fact, Susan was entitled to earn $125 an hour, out of Ari's funds, for her work as conservator, yet she declined to charge Ari's estate *anything* for her time.) Sometimes things got a little tight, but Susan and Ari were doing just fine, and Susan was excited to show the court how careful she had been.

On the way to the courthouse for the review, Jimmy Sandlin assured her yet again that the proceeding would be a mere formality that would likely be over in just a few minutes.

But that was *not* how the hearing went.

As Susan remembers it, "I'd barely finished saying hello to Jimmy and putting my purse down, you know, just settling in, when the judge walked in and greeted everyone and it all started happening."

To Susan's shock, Ari's guardian ad litem marched straight up to the judge's bench and said, "Mrs. Garmany needs to come to the witness stand to testify. I have serious questions and concerns. I want Mrs. Garmany to be sworn in and I want this hearing to be recorded."

Utterly blindsided, Susan took the stand.

"I've looked at what you're spending Ari's money on and I have some *major* problems," Susan remembers the GAL saying right at the start. "You are spending a *ridiculous* amount on *dogs*. Just how many dogs do you have at your house?"

"We have four," Susan said softly.

"*Four dogs?* That's excessive! That's not what Ari's money is for. The money is for *her*, not for your dogs."

"Three of the dogs were Ari's before—"

"You're the one in control here, Mrs. Garmany, not Ari. You're the one who is supposed to be protecting her and conserving her money, not throwing it away on a bunch of dogs."

Susan could barely summon the breath to answer. The illusion that she might have been congratulated by the court for her financial diligence had been cruelly shattered, and now she couldn't even finish her thought about the three dogs before more challenges, more harsh questions, came her way. On the stand, Susan realized she was trembling.

The GAL then accused Susan of spending too much money on Ari's Christmas gift—a $600 iPad that Ari had really wanted, and which her parents would surely have bought for her if they could have. The GAL questioned Susan's knowledge of the management of the chicken farm and pushed her to admit she had no formal experience handling business or financial matters, in a way that suggested Susan had never been a professional or held an important job, all to her great detriment.

Now Susan began to get angry.

"That's right, I haven't," she responded smartly to the GAL. "I was always *just a mother*."

A pregnant Jennifer Hallmark comparing belly size with her grandfather in 2004. I think she won.

Like father, like daughter: Here's Ari with her daddy, Shane, when she was just a year old.

Ari and her mamma, Jennifer, were so alike, Ari's grandmother called her a "mini-Jennifer."

Having a family of her own was Jennifer's deepest wish ever since she was young.
Courtesy of Cindy Mitchell Photography

Three generations: Jennifer, Ari, and Ari's grandmother, Susan (who she called Nanny).

Jennifer and her sister-in-law, Mandy Garmany, near the end of nursing school in 2011. Jennifer finished as the class valedictorian.

The massive EF4 tornado at the precise moment it tore through the Ruth community in Arab on April 27, 2011. Courtesy of the Arab Tribune/Charles Whisenant

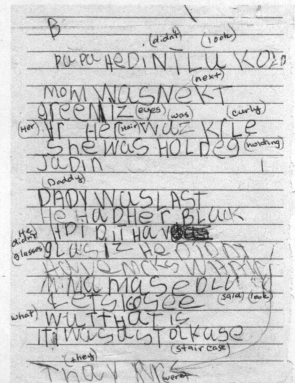

In the summer following her kindergarten year, Ari wrote about her experience immediately after the tornado. This is a copy of the first page.

Ari used markers to draw this depiction of Heaven while she was still in the hospital (the wavy lines represent the very bright light she said was all around her).

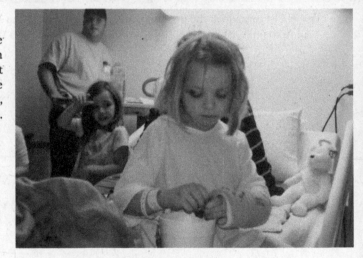

Ari at the Huntsville Hospital for Women and Children just after the storm. She spent five days there, three in the ICU.

Five black hearses outside the Union Hill First Congregational Methodist Church in Arab on the day of the visitation. Courtesy of The Huntsville Times/Bob Gathany

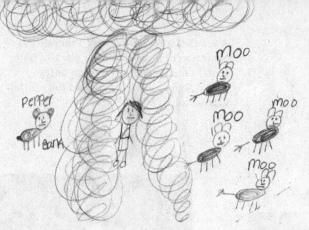

pepper

bark

moo

moo

moo

moo

In the weeks following the storms, six-year-old Ari shared her story the best way she could: by creating dozens of sketches of the tornado and her time in Heaven. (The swirls in the heaven drawings represent a bright, enveloping light.)

mawmaw side look lets go see what that is!

Angel Papa maw mike mauv Papa bilmark Mom daddy Ari Jayden

MY daddy did not have his glasis. And he did not have the marks were tha y were.

A few days after her parents' funerals, Ari bravely went in her mother's place to both a traditional pinning ceremony at the Snead State nursing school and the official graduation in Huntsville in 2011.

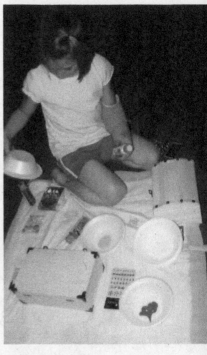

After all the public memorials, Ari privately honored her parents by creating treasure boxes, which she filled with items that reminded her of each of them.

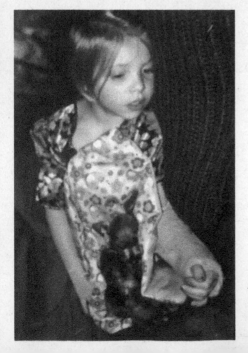

Ari with Chloe, the orphaned puppy she received as a gift after the tornado. They helped each other heal.

Ari visiting her grandmother, Susan, for a little reassurance in her new school. Susan worked in an adjacent classroom with Ari's friend Julia, who is blind.

The legendary Larry Gatlin brought Ari up onstage in 2012 when he raised over $20,000 for a nursing scholarship in Jennifer's name.

Football star Bo Jackson won over a new fan in Ari when she met him at the first Bo Bikes Bama fundraiser for tornado victims in 2012.

Ari was so proud to show off her book that I helped her write about Heaven at the first annual Jennifer Hallmark 5K Memorial Scholarship Run in April 2012.

Ari at the 5K Memorial Run with her kindergarten teacher, Laura Byars, who all the kids called "Momma Byars."

Ari crossing the finish line after running more than three miles to honor her mother (she didn't even practice!).

Ari started out in her first pair of high-heeled shoes at her book signing, but by the end of the evening she'd kicked them off.

Ari raised money to help two large families in Kenya, including this grandmother raising sixteen orphans. Photo courtesy of Grace Jepkemboi

Ari with my colleague, Dr. Grace Jepkemboi, who created the foundation through which Ari helped collect school supplies for Kenyan orphans.

Ari's grandmother bought new raincoats for her and her cousins so they could frolic in the rain (and so Ari could become less afraid of storms).

Ari with her little army of dogs (from left): Foxy, Chloe, Quigley, and Goober.

Here's Ari filming a special with a crew from the Weather Channel. During the shoot we found the unbroken Christmas ornament in the footprint of the tornado.

In 2014, Ari shared her story of Heaven with Neil Heslin, whose six-year-old son Jesse perished at Sandy Hook Elementary School in Newtown, Connecticut.

Ari with her community softball team. She was every bit as athletic as her mother, Jennifer.

Ari played a lot of different sports but she really excelled at gymnastics.

An elated Ari and Susan sitting at the judge's bench as Ari's adoption was finalized in 2017.

Ari's adoption lawyer, Sam McClure, promised he'd walk on his hands if he won the case—and he kept his promise!

A full crowd turned up to hear Ari speak at the dedication of a new storm shelter in Arab named after her family.

Ari loved answering questions after her speech. It always made her feel good to share her message with others.

Ari giving a speech at the New Beginning Church in Florence in 2021, and me helping her with an audience Q&A afterward.

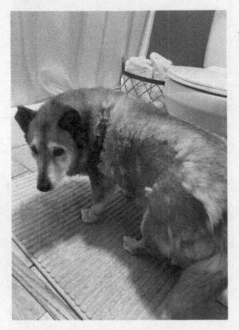

Ari's dog, Foxy, who was four when the 2011 tornado struck, still hides in the shower eleven years later whenever she senses bad weather.

Ari with her newest puppy, Stetson, who she named for the cowboy hat her father bought for her when she was little.

Eleven years after Kenny Chasey found Ari in this field after the tornado, she met him there to ask him questions and to replace the sweatshirt he took off to support her neck and head in 2011.

Susan, Ari, and I make a pretty good team. We aren't just friends, we are family.

Ari and her best friend, Mary Elizabeth, at high school cheer practice at the start of their senior year.

"God has a plan for me," says Ari at the beautiful house her parents built for her in Arab.

"Well, as Ari's conservator you should know all these things," the official said. "You are not doing your job. *You're not protecting Ari.*"

I can't imagine the GAL could have said anything worse than that to Susan. And after she said it, Susan began to cry.

The official asked the court to remove Susan as Ari's conservator and appoint a special conservator to conduct a full review of Susan's accounting. A hearing was set to decide if Susan should continue as Ari's conservator or be permanently replaced, pending the result of the accounting review.

Everything happened so quickly that even Jimmy Sandlin—who had presided over more than eighteen thousand cases as a family court judge—was caught off guard and didn't see an opportunity to turn things around. The judge granted the GAL's request, temporarily removed Susan as Ari's conservator, and appointed a lawyer to be Ari's special conservator for the six weeks it would take to review Susan's accounting. The review would be conducted by the lawyer newly appointed as special conservator by the court.

Just like that, everything had changed.

The six weeks passed, and the day of the hearing to discuss the special conservator's accounting review arrived. And once again Jimmy Sandlin assured Susan the court would almost certainly return the conservatorship to her, perhaps even with an apology. Susan tried her best to believe him. But things didn't go any better than at the first hearing.

The hearing began with the special conservator making a pointed statement as he walked up to Susan in her chair.

"I see you like to get your nails done," he said.

The question that followed: *Did Susan use Ari's money to get her nails done?*

"I do my own nails," Susan responded with anger in her voice.

What about a propane gas delivery? Was that for Ari or Susan? (It was for Ari's house.)

What about the Walmart picture frames? Were they for Susan?

"*No!* I framed photos of Ari's parents for her so she wouldn't forget what they look like!"

The conservator held up one receipt for $68 that had the word *train* written on the back.

"What does 'train' mean?" the conservator asked. "What kind of train did you spend Ari's money on?"

"I never bought any kind of train," Susan said.

"So then why did you write down 'train'?"

Susan racked her brain, but she just could not remember why she'd written the word or what it meant.

"So did you buy one of your other grandkids a train with Ari's money?"

"*NO!*" Susan answered in utter despair. "I would *never* do that."

There was no letup. The accusations kept coming. Question after question. A receipt for a $30 trash can—did she buy it to use for her own garbage at her house? Susan's integrity and character were repeatedly and harshly questioned and again she broke down in tears on the stand. The accounting review itself was never even mentioned. But the accusations continued nonstop.

Finally, Susan simply could not take it any longer.

"*I CAN'T KEEP DOING THIS!*" she cried, throwing up her hands.

The courtroom fell silent.

"I can take care of Ari, but I can't keep doing *this*," Susan went on in a broken voice. "Coming to court over and over and getting attacked. And I know all these hearings are costing Ari money. I can't do it, I just can't, not year after year. Let someone else take care of Ari's investments and I'll just take care of Ari."

It was an emotional reaction to the very personal nature of the questioning, and Susan had no idea what her statement would entail.

"What I meant was that they were tearing me apart and I couldn't win against them," Susan explains. "The court stuff really upset me, and I felt I was harming Ari by being so upset about it all the time. I wasn't trying to say I'm this great person. I was saying that I'm human, a sinner saved by grace, and I do the best I know how to take care of Ari, and I would *never* do anything to harm her or take advantage of her."

But what Susan meant to say did not matter.

The judge never even asked about the forensic accounting review that Ari was forced to pay the special conservator more than $9,700 of her own money for. No forensic accounting document was ever displayed in court, or made available even after repeated requests by Susan, and as far as I can tell, it was never put into Ari's case file. In its final decision the court officially accepted Susan's accounting—but the court also accepted what they called Susan's "verbal request to be replaced as conservator." The court then granted permanent conservatorship to the special conservator who had conducted the mysterious accounting review, giving him complete control over all of Ari's finances.

For the sake of clarity, I will call this lawyer the steward.

After the hearing, Susan went home and racked her brains and tried to figure out what in the world the "train" receipt was for.

Finally, she found her copy of the receipt and saw it had a Walmart serial number on it. She checked the Walmart website and finally figured out what "train" meant.

"It was for a training collar to help with little Chloe's barking," Susan says. "Chloe would bark all the time and Ari and I talked it over and decided to buy this special collar for her. 'Train' was for *training.*"

That was the simple explanation for the "train" receipt. But simple or not, it did not change the facts.

Ari's future was no longer in her and Susan's hands.

CHAPTER EIGHTEEN

My heart just broke in half for Susan, who felt so guilty after giving up the conservatorship. She'd been through so much herself, and now she blamed herself for what went on in court.

But she was *not* to blame. At first, she had no idea of the consequences of giving up the conservatorship and truly believed it would simplify things for everyone, especially Ari. As someone who has reviewed basically every document in Ari's six-inch-thick case file, I can say without hesitation that Susan did *nothing* wrong, and in fact she did everything right. Susan's accounting of Ari's finances passed the scrutiny of a pricey forensic accounting review, and exactly *zero* errors were noted. The one-year accounting she filed with the court was perfectly thorough and transparent and included aggregate details of every single item purchased for Ari. There was no discernible reason for the court to demand an expensive financial review that Ari was forced to pay for. Susan was nothing less than heroic on Ari's behalf.

So how did she lose the conservatorship?

Many years later, the steward explained to the court that the reason Susan lost the conservatorship was because "she just quit—while she was on the stand." As for me, I believe that, in very simple terms, Susan was outmatched. All she brought to court, beyond her professional-level accounting, was her love for Ari and her faith in the power of goodness and the power of God—the kind of faith that will see you through your worldly battles.

And, true to form, though this was a terrifying time for Susan, she shielded young Ari—then only eight years old—from all of it.

But in the end Susan faced formidable forces that turned what should have been a routine accounting review into a pitched battle.

As I mentioned, my only goal in writing this book is to help Ari share her experience and message. What other people were thinking, or what their motives or agendas might have been, I simply do not know.

Everything I describe are things that happened to Susan and Ari, and which they shared with me or that I observed. The court's rulings had serious consequences that very much impacted Susan and Ari, and I will describe certain moments that came to define their strength and courage and determination over the years that followed.

But I will only glancingly describe the most significant court happenings and will not attribute motives to anyone involved in those happenings, aside from myself, Ari, and Susan. All that matters, in the end, is that the years and years of court proceedings created another unfortunate hurdle that Ari, already physically and emotionally devastated by all she had suffered, had to fight to overcome.

And anyway, the things that happened in court are not the most notable parts of the real story of Ari Hallmark.

The real story is far more powerful and amazing.

During this time, sharing her Heaven story seemed to be healthy for Ari. "Just talking about what I experienced and telling you about it and writing it down, it was kind of like therapy for me," Ari says now. "Seeing the first few people I told my story to, and how much it was impacting them, that got to my heart and made me realize this was something that could really help people."

To produce Ari's little book, I mounted her pencil drawings on colored construction paper and typed up captions, in Ari's words, to go along with them. The title we chose was *To Heaven After the Storm.* My local Office Depot put it all together and, on the one-year anniversary of the tornadoes, April 27, 2012, we had a few copies to hand out to Ari's family at the first annual 5K Memorial Run, a fundraiser for the Jennifer Garmany Hallmark Endowed Scholarship Fund at Snead State Community College. More than two hundred people ran in the roughly three-mile race, and one of them was Ari.

A natural athlete just like her mother, Ari finished the race without stopping, and when she crossed the finish line all the spectators erupted in cheers. At first Ari was anxious being around so many people, but as the day went on she began to relax and even enjoy herself. We gave out the handful of copies of Ari's book that we had, and as other attendees heard about it, just about all of them asked for a copy.

And when someone at a Christian bookstore in Arab heard about it, they asked us if Ari would do a signing there. Susan and I sat down with Ari and asked her if that was something she wanted to do.

Emphatically, Ari said yes.

When I got to the bookstore on that August evening of the

signing, there were already several dozen people lined up outside, waiting to get in.

Inside, Ari saw me enter and ran right up to me in her pretty fuchsia blouse and fancy black pants, bubbling with excitement.

"I have my first high heels on!" she squealed, pointing down.

Ari had been shy at the 5K run, but now that shyness was gone. In fact, Ari was happier and more energetic than I had seen her in the entire time I'd known her. Far from being an event about death and grief, the signing, I realized, was a celebration of life and loved ones. Volunteers created a huge crepe paper rainbow and prepared three big tables with all kinds of colorful refreshments, including an amazing array of candies. Ari found the ones she liked best—strips of sugared sour candy that looked like flat rainbows—and pretty much didn't stop eating them all night.

Ari's art teacher, Kim (who helped us design the cover), and I sat on a small sofa with Ari as people lined up to get their books signed. I was a bit on edge; I didn't know how Ari would react to a constant stream of people saying hello and asking her how she was and wishing her well. To my surprise she seemed to enjoy every minute of it. She spoke to anyone who spoke to her, and she charmed everyone with her maturity and matter-of-factness, and she answered occasional questions about Heaven, and she signed every copy with her name in pink Sharpie ink and her special little pink heart above the *i* in Ari. I'd even ordered a self-inking stamper with Ari's signature that she could use when she got tired. But she never got tired.

As the evening wore on I kept looking at the clock, expecting that Ari would eventually hit a wall. But she never did, even though the volunteers kept bringing her more cookies and more rainbow strips and all that sugar gave her quite a rush, and she did get a little bit loopy toward the end. But she was never bored, and she never tired of having people come up to her and compliment her outfit or her high-heeled shoes (which she eventually ditched in favor of bare feet), and she made it through an entire *three hours* of signing her little book.

I realized that interacting with all those people and sharing her Heaven story with them was *fun* for Ari, probably more fun than she'd had in a long time. This was Ari's true personality—outgoing, adventurous, playful, loving, like her mother, Jennifer—and though the tragedy of April 27 had threatened to snuff out these qualities, the signing allowed them to shine through again. Ari was *happy*. She was actually *crazy* happy. Talking about Heaven energized her and seemed to fill her with purpose. It was an astonishing thing to witness, almost a kind of rebirth. Selfishly speaking, seeing Ari so happy and engaged was just so much *fun* for me, too. It had been an unthinkably hard year for her, and to see her so enthusiastic was nothing short of magical.

At the same time, I realized something else.

Seeing Ari happy *was good for the whole town.*

It seemed like, even after having their copies signed, people did not want to leave the event. Most everyone hung around and ate and talked and just savored being with each other and being around Ari. The Arab community is a community where everyone knows everyone, or knows of everyone, and the tornadoes were about as heavy a thing as had ever happened in the area, and gathering at this special event and seeing one of the storm's most fragile and tragic victims running around with a smile on her face was really, really healing for everyone.

I thought, *How lucky is Ari to live in a community that embraces her and shows her this much support and love?*

And—*How lucky is this community to have a kid like Ari?*

When it was finally over I said good night to Ari and walked toward my car. But before I could get in, Ari came barreling at me, a big smile on her face. She had a simple question for me.

"When are we going to do this again?"

It was around this time that I was contacted by someone at the Weather Channel, a widely watched national outlet. They asked if Ari would take part in a documentary about tornado survivors. Once again Susan and I sat Ari down to talk about the request. We wanted to see if it was time for Ari to take a break from publicly sharing her story.

Once again, Ari was emphatic. She wanted to do the interview.

Neither Susan nor I were surprised. It was obvious the experience of sharing her Heaven story was extremely positive for Ari. Perhaps it made her feel closer to her mommy and daddy to talk about seeing them go to Heaven. Perhaps the idea of helping others with her story and seeing how it impacted them did, as Ari would later say, "really get to my heart." Perhaps it was both these things, and more. But there was no ambiguity that Susan and I had to try to puzzle out from Ari's moods or words. We had given her a number of exit ramps and she never took one.

She wanted to keep talking.

Early on, it looked like Ari would only be featured in the Weather Channel documentary for a few minutes. As it turned out, her segment went on for thirty minutes. A TV crew from California came to Arab for two days and filmed Ari, Susan, Laura Byars, me, and some others talking about the events that led up to and followed April 27, starting with Ari's dreams about her parents dying. Ari was thrilled that a crew member let her do the three-two-one countdown and click the fancy digital clapboard to start a take. For one of her tapings, Ari sat at the foot of her bed in her bright pink-and-green bedroom, wearing a turquoise dress and matching hair bow and surrounded by her stuffed animals. Scruffy little Chloe, a red bandanna around her neck, sat right by Ari's side, in case she had to leap into action and "protect" Ari from the TV crew. (In fact, Chloe did not leave Ari's side for the entire two days the crew was there.)

"I believe I went to Heaven after the tornado," Ari said in her precise Southern accent, so poised and assured for an eight-year-old discussing such a topic. "I saw Jesus and all the family that passed."

The crew also filmed Susan, Ari, and me walking through the flat field near Ruth Road where Ari was found on April 27.

The property had been completely cleaned up and no real evidence of what had happened there remained. But suddenly, as we walked, Ari spotted something on the ground.

She squatted to look at it and gently dug it out of the moist dirt. It was a small Christmas ball, a fragile little fuchsia ornament caked in dirt and faded on the side exposed to the elements, but miraculously, still unbroken. We all looked at it with utter amazement.

"That had to be one of Maw Maw's," Susan said.

Finding the ornament not far from where Ari was thrown, and seeing that it had not been broken, not even by a ferocious EF4 tornado—seeing that it had survived, just like Ari—was absolutely surreal. It was like an early Christmas gift for Ari, straight from Heaven. Even one of the cameramen teared up.

"God knows how to do these things," Susan said as we all walked on through the field, "right when you need them most."

Ari handed me the precious treasure as we walked and said, "We'll have to put it on the Christmas tree."

The segment ended with Ari's poignant and powerful message, filmed near the spot where the tornado hit. Ari's message had not faltered, it had only deepened.

"Everything can just change totally in one day, and I believe that God had helped me survive through the tornado to tell people that have gone through what I'd gone through, 'That's okay,'" Ari said. "Because you're going to see them again, It may be a while before you see them, but you're *gonna* see them eventually again."

The segment closed on those very words.

Certain disasters, like the April 27 tornadoes, transcend geography and become national or even global tragedies. Such a tragedy happened again on December 14, 2012, about twenty months after Ari's parents passed away. This time, it was a school shooting at the Sandy Hook Elementary School in Newtown, Connecticut.

A very troubled twenty-year-old used his mother's Bushmaster rifle to shoot and kill a staggering twenty-six people, including twenty children between the ages of six and seven, the same age as Ari at the time. It was, like the tornadoes, a nearly unimaginable horror, beyond all understanding or tolerance, and the pain it caused was too deep and too enduring to contemplate. I don't believe anyone anywhere was untouched by the news of what was lost that day.

Ari learned about the shooting in the way that children learn about these things, through a teacher's gentle lesson and by asking questions. I can only imagine how someone that young even begins to process something like that. Ari thought a lot about the shooting and came to a decision that she announced to me one day.

"I want to go to Sandy Hook and talk to those parents," she said. "I want to tell them that their children are okay."

CHAPTER NINETEEN

As usual when I'm around Ari, I was impressed by her heart.

Hers was, to me, a remarkable reaction to the school-shooting tragedy. Instead of trying to block out the horror of the massacre, Ari's instinct was to run straight into it—*because she believed she had a message that would truly help those parents who were hurting to heal.*

What an amazing amount of love and empathy for a child who just turned eight to express. Of course, Ari herself was the victim of unfathomable tragedy, and she knew better than most what healing from seemingly unhealable wounds might entail. She knew what kind of thoughts and gestures mattered, and how small expressions of love and compassion could make all the difference. The more she thought about it, the more she believed with all her heart that she could help ease the parents' pain by sharing with them what she'd learned in her own moment of tragic loss:

They would see their children again. Their children are okay.

I sat down with Ari to talk it over. I told her it would be really hard for us to be able to meet the grieving parents, simply because they needed their privacy and their community would be very protective of them. We might not ever be able to talk to the right people who could arrange a meeting, despite Ari's beautiful and sincere intentions.

But even if meeting with the victimized parents was possible, Ari had to understand that she'd be entering into a situation fraught with more emotion and suffering and sorrow than I thought any child should voluntarily be exposed to, especially one who had already had to confront that kind of darkness, and so recently. Ari needed to know just what she'd be walking into.

"Ari, these parents are going to be *so* sad," I warned.

Ari looked at me in her familiar matter-of-fact way.

"I'm not afraid of sad," she said.

I followed up on Ari's request and reached out to at least twenty different people, with no luck. As for Ari, she just wouldn't quit about it, and she asked me about it every time we saw each other. She was determined to go and share her story, more determined than I'd seen her about anything. She'd spoken about it with her counselor, who met with Ari at least twice a month to help her navigate her difficult journey, and the counselor gave the okay for her to go. Susan was on board, too. As far as Ari was concerned, it was going to happen.

For a while, however, it really did appear as if scheduling a visit to the school might not be possible.

But—it *was* possible.

It took me many, many months and dozens of phone calls, handwritten letters and emails, but I finally spoke with Kaitlin Roig, a first-grade teacher who was at the school the day of the shooting. Kaitlin listened to me sharing Ari's story and describing what Ari wished to do at Newtown. She then connected me to the new superintendent of the Newtown school district. From that point on, everything just fell into place. A wonderful benefactor, Tiffany Jones—an Arab entrepreneur and a true angel—agreed to cover some of the costs of Ari's trip to Sandy Hook (Susan and I traveled with Ari at our expense).

The three of us flew to Connecticut. It was Susan's first time on a plane and she got a little light-headed when we landed (somehow, a wheelchair no one ordered turned up for her to use). We took a cab to the scenic small town of Newtown in Fairfield County, and the next day we met with an amazing little girl named Lauren, a first-grader who survived the shooting but was mourning the loss of many of her friends. Ari and Lauren sat down together and Ari assured her that her school friends were very happy in Heaven, and *not* the way Lauren remembered them in their last moments on earth.

We also met with Newtown's superintendent of schools, Dr. Joseph V. Erardi, and later with Kaitlin Roig, who had made the whole trip possible. She spent the afternoon driving us around town and sharing her powerful story. On the day of the shooting, as the gunman shot his way into the school, Kaitlin rushed all fifteen of her first-grade students into the tiny class bathroom and locked the door. Soon they heard more gunshots ringing out from the adjacent classroom. By hiding her students and telling them, "We have to be absolutely quiet, but it's going to be okay and I love every one of you," Kaitlin saved their lives.

But Kaitlin was so traumatized by the event, by hearing the invader's gunshots and waiting for him to blast through the bathroom door, that when she finally went home the night of the shooting, she told us she wasn't sure if she was alive or dead.

A Newtown parent named Neil Heslin, whose first-grade son,

Jesse, lost his life during the shooting, was not around to talk with us in Connecticut. But he was so interested in meeting Ari that he arranged to see us when we went to New York City after our Newtown visit for a two-day mini vacation (the expenses were on me). Ari was excited to meet Neil and even did her hair in a different style. We sat with Neil in a little deli and he and Ari spoke for about an hour. The story of Neil's son, Jesse, was incredible.

Jesse was an imaginative boy who loved pretending to be a soldier and putting on his uniform, helmet, and boots and regularly marching around the perimeter of his family's property, defending it from bad guys.

The day of the tragedy, Jesse indeed acted heroically—when the shooting started he stood beside his teacher as she closed the door, while the other students huddled in the corner as the teacher told them to do. The gunman opened the door to the classroom and fired at the teacher, killing her. Then he ran out of bullets and had to reload.

Jesse took that brief opportunity to scream at the huddled students to *RUN!*, and because they did, nine more children survived. Jesse charged at the shooter, and that was his final brave action on earth.

Nearly two years after the shooting, Jesse's father, Neil, was still deeply haunted by the events of that day, and in particular by how he had dropped his son off at school that morning not long before the shooting started. The thoughts that haunted him were *Why couldn't I have been later that day? Why didn't I do something differently? Did I pass the shooter in the parking lot? Could I have ended this whole thing before it started? If I'd been just a little later, maybe I would still have my son, Jesse, with me.*

The Girl Who Saw Heaven

After telling us about Jesse, Neil asked Ari about her story and hung on every word. He asked question after question about Heaven, and Ari answered them all in her easy, comforting, matter-of-fact way. (Neil went on to become a passionate and effective advocate for school safety improvements, and on behalf of the victims of school shootings and their families.)

For me, Neil's story was very difficult to hear. I thought of my own two sons, and the hundreds of times I'd dropped them off at school, never once imagining that as I watched them turn a corner and wave goodbye to me, that could be the last time I'd ever see them. Trying to fathom the pain and anguish that Jesse's father felt was impossible, and I worried about how someone as young as Ari was handling his story.

When our meeting with Neil was over, Ari turned to me and, in a tender way, said, "Jesse's dad is the saddest person I've ever met in my whole life. I'm going to pray for him."

While I'd been worried about Ari, Ari was worried about Neil.

Yet again, I was impressed by Ari's capacity for empathy. How could someone so young who'd lost so much be so full of compassion for others who, like her, were suffering?

Of course, I already knew the answer to that.

It was Ari's experience in Heaven that allowed her to be so assured in the face of such darkness. Ari looked at death in a different way than others; in fact, though she missed her parents terribly and had to fight through many moments of anger and sadness, Ari did not even believe that her parents were "dead." She knew precisely where they were, and she understood that she could not be with them—for now.

But she also believed—no, she *knew*—that she would see them again. And as long as Ari was sharing that powerful message with others, Ari was okay. Actually, she was more than okay. She was happy because she was doing what she believed she was meant to do.

On our trip to New York City we met with someone who was taken with Ari's story, and an opportunity arose for Ari to consider turning her little illustrated book about Heaven into an actual published book that would tell a broader account. At first, I wasn't sure that would be in Ari's best interest. I had no doubts about how helpful and healing telling her story was for Ari, and how much it helped other people, but I was afraid she might not be ready to put herself out there in the way that a bigger book might require.

But Ari wouldn't hear it. She wanted the book to happen. We agreed to have another, more formal "meeting" to discuss the matter further, which we designated the "Big Book Meeting."

We scheduled the meeting for the following week at Ari's house, and I said we should all think more about it until then. I reminded Ari that we were only talking about it *maybe* being a *possibility*. That was all it was at that point. The day of that "meeting," Ari invited her best friend, Mary Elizabeth, over to help her decide, and both girls were fully dressed up in their finest dresses and shoes. Ari was showing us how seriously she took the matter (though both girls were so adorably cute, I couldn't help but take about twenty pictures of them, for which they gladly posed).

Once more, I did my best to tell Ari all the possibilities I could think of and to inform her about the possible pitfalls of doing the Big Book, and I assured her we could always do it later on, when she was older. Basically, I did my very best to talk Ari *out* of it.

I should have known better. After all, Ari had put on her power dress for the meeting, and she meant business. She wanted to talk about what we might be able to do with any profits from the Big Book.

"Well, what would you *want* to do with them?" I asked.

"I want to help get clean water to the people we've helped in Kenya," she said. "I know a lot of little kids die there because they don't have clean water."

Susan and I looked at each other as if to say, *Huh?* Neither of us knew where Ari got that idea, and to this day I still don't know. But that was her plan, and she stuck to it, and just like that, we'd moved past deciding whether or not to *write* the book and were already discussing what would happen *after* we wrote the book.

She's good, I thought, somewhat in awe of Ari's decisive spirit (and her negotiating skills). *This child is really good.*

As a courtesy Susan and I sent an email to the court officials involved with Ari's conservatorship to tell them Ari was interested in having a book written and donating the profits to charity.

Just thought we'd let you know, we wrote.

Not long after that, the court contacted Susan.

Apparently, the court had concerns with the idea of a book, and about Ari's plans to keep publicly sharing her story, and they ordered Ari to see a counselor of the court's choosing. Susan was told this counselor would evaluate Ari and make the final decision about whether she could continue to share her Heaven story. I cannot explain why court officials felt this way. The most charitable interpretation is that they truly believed it was harmful to Ari to be talking about the events of April 27 and acted according to those beliefs.

Even if that was true, I was shocked when I heard about their call with Susan. Ari already had a counselor who knew her very well and had seen how fulfilling telling her story was for her, and this counselor had approved *all* of Ari's efforts to share her message, including in the bigger book. Anyone who knew Ari even a little bit could tell how beneficial it had been for her to talk about Heaven. She went from being sad and somber, a shadow of her funny, playful, energetic self, to, in the simplest terms, being herself again. That's how important the story was to Ari. It was nothing less than the linchpin of her grieving and healing process.

And now, a counselor who had never met Ari would decide her future after a single sit-down session? This stranger would decide the proper way for Ari to grieve her loss?

This was the first time I realized how truly disastrous it had been to let go of the conservatorship. Literally any decision involving Ari and her finances was no longer Ari's or Susan's to make. They would always be at the mercy of the court. Decisions would not be made by anyone who actually knew and loved Ari, or by Ari herself—who, as we were aware, had no problem articulating what she believed was in her best interest. But this was the reality of Ari's situation at the moment, and we had no choice but to send her to see the court's counselor.

Susan went with Ari to the counselor's office, which was out of town. Susan was seething inside, but remained stoic. Her role that day was to be with and protect Ari, and to give her all the support she might need.

Before the session began, the counselor turned to Susan.

"You will have to wait outside," he said.

Reluctantly, Susan left Ari with someone she didn't know—a situation Susan knew would make Ari uncomfortable.

The closed-door session was very short, less than twenty minutes. When the door opened Ari stomped out, wearing a grimace Susan knew meant she was mad about something. Ari, I have learned, is a very astute judge of when someone is not being open with her, or not listening to her, and her reaction to that is to shut down and write them off.

"He just asked me some questions and I didn't get to say much at all," Ari later told Susan. "He didn't talk to me or let me talk to him and it just makes me so *mad*."

When the counselor brought Susan into his office to talk—and made a very unsettled Ari wait by herself out in the hallway—the counselor was, according to Susan, just as dismissive with her.

The counselor's decision came a few days later, in the form of a phone call from a court official to Susan.

"The counselor doesn't think it's normal or healthy for Ari to be going around talking about death and dying all the time," he said. "She needs to be doing more normal things that other kids do, like playing softball."

And that was that—the court essentially stopped any further discussion about Ari publicly sharing her story of Heaven. It was not a formal order or directive, but for us, it had the same effect—there was simply too much at stake to go against the court's stated position that Ari talking about Heaven was "not normal or healthy."

Ari was crushed by the decision. I drove to Arab to speak to Ari afterward, and as she talked about it I saw tears in her eyes.

I had almost never seen her cry before.

"Why do I have to have all these lawyers?" she pleaded. "They just mess up my *whole life*! I wish I didn't have *any* lawyers!"

As for me, I wanted to fight for Ari—I was *furious*. When Susan first told me what the court had decided, I called the counselor myself. I wanted an appointment so I could hear his reasoning and ask him what type of evaluation he'd performed on Ari and find out what he knew about early childhood grief. I wanted to know if he'd used a sample group of young, traumatized children who'd lost both their parents to come up with his definition of "normal or healthy" activities.

I wanted to ask, "How did you come to such a consequential conclusion about this little girl's life in only twenty minutes?"

The counselor never returned my calls or emails.

Every instinct in my body told me to keep fighting for Ari, because I knew we were in the right—I knew *we* were the ones with her best interests at heart. But the truth was, there was much more at stake than just Ari's right to share her story.

Up until then, the court officials overseeing Ari's conservancy tended to not communicate very well, if at all, with Susan, as was the case when they tried to sell Ari's house. Susan had also been falsely accused in court of different transgressions on several occasions. From what we could tell, the officials never gave any serious consideration to Ari's wishes or feelings. (In fact, when Ari was twelve and finally came face-to-face with her conservator, he did not even know who she was, even after she told him her name, and then told him that he was her conservator. "I am?" He responded with a blank stare.)

So it was easy for us to envision a similar scenario happening now. If Susan or Ari rebelled against the court's decision, what was to stop the court from accusing Susan of not protecting Ari and removing her guardianship and granting it to the other couple still involved in the matter of Ari's future? It was not that difficult to envision a scenario where Ari might be taken away from Susan, and forced by the court to live elsewhere, and with someone else. That was something we could *not* allow to happen.

After the counselor's decision, Susan and I sat down and had a very serious talk. We agreed there was nothing more important than keeping Ari with Susan. That was what her parents wanted for her, and it was all that really mattered in our eyes. Letting anyone take Ari away from her Nanny would be compounding one unthinkable tragedy with another.

The next decision we made was to shut down any project involving Ari's story. We wouldn't tell anyone we were stopping or explain why—we would simply move on to other things. That was the safest thing to do for Ari, and thus the right thing to do. Still, it was one of the hardest decisions Susan and I ever had to make.

And, as we expected, Ari was angry when we told her the plan. More than angry—*devastated.* We did our best to sit with her and explain why things had to be this way, at least for the current time.

"The lawyers don't think it's the right time for you to worry about a book," we said.

"Stupid lawyers," Ari protested.

"They think it would be better for you to do regular things."

"I already do regular things!"

But even as we spoke the words, we knew we weren't telling Ari the whole truth, because we couldn't.

We could not let her know that our real fear was the possibility of her being taken away from Susan, and that was why we were caving. Not being able to tell Ari the real reasons why we had to stop everything was utterly heartbreaking, and to me it felt like I was lying to her. There were other times when we'd shielded Ari from something to protect her, but this was the first time it felt like we were deliberately deceiving her. And that was a rotten feeling.

Ari's reaction, after getting over the initial anger, was familiar. She was not a crier. She just kind of wadded up and got pouty and withdrew. Ari knew how to disappear into herself when things were bad.

And now, she began to withdraw again.

The upshot of the court's decision was that Ari could no longer share her Heaven story with, really, anyone. Over the next few months she received several invitations to talk to different groups and people. She was even selected for an annual award by a local civic group to honor all the charitable work she'd done with the proceeds of *To Heaven After the Storm*. But Ari was not able to receive that award, nor did she accept any of the other invitations. Susan would not allow her to.

"But the lawyers will never know!" Ari sometimes protested.

The risk, however, was just too great to take.

And then it happened. I watched it happen, a little more every time I visited Ari in Arab. Now that she could no longer talk about Heaven and help people dealing with grief, Ari changed. Her demeanor, her disposition, changed. She slowly became sullen again, and as she grew older, she was occasionally difficult for Susan to handle. The sadness returned. Fundamentally, Ari's personality was transformed.

The joy, the happiness, disappeared.

CHAPTER TWENTY

And I say, "Oh, if only I had wings like a dove, I would fly away
and be at rest. Yes, I would go far away. I would live in the desert. I
would hurry to my safe place, away from the wild wind and storm."

Psalm 55: 6–8

For a long time after April 27, 2011, Ari was terrified of storms.
When she lived with Susan on the chicken farm for more than two
years after the tornado, any hint of severe weather filled her with
panic.

"Nanny, let's go to the shelter! We need to go now!" she'd cry.

There was a small dirt-topped shelter dug into the side of a hill
across the street from Susan's house, but it took on water when it
rained and collected spiders and crickets when it was dry and was
generally a dark, spooky little place. Ari still preferred being in it to
being unprotected, even during storms that weren't nearly as bad
as April 27.

"I always took her to the shelter whenever she asked, always,"
Susan says. "It was scary in there, but I knew that's where she needed
to be."

Ari also panicked when TV news shows or the Weather Channel began their drumbeat of urgent alerts about coming storms. Ari would stay glued to the TV—sometimes all night long—so she could track precisely where a storm was heading and how powerful it would be. She wasn't interested in general predictions: she needed to know *exactly* where a tornado was going to hit.

"I would let her do it," says Susan. "I'd let her stay up all night if that's what she wanted. I knew she needed to know how bad it was going to be. Truth is, I wanted to know, too. I never, ever got panicked around Ari when the weather was bad. I was never like, 'Oh, Lord, we gotta go, here it comes.' Nothing like that. But after everything that happened, I understood why she needed to know, and I wanted to know, too."

The other situation that truly frightened Ari was being caught driving somewhere with Susan when bad weather struck. One evening they were on the way home together after a doctor's visit when the sky darkened and lightning split the sky and a hard rain began crashing down on the car. Ari, seat-belted securely in her back seat, flew into a sustained panic. "She was crying and yelling and saying, 'Nanny, I'm scared, I'm really scared,'" Susan says. "I was afraid I wouldn't be able to keep her in the car, that's how panicked she was."

Susan realized she had to pull over soon, so she drove to her sister, Cindy's, home instead of her own, which was farther away. As they pulled into Cindy's driveway, Susan told Ari, "Sit still and I'll come round and get you." But before she could even fully stop the car, Ari unbuckled herself, shot out of the car, ran to the front door, and banged on it so hard "she beat the screen out of it," Susan says. "Cindy's son, Cad, opened the door and before he could say a word, Ari jumped up in his arms and wrapped her arms and legs around him."

As Cad gently rocked her and Ari slowly stopped crying, she began saying the same thing over and over, in the saddest whisper.

"I just want to see them one more time. Just one more time."

"It was heartbreaking to watch," Susan says. "To me it almost seemed like PTSD."

When Susan told me about Ari's fears, I brought it up with Ari one day just to see if there was any way I could help.

"Ari, maybe this is something you can learn how to let go of and make your life easier, so you don't have to be afraid," I suggested.

"You know what?" Ari said, looking up at me with a serious face. "I think I've earned the right to be afraid of storms."

There wasn't much I could say to that, so I just nodded.

It was Susan and Ari's counselor who, after nearly two years had passed, came up with a way to help Ari conquer her justifiable fears.

Whenever it rained—but without any thunder or lightning— Susan would gather up Ari and her two little cousins AnnaClaire and Addi and help them put on their sweet little raincoats and colorful rain boots, and give each one a tiny umbrella, and take them out to the yard so they could play and frolic and take pictures in the rain. Which they *loved* doing. (Susan, meanwhile, supervised them from the dry safety of the front porch—no sense in her getting drenched, too.) Over time, Ari became more and more comfortable with rainstorms, and eventually with more serious storms as well.

For me, the most beautiful thing was seeing how completely accepting Susan was of Ari's journey and all that it entailed. She was always there to help Ari with anything, and she allowed Ari to feel her feelings and be afraid and she never judged her in any way, and she understood the value of just being there for Ari and letting her work through her fears herself. I got to watch Ari gradually let go of the terror and, with each passing day, heal just a little bit more.

Susan and Ari had a wonderfully accepting and loving relationship. I'd see how Ari looked up at her grandmother and reached up to put her hands in Susan's hair, and I'd see how they sat squeezed together in one chair, quietly there for one another. In this way, they helped each other recover from the events of April 27.

They helped each other find a way to get through the storms.

We all face storms that scare us and sometimes even terrify us, storms we might need help getting through. I think we must all eventually confront the dark specters of death and grief. I have faced my own storms in life. Perhaps the worst one happened when I was in my late twenties and chasing a treasured goal—becoming a mother.

This had been my ultimate and most pressing goal in life since I was *very* young, and one that I'd carefully orchestrated my life around. I'd accomplished all my self-imposed "prerequisite" goals—screenings for immunity to potentially catastrophic diseases, completing my master's degree, moving back home to Alabama, and getting married.

In fact, I married the man I dated in high school, Keith Moses, and we decided to have a child right away. But—despite having already bought a bunch of maternity clothes—it didn't happen. After a time it became clear I would need fertility help to get pregnant. It felt like a long, difficult process, and I prayed a lot about it, and finally I was able to get pregnant.

I was *so* excited. I mean, I really loved being pregnant. And, being the meticulous, list-making person I am, I read loads of books about pregnancy and filled notebooks with daily entries about my baby's growth points and basically threw myself into every detail of having a child. I was tickled that, because of the fertility regiment, I knew the exact date when my baby would finally join us—August 20, 1992.

And I was *elated* when the technician for my midpoint ultrasound allowed me to watch the monitor as she showed me all my baby's major organs and assured me everything was just as it should be. I learned I was having a girl—a child we decided to name Ashley Michelle Moses. After that, I talked to Michelle every day, and I sang the ABCs to her and spelled her name in a singsongy way as I walked in the fields around our house.

Early on the morning of August 19, one day before Michelle's due date, I was getting ready for work when I felt her wake up with a wild start. It wasn't an ordinary movement; it was almost as if something had really scared her and she flung out her arms and legs.

"It's okay, Michelle," I assured her, wrapping my arms around my belly. I felt her relax, and so I got dressed and drove to work.

It was only after I came home from work that evening that I thought, *Gee, Michelle sure has been still today.*

I'd heard that babies can sometimes get very still just before being born, so I was sure that was the case. I started having mild contractions that evening and slept on the couch so I could log the time and length of each contraction. This was my first baby and I was *so* excited thinking she was going to be born on her exact due date.

Early the next morning, August 20, my husband drove me to my doctor's office and waited in the truck while I went inside. I told the receptionist my baby's due date was that day and I was having regular contractions. I also mentioned that I hadn't felt her move in a long while, so I was sure she was ready to be born. The receptionist led me straight to an examining room. A nurse came in and we chattered away as she ran the cold fetal Doppler over my belly. Then the nurse fell silent, and so did I. I couldn't hear the familiar sound of Michelle's heartbeat.

The nurse put the Doppler away and said, "Let me go find Sharon."

I thought: *Someone must have dropped that Doppler and broken it.*

Sharon was the ultrasound operator who had become a friend. She came into the room with an ultrasound machine. She dimmed the lights and smiled at me and started the process, saying nothing. I remember how quiet it was, and I remember some other people quietly slipping into the dark room and standing behind my head. I felt Sharon push down harder on my stomach than she usually did. I tried to sit up so I could see the monitor, but Sharon swiveled it away from me, while someone behind me gently laid me back down and lightly kept their hands on my shoulders and patted me.

"Sharon, can I see the monitor?" I asked.

There was no reply.

"Sharon, please, let me see. You always let me see."

Reluctantly, Sharon turned the monitor so I could see it. We were looking at one of Michelle's organs that I didn't recognize. I thought it might be her bladder and I asked Sharon if it was.

"I'm just looking for any movement at all," Sharon said softly.

At that moment, it hit me.

We weren't looking at my baby's bladder.

We were looking at her heart. And her heart wasn't moving at all.

No movement at all was the thought that appeared over and over in quick succession in my brain. *No movement at all. No movement at all.*

That was the thought that slowly helped me understand the reality of the situation.

Michelle was gone.

I don't even remember what happened next. I remember Keith coming in, and I remember a doctor telling me I did not have to deliver the baby naturally; instead, he could perform a C-section.

"No," I said. "I want to deliver her."

"It will be hard. The baby won't be able to help you."

"That's okay. I want to deliver her."

Keith drove us to the hospital, the same hospital where we'd both been born. As we walked out of the parking deck and across a walkway and down some stairs, a group of people congratulated me. Then another, and another. It took all I had not to burst out crying and tell them my baby was gone. Only after I was in the labor and delivery wing did I lose control and melt to the floor and start sobbing uncontrollably.

The delivery, as the doctor had warned me, was slow and long and horribly difficult. My regular OB came into the room while I was in early labor and told me she would stay there with me to deliver Michelle. She was pregnant, *very* pregnant, in her last trimester, and I knew this was going to be incredibly hard on her. I saw in her face that she took this loss personally. We'd been through so much together and we'd made it nearly to the end. We had come so close.

A nurse stayed with me the entire time I was in the labor and delivery room, the equivalent of *three long shifts* for her. The comfort of her presence, her kindness and soft touch, are wonderful gifts I will never forget, though to my shame I cannot recall her name. She held my hand during the delivery, as I secretly hoped that maybe, *maybe* someone had made a mistake. But they hadn't.

Michelle was delivered on her exact due date, August 20.

She weighed seven pounds, fourteen ounces, and had a headful of dark hair.

During the quiet night that followed I reflected on the fact that I knew the precise instant when Michelle left me and went to Heaven—it was early that morning when I felt her lurch. Yet my overriding thought, the feeling I could not escape, was how unfair it was to get all the way to the due date—*exactly* to the due date—only to find out she was gone. I could not keep her.

What made it even worse was that, at first, there was no obvious cause of death. But late the next day, a doctor stuck his head into my hospital room.

"I've got some good news," he said. "We think we know what killed your baby and we think we can keep it from happening the next time."

Then the doctor walked away.

Good news? I thought. *Really?* I wanted to scream, *Why didn't you know about it* this *time? Why couldn't you stop it from happening* this *time? And what was* it *anyway?*

The death was caused by a Group B streptococcus infection (GBS). Group B strep are bacteria that are generally not harmful, but that can cause deadly infections in some babies as they are being born. The bacteria often lead to meningitis, which can cause an otherwise healthy baby to die or have lifelong disabilities. The presence of GBS is easily detectable by a simple and very inexpensive test, and generally the baby can be protected with amoxicillin given to the mother.

In other words, it is generally easily preventable, and a screening to detect it is very inexpensive.

But at the time, the GBS screening was not administered as a matter of protocol in the United States. The American College of Obstetricians and Gynecologists (ACOG) protocol only recommended the screening as a "best practice." In the large medical practice that cared for me, they did not routinely screen expectant mothers for GBS and instead waited for the presence of several risk factors to screen, a practice I later learned was encouraged by insurance companies. I, like most mothers, did not even know to request the simple twenty-dollar test.

When I learned all this, I was crushed. A simple test and a little amoxicillin could have saved Michelle's life? The thought was almost too horrifying to bear. I struggled with my anger. A great deal of anger. Anger at all the mothers around me who knew about GBS but didn't tell me. I just kept hearing about people and babies impacted by GBS and I kept wondering, *Why didn't somebody tell me?*

And after a few days of continuing my angry internal tirades directed at unknown people who should have told me, I realized that I was now *one of those people.* One of the mothers who knew.

Who needed *me* to tell *them?*

Not long after receiving Michelle's autopsy report, I wrote a letter to the editor of my local paper about Group B strep.

"I wish I had known," I wrote. "I wish I had been given the chance to spend \$20 for the test."

The letter caused a stir in the area, and I was told the local OB-GYN clinic had to hire someone to answer all the questions it was receiving about GBS (to their credit, my clinic implemented routine GBS screenings within a few weeks). I further learned that the American Academy of Pediatrics *wanted* routine screening to become ACOG protocol, because pediatricians were often the ones left with seriously ill newborns after what looked like a healthy birth. A much-loved and respected OB-GYN doctor in a neighboring city eventually explained to me that insurance companies were reluctant to adopt any type of routine screening.

Over the next several months I became heavily involved in the Group B Strep Association and worked with other parents to get ACOG to adopt routine GBS screening as part of their protocol. Around the time I entered this fight, my mother-in-law, Ann Moses, bought me a necklace, and I put Michelle's baby ring, which my grandmother had given me, on the necklace. Then I vowed not to take the necklace off until our side had won—until the screening was standard protocol.

I wore Michelle's baby ring for *four years.*

By the time GBS screening became part of the ACOG protocol and I finally slipped off the necklace, Michelle's little baby ring had been joined by two others. One for each of my beautiful sons, Tyler and Michael.

Years before I ever got pregnant, I'd studied the subject of grief and even presented at several conferences and workshops about it. This background is one of the reasons I was able to step in and help Ari. But back then, before I lost Michelle, my belief that I understood grief was, I would soon learn, a delusion.

The fact was, I knew *about* grief, but I did not *know* grief.

After losing Michelle, for instance, I understood for the first time that grief can be a *physical* experience. At first, grief made me exhausted, drained of energy, very forgetful, and unable to focus on even simple tasks. Then I experienced unusual pain from various sources in my body. My body frequently hurt, for different strange reasons. One day my feet ached so badly I could hardly walk; the next day the pain was gone. For several weeks one of my knees throbbed with terrible pain, though I'd never had knee pain before and an X-ray revealed no injury. I often suffered intense, grueling headaches. Strange things were happening to my body, with no apparent causes. *Grief can't make my body hurt*, I thought. *But I'm not making this pain up, either.*

Another thing I knew nothing about was how long the heavy parts of grief last. Six weeks after losing Michelle, I believed I should have been further along in my healing process than I was, so I went to see a counselor to find out what was wrong with me.

"That is grief," the counselor said. "All you can do is walk through it, and that's what you're doing."

Around this time, I came to another realization at a University of North Alabama football game I attended with my friends, the Browns, six weeks after Michelle's stillbirth (I still hate that word).

On the way to the concessions stand, as Susan Brown and I walked in front of all these people sitting in the bleachers, I realized that, from the outside, not one soul could tell I'd just gone through the worst tragedy of my life. They couldn't tell I'd gone through anything at all. I didn't look like I'd been pregnant, nor did I have a baby strapped to my chest, so there was no evidence of my ordeal at all, and thus no one could tell that something precious and irreplaceable had been stolen from me, damaging me to my core. Outside, everything looked fine. But inside—*total disaster.*

Something inside wanted at least one person in the crowd to look at me and just *know* what I'd been through and acknowledge my grief.

That's when it hit me.

If no one could tell what I was going through, then what didn't I know about *that* person, or *that* person, or anyone who crossed my path? What do any of us know about what the rest of us are carrying? Sometimes we're just not very good about finding out what is really going on with people. We don't like to talk about grief, and instead we usually pretend everything is fine. That's the same as ignoring each other's tragedies, when we could be helping each other get through them.

I was discovering the hard way what grieving was all about.

There was one other thing I struggled with after losing Michelle— the human desire to find a reason for bad things happening. After Michelle died, and I was very public about trying to change the policy regarding Group B strep, people sometimes came up to me and, with every best intention, said something along the lines of "That is why God let this happen to you—so you could do all this work and help other mothers save their children."

I'd always smile and thank them, but inside my reaction was *Really? So if I'd been a lazy person who wasn't interested in helping others, this would have never happened to me? Well, three cheers for being a hard worker!*

Maybe on some level that I can't understand, they were right. I certainly know there is more that I *don't* know than I *do* know about life.

It was these comments that likely led me to have a conversation with God when I got pregnant again the following year.

God, if You let something like that happen to another one of my children, I promise You, I will not do anything to fix anything. Nothing at all. Just so you know, God, I won't do it again. I'll just sit here.

I'm not particularly proud of my tone in that conversation with God, but I've always believed that God is very real and that is why I felt it was okay to talk to God and tell Him, *Don't let that happen to me again.* I think it's okay to get mad at God once in a while because our relationship with Him is a *real* relationship, an *honest* relationship, and in any relationship there are times you're going to get mad. He already knows what you're thinking anyway, so you might as well say it.

And as God blessed me with a healthy baby boy I named Tyler, and two years later another healthy boy named Michael, I had lots of conversations with God to thank Him for watching over us. *And* I apologized for my earlier bad attitude.

I believe in God and I believe that God is good.

And I know that God helps us all make it through our storms.

Before the 2011 tornado, Ari's father, Shane, had plans to pour a long driveway and lay in a walkway leading up to the front door of the new home he was so proudly building for his family. Sadly, he never got to that task and a few others, like moisture-proofing the house and putting up shutters. Most important, Shane envisioned a state-of-the-art storm shelter that never got built. As Ari and Susan prepared to move into the new home, building the shelter became the top priority. At that time, Susan still held the conservatorship and the court had approved the money for building the shelter. It should have been as simple as that.

But it wasn't.

Not long after the approval, the conservatorship changed hands. Susan and Ari moved into Ari's new home right around then, and the court asked Susan to provide estimates for the shelter's construction in Ari's new house. Susan promptly sent them in. But weeks passed, and weeks turned into months, and tornado season came and went without a shelter.

There was no explanation from the steward for the delays, and to this day I don't know why a preapproved project would take so long to happen—over half a year with no progress. This wasn't a request for something frivolous; it was for a storm shelter for a child who just lost her parents in a tornado, and who had been seriously injured by the tornado herself! What could possibly be more important than addressing Ari's fears and helping her find some peace of mind?

Even so, as storms continued to roll into the Arab area with no sign of a new shelter for Ari, and with no existing shelter anywhere nearby, Susan was forced to drive Ari to someone *else's* shelter whenever she got scared by the weather.

After all that waiting, Susan decided she'd had enough.

"There was an off-season sale on storm shelters, and I just called them and said, 'Start building,'" Susan remembers. "I paid for the whole thing with my own money, which I didn't really have much of. But I just got tired of waiting, and I finally said, 'I've got to do this for Ari.'"

Later on, Jimmy Sandlin persuaded the court to reimburse Susan for the shelter.

The unpleasant incident raised a troubling question:

Was this what Ari's future was going to be like? One big struggle?

CHAPTER TWENTY-ONE

When Susan was a young girl growing up in Arab, her mother, Marlene, taught her a lesson that, years later, Susan shared with Ari.

Whenever you feel really sad, think about people who have it worse than you, and ask yourself what you can do to help them.

That spirit of empathy and generosity came to define who Susan is as a person. And now it defines Ari, too.

Exactly three years and two days after the 2011 Super Tornado Outbreak, another series of monster tornadoes ripped through northern Alabama. It was another one of those multistate, multiday weather events that produced wave after wave of heavy hail, flash flooding, powerful winds, and violent tornadoes, and in their wake great damage and suffering.

Tom and I were married in 2012 and were living in a small town just north of Birmingham at the time, and my youngest son, Michael, was living with us while he attended the University of Alabama at Birmingham. We had a storm shelter we'd never used and we didn't expect to use it that day, either—until, in the middle of the night, we heard the storm rumbling in. The sound of it—the *feel* of it—was different, eerier, more intense. We not only scampered down into the shelter, but we all strapped on helmets we'd stored there for just such times. That my teenage son was willing to put on such an uncool helmet showed how serious we thought things were.

The tornado missed our town, but slammed into the town of Kimberly, two miles away. It damaged the fire station and took the whole roof off the Kimberly Church of God and dropped it in the parking lot.

That same day, seventy miles northeast of Birmingham and just past midnight, an EF3 tornado with 150 mph winds touched down near Brow Road, four miles east of Sardis City, in the small valley town of Owens Creek. It lifted a home off its block foundation and set it down about eighty feet away, taking with it most of the home's roof.

At 1:17 a.m., a slightly less intense, shorter-lived tornado touched down on Egypt Road in Boaz, and traveled a two-hundred-yard-wide, six-mile-long path straight through Sardis City, where it downed trees, destroyed a wood barn near Mountainboro Road, and badly damaged several houses.

Susan's brother, Tommy, lived in Sardis City, and his house was torn to shreds. Tommy's son lived close by, too, and his house was severely damaged, but still intact. Thankfully, there were no fatalities in the area, though the four-day 2014 Tornado Outbreak did claim thirty-five lives in the US.

The following morning, Susan called me with a question. She was going to Sardis City to help her brother and nephew with the cleanup, and Ari—then just nine years old—wanted to come along. She didn't just want to go, she *insisted* on going. Susan thought it would be okay and she wanted to know what I thought.

At the time, Ari had not yet conquered her fear of storms and tornadoes, and the presence of bad weather could still cause her to panic. But Susan said Ari did not seem worried or upset by the prospect of walking through rubble and wrecked structures and damaged homes. Susan put the call on speaker so Ari could join in, and I asked her what her thoughts were about going.

"I wasn't able to help clean up after my tornado," she said. "So I want to go with Nanny to help clean up after this one."

I said I agreed with Susan that it was fine, and Ari asked if I could come, too, and we arranged to meet in Sardis City. We also agreed that if any of us wanted to leave at any time for any reason, we'd all leave together. It was a way to give Ari a way out if she needed it.

"I thought it would be a good way for Ari to see what happens *after* a tornado, when people come together and help whoever was affected," Susan says. "To see how a community becomes a family."

I rushed to get there first in case Ari had a bad reaction right out of the car. The damage to Sardis City was severe. The tornado took houses and turned them into hollowed-out wrecks, blowing big planks of wood and building materials everywhere and strewing people's most intimate possessions across hundreds of yards. Family photos, checkbooks, clothes, money, just lying muddy on the ground—entire lives ripped open for all to see. Walking through the sad debris, I was taken aback by just how much of a person's life gets exposed by the destruction: what kinds of magazines they read, the pajamas they wear, all now just debris being picked up by your neighbors. I'd never considered that kind of vulnerability before.

The scene of a tornado is not a pleasant place to be.

And yet Ari was okay. She was somber and quiet the whole time, but she did not cry or ask to leave. One of the first things we saw was the body of a cow impaled on a wooden fence post. We turned away from it, but I think Ari saw it anyway. I would say she bravely carried on, but Ari would hate me using the word *brave* to describe her.

All she did, she would say, was pitch in.

Our job was to drag pieces of debris into different piles—things that could be saved or recycled, precious things to be reclaimed, things to be burned or thrown away. At one point we walked through Tommy's son's fenced-in pasture and picked up stray boards with big construction nails in them so the cows that survived didn't end up stepping on them. I remember Ari dragging a board that was almost bigger than she was into a pile.

What truly amazed and impressed me, though, was watching how people in the town of Sardis City came together that morning. Dozens of friends and relatives and neighbors were there, and things got very organized very quickly. People who'd been through it before knew what to do—send someone for food, have someone bring this or that, figure out what could be sold for scrap metal, raise funds for whatever was needed. People were *not* wandering around crying. That was not the purpose or mood of the day. Everyone was sad and respectful of the tragedy, but at the same time they were there to *work*, to get things *done*. The tornado happened. Homes were destroyed. *Okay, let's get to it.*

In a way, everyone there was doing okay because we were there *together*. They'd survived the tornado, and that was what mattered. Things could be replaced, but not friends or aunts or uncles. One story I heard about the day of the tornado was that Susan's brother, Tommy, and his wife left their home just before the tornado hit so they could check in on Tommy's son. Because they did, they were not in Tommy's home when it was destroyed, most likely sparing their lives.

This was something to be grateful for, not bitter about. So the people of Sardis City *were* grateful for having made it through the storm, and for having each other.

And the people who lost their homes and possessions, people like Tommy—I saw them stand there in the rubble of their lives and just *absorb* all the community's generosity and support and love and be strengthened by it. It was quite a beautiful and touching thing to watch, especially in the face of so much destruction and suffering.

Tornadoes take, but people give.

And Ari was right there with everyone, doing her part. She did not want anyone to take her picture or anything like that; she just wanted to blend in and quietly go about her business. Once again I witnessed her unique poise and fortitude. The more I thought about it, the more I believed Ari had wanted to be there for two reasons.

One was to help people who needed help, as her Nanny had advised her to do.

But the other reason, I believed, was to prove something to herself.

Ari was not going to let the 2011 tornado and its aftermath define her life, nor would she permit her fears to stop her from helping others. Her determination to go to Sardis City was a determination to overcome, in a way, the great burden of everything she'd endured, or at least not let it become something that held her back in life.

Alabamians are known for their hospitality and communal spirit. When something happens to one of us, it happens to all of us. One of the most famous Alabamians ever—the superstar athlete Bo Jackson—proves this point about as well as anyone.

Bo was the eighth of ten children born to Florence Jackson Bond in Bessemer, Alabama, about eighty miles south of Arab, and he went on to win a Heisman Trophy as a running back for our Auburn Tigers. He then became the only athlete *ever* to be named an All-Star in both the National Football League and Major League Baseball, a testament to his incredible drive and athleticism. On top of all that, Bo is also one of the best human beings you'll ever meet, and Alabama is proud of him.

Bo was not in Alabama when the tornadoes crashed through the northern part of the state in 2011, but he watched the TV news reports and immediately knew he had to do something to help. To honor the victims of April 27 and inspire people across the country to lend their neighbors a helping hand, Bo decided in 2012 to mark the first anniversary of the tornadoes by taking a five-day, three-hundred-mile bike ride through some of the devastated towns in northern Alabama, raising funds and meeting survivors along the way.

"I told my wife I was going to ride my bicycle across the state," Bo recalled, "and she looked at me like I had lost my mind . . . *again.*"

Bo's effort became known as Bo Bikes Bama and was a huge success. Bo rode with famous friends like Scottie Pippen and Ken Griffey Jr., but also with regular folks from Pleasant Grove, Cordova, Tuscaloosa, and other towns that suffered grave losses. When Bo and the bikers passed near Arab, Susan took Ari to meet him, and he hugged her and gave her an autographed football.

The next year, 2013, Bo returned for the second annual Bo Bikes Bama in Cordova. He had not forgotten Ari. Bo arranged to meet her again in Birmingham, at a charity auction tied to the bike ride, and this time, my husband, Tom, and I went with Susan and Ari.

I got to watch as Ari gave Bo a copy of her small book, which he warmly thanked her for. But that wasn't all he did. He had a surprise for Ari that he'd cleared with Susan beforehand—presenting her with a brand-new, custom-made pink bicycle, which perfectly matched Ari's pretty pink dress.

After the ceremony and auction ended, a whole bunch of reporters and TV crews gathered inside the media room to ask Bo questions, but he wasn't in any hurry to get to them. Instead, he sat down on a nearby couch and talked with Ari, with his back to all the cameras, reporters, and anxious news anchors. Bo leaned forward so he could talk to Ari at eye level and they had a really sweet, unforced conversation. You could tell they were enjoying talking to each other. At one point they talked about their mothers, who had both passed away and gone to Heaven.

"I bet that right now *my* mother is talking to *your* mother about me talking to *you!*" Bo told Ari.

Ari smiled and nodded, as if to say, *Yeah, I bet that, too.*

The next year, in 2014, Ari rode her new pink bicycle in the third annual Bo Bikes Bama event, which so far has raised more than $2 million for the Alabama Governor's Emergency Relief Fund, leading to the construction of sixty-eight storm shelters, ten warning sirens installed, and over six hundred homes repaired in the state.

As Bo Jackson put it, "I am my brothers' and sisters' keeper."

Ironically, Ari herself was having trouble accessing funds for even the smallest and simplest of needs. I hadn't been fully aware of just how tight things were for Susan and Ari financially until the day I took a drive with both of them. I sat in the back seat and listened as

Susan and Ari spoke casually about different things. At one point, the talk turned to Ari's bedroom.

Ari felt she had outgrown the bright pinks and greens her parents had used to decorate her bedroom. These colors were too "babyish" for her, she decided, and now she wanted to paint the walls a different color.

"Nanny," Ari asked, "when am I gonna have enough money to buy a gallon of paint?"

"Well, we'll have to see about that," Susan replied.

I was shocked. With everything her parents had left her, Ari couldn't afford to buy a gallon of paint or two? It didn't make any sense to me, and when I looked into it later, I went from surprise to anger.

When Susan gave away the conservatorship in 2013, the court took away the $20,000 expense account that had been set up for Ari's care. The court also removed Ari's access to her monthly "orphan" check (from an insurance policy her father had) and the income she received from the farm. This meant she and Susan basically had to survive on the portion of her father Shane's monthly social security check that the steward decided was enough for her, and Susan's modest income as a school aide.

Susan could, of course, petition the court to approve an expense, but by then Susan and Ari realized that getting any funds released usually entailed, at best, a long delay and multiple lawyer fees. I realized it, too, and that's why I told Susan and Ari I would help them update Ari's bedroom. We all got together and walked through the bedroom, which was indeed painted an adorable shade of green with fuchsia pink accents—which Ari kept emphasizing was "a little girl's colors." We talked about what colors might work for Ari and I told her I would soon stop by with some paint samples for her to choose from.

Before I left, I noticed something odd: two thick, dark, maroon-colored velvet curtains blocking the entry to the home's upstairs. It looked like something you might see at a funeral home.

"Why is this here?" I asked Susan.

She explained that, even though Ari's parents had built and furnished a big, whimsical playroom for her upstairs, she and Ari could not afford to heat or cool the second floor and had to block it off to keep the utility bills as low as possible.

The dark curtains were an eye-opener for me. Because of court decisions, Ari often ran up against financial constraints, even though her parents had left her more than enough money to do things like paint her bedroom and heat the second floor. Susan shared another story with me about the wood boards in Ari's living room floor, which were beginning to buckle. Susan hired someone to fix them, but they found a bigger problem—moisture seeping into the house from the basement, the result of Shane not getting the time to finish installing a moisture barrier. Incredibly, Susan withdrew *$11,000* from her own retirement fund, making a significant dent in it, and had the moisture barrier work done. Some family members and friends helped replace the damaged boards.

Ari's loved ones and her community are standing up for her and helping her when she needs help, I thought. *This is what communities do.*

I told Susan we would figure out some way to reclaim Ari's upstairs playroom for her—*and* a way to pay the electric bill.

First, I recruited a small team of helpers—my son Michael and his girlfriend, Sarah, as well as Susan and her brother-in-law, Randy. We ordered plywood and materials and we set aside a full day and we showed up at Ari's home early in the morning with a bunch of supplies. Michael symbolically ripped down the curtains.

We found the upstairs playroom just as Shane and Jennifer had left it—beautifully painted and decorated and filled with toys and stuffed animals. To the left there were little pretend stoves and ovens and pots and pans for Ari and her friends to play with, and against another wall big bookshelves were stuffed with children's books. Everything was perfectly planned and appointed. It was every little girl's dream room.

But in the fall of 2017, as Ari, then nearly a teenager, had pointed out, she was not a little girl anymore, and so this room needed updating, too. Ari decided she was ready to move her bedroom from downstairs, where she was near Susan's bedroom, to the second-floor playroom, which had been her parents' plan all along. So that's what we did: we turned the playroom into Ari's brand-new, big-girl bedroom.

Michael and Randy handled the main construction project—flooring an adjacent attic space that Shane had not finished. When that was done, we moved everything from the playroom into the attic, so Ari could later pick and choose what she still wanted to keep, and what she had outgrown. We decided we didn't want Ari to see us doing it, because, in a way, we were literally dismantling her childhood. So Susan and Sarah took Ari to buy some new pillows and a comforter for her bed.

Then we moved Ari's bed and furniture upstairs and painted her bed frame a wonderful duck-egg blue, which Ari had chosen. Ari, Sarah, and Michael also painted one wall with a special black paint that turned the wall into a floor-to-ceiling chalkboard, where Ari and her friends could write each other little notes and messages.

We decorated her bathroom, set up a well-lit makeup area for her (with a little hanging chandelier), and organized her closet. Susan brought in a really nice acrylic painting of a cow she'd planned to give Ari as a Christmas present, but chose to hang on the wall for her now, since Ari loved cows and pigs and, really, all animals. It was a long day, and it was a typically broiling late-summer day, too, but by the time we were done, Ari had a truly magical new bedroom—just as her parents would have wanted.

You could tell Ari was very, very happy about her new room. She wasn't ecstatic—Ari doesn't quite get ecstatic about anything—but we could all see how important it was for her to have this space for herself, and to have it just the way she wanted it. She had lost control of so many parts of her life, but this would be a safe place for her, a place full of happy memories of her parents, and a place she could continue to make *her own*.

Even so, Susan wondered if Ari—who since the tornado had slept either in Susan's bed with her or, later, in her own downstairs bedroom near to Susan—was ready to move up to the second floor all by herself. But the very day we finished the room, Ari moved in and slept there through the night and never looked back—not even on nights when big noisy storms might have scared her back into Susan's bed.

Ari was right—she wasn't a little girl anymore.

CHAPTER TWENTY-TWO

The courts had instructed that, instead of talking about Heaven, Ari should focus on doing "normal" childhood things, like softball. That implied Ari couldn't do both, which doesn't make much sense. It also showed that the court did not have the slightest idea who Ari was. It didn't take long after Ari returned to school in the fall of 2011 for her to begin to show flashes of her naturally social, outgoing, athletic self. By 2012, she was involved in all kinds of activities. The fear that talking about her experience on April 27 would have somehow steered her toward an *abnormal* childhood was completely unfounded. And it was a huge underestimation of Ari's mind, spirit, and soul.

As it turned out, Ari *did* play softball. But she didn't stop there. Once her physical recovery advanced to a point where she had more mobility, she continued with gymnastics and soccer. As she moved from childhood into adolescence, she also performed ballet, ran track and field, cheered, went hiking and shot trap, attended church, entered beauty pageants, volunteered several hours a week, and took part in technology competitions, among *many* other activities. She showed herself to be an uncommonly gifted athlete, and she routinely won first place in events like running and the long jump. When Ari competed in a state track-and-field event, more seasoned competitors from other schools approached her at the starting line and warned her not to beat them in that day's race, or else.

Ari, not one to shrink from a challenge, whipped them anyway.

The only thing that threatened to hold Ari back was finding the money for all the gear and supplies she needed for her activities. For example, when she was in the seventh grade, Ari was so excited about winning a spot on the cheer squad, which, at least in the South, is a *very* big deal. Cheerleaders have to perform strenuous and sometimes dangerous routines, and hours and hours of practice are required. So is special gear and uniforms that can, to say the least, get expensive. To even be accepted on the cheer squad, Ari needed to buy lightweight, impact-absorbing cheer shoes, which were quite costly.

But the steward denied Susan's request for funds for the gear Ari needed and told Susan that she'd have to save a little bit out of each check until she could afford to buy the "extra" things Ari wanted.

I mentioned this in one of my conversations with Charles Whisenant, who had become a good friend of mine and someone I could occasionally talk to about some of Ari's problems with the court. Charles went through something similar, under tragic circumstances. In 2000, Charles and his wife became the guardians of a five-year-old and a seven-year-old and raised them as their own. Charles had experience with conservators and guardian ad litems and other custody matters, and from time to time he allowed me to pick his brain about court procedures, bounce ideas off him, and otherwise vent about Ari's problems. I felt kind of bad because whenever I called Charles I was generally pretty angry, but he understood why and he always patiently talked me through everything.

At the time, Charles was also the chairman of the Arab Emergency Relief Fund, and he helped raise funds for Ari and other members of the Hallmark family. As I mentioned, he arranged for Ari and Susan to spend two days at the Smoky Mountains in Tennessee. "We wanted to do something to get Ari's mind off things," Charles says. "Afterwards, Ari mailed me a thank-you card that said *Kind Deeds Are Like Little Prayers.* She signed it, *Love, Ari.*" Charles still keeps Ari's note on his desk.

When I told Charles about Ari's difficulty paying for cheer shoes and uniforms, he said, "That's ridiculous," and sounded almost as angry as I was. Then, very quietly, he paid off the entire bill for cheer gear that Susan had been chipping away at. He didn't want it to be a big deal, he just took care of it. I learned he did similar things for a lot of people in Arab, often anonymously. Like I said, that's just what people in Alabama do—in dark times, they help each other get through.

While Ari filled her life with sports and cheering and friends and other "normal" things, she did not block out her experiences on April 27.

She could no longer do what she wanted to do, what she called her "purpose"—sharing her hopeful message with others—but she did continue to write about all the facets of her life, including her time in Heaven. She did not dwell on it, or obsess over it; in fact, in the rare instances when she did mention Heaven, it was in her usual matter-of-fact way, as if she were talking about cheer practice or next week's track meet. But neither did Ari try to erase the events of April 27 from her mind, as if she could have anyway. Ari kept writing down her thoughts in her little notebooks—thoughts about the changing seasons, messages to her parents and memories of her time with them, observations about what she saw in Heaven. It was like she was continually working her way through her feelings.

For about a year or so, when Ari was around twelve years old, she had an especially hard time coping with her situation. Most of her frustration had to do with all the court-imposed restrictions on her freedom, such as rigid, mandated visits with the couple involved in court. She also resented the court's control over seemingly everything in her life. For instance, whenever she and Susan ate out, Susan had to ask waitresses for separate bills so Ari's receipt could be copied and mailed to the court. This not only embarrassed Ari, but served as a constant and unwelcome reminder of the absence of her parents. That the waitresses often seemed confused or irritated by the request didn't help.

"Why do I have to have lawyers?" she would ask. "None of my friends have them. They mess up *everything*."

For the first time, Ari began giving Susan a bit of a hard time. It wasn't too serious—more or less the typical rebellious phase most preteens and teenagers go through—but it was very out of character for Ari. Suddenly she could be snippy and defiant when talking to Susan, or she would answer back smartly or snap over little things.

"What happened to my sweet little Ari?" Susan once asked.

"The lawyers," Ari answered.

Susan was patient and forgiving, up to a point. "We had to have two or three come-to-Jesus talks about her behavior and such," Susan says now. "But it really wasn't that bad. I don't know if not being able to talk about Heaven was the cause of it, but it sure didn't help."

I believe that not being able to share her story, and to help people with that story, had a detrimental effect on Ari. Her Clean Water Kenya project, for instance, had been such an energizing project for her, and she really missed it when it went away. Ari had come out of a truly horrific tragedy, and telling her story was her unique and special way of working through it. Helping others find hope *was* Ari's way of healing—her way of not being swallowed up whole by her grief.

And then it was all taken away.

At the same time, being deprived of the chance to shape her own narrative about her parents did not prevent Ari from having to answer constant questions about them. "What do your mom and dad do?" is a common question kids ask each other when they first meet, and Ari patiently answered it over and over with a standard response.

"My parents can't be with me right now, so I'm staying with my Nanny, and she's a teacher."

Ari was always being reminded that, unlike nearly every other student at school, she did not have a mom or a dad. She would see her classmates' parents show up at track meets and school events, at birthday parties and Sunday lunches, and the pain of not having her own parents there would inevitably resurface. It was an awful lot for a girl her age to have to handle, and it's not surprising she had a hard time of it.

"I kind of lost my way," Ari says now. "Being a girl in junior high is hard enough, and I lost sight of what I was doing with my life. I got to thinking, what is my purpose anymore? And it was probably around that time that, one day, I realized that I had forgotten what my dad's voice sounded like. That was probably one of the hardest and worst things for me—forgetting little things like that about my parents. You never think about stuff like that until you don't have it anymore."

It was, Ari says, "very, *very* frustrating. I could remember everything else about my dad, but I just couldn't remember his voice. So I prayed about it and I said, 'Please tell me what I need to do.'"

About two months later, Ari had a dream.

"Well, it was more of a flashback than a dream," Ari says. "A flashback to the day of the tornado."

In her dream, Ari flashed back to a specific event that happened early in the morning on April 27, 2011.

Ari was still in bed, just waking up, which is when her father usually brought her a glass of chocolate milk. It was one of their many sweet rituals—one of the many small loving things Shane did for his little "princess." But on that day, Ari had a special request.

"Could I have strawberry milk this morning, Dad?" she asked.

It was going to be a busy morning for Shane, with the big storms coming through and farmwork to handle and a million chores still to take care of in the family's new home. As Ari remembers it in her dream, Shane wasn't too happy with the idea of making an extra trip to the store that morning. And yet he did it anyway.

And then, in her dream, Ari heard her daddy's voice.

"You know I love you if I'm going to the store and getting strawberry milk and I've got to be at work in ten minutes," Shane said.

"I can still hear him saying that," Ari says. "I can remember his voice now. The dream was pretty much my dad telling me he loved me."

In this way, Ari's father not only reminded her of what he sounded like, but he also helped her begin to find her way back.

CHAPTER TWENTY-THREE

As the years went on I became more involved with Ari's court battles, trying to hold the steward accountable for what I thought was legal cause to have him removed as conservator, and have Susan reinstated. This was, I believed, the only way to gain back Ari's freedom.

Susan was tangled up in the court battles as well, but dealing with lawyers and trying to fight through the bureaucracy wasn't her strong suit—nor should she have been burdened with it. She had her hands full just trying to raise Ari and get her through school and handle all their finances. As for me, I did have some experience with legal matters, at least as they related to education, and I was happy to learn more so I could help Susan and Ari—without realizing, when I first stepped in, that I'd end up spending literally hundreds and hundreds of hours over the next few years working on Ari's court cases.

One of the stickier issues was the ongoing matter of who, ultimately, would have legal custody of Ari until she turned nineteen. The court forced Ari to maintain a rigid visitation schedule with the couple who petitioned for guardianship and custodianship of her—visits that, Ari had made very clear to the court and to others, she found disruptive. Still, as Ari's official guardian, Susan had full legal custody, but the court, we knew, could always decide to change that arrangement. The court's ability to take Ari away from Susan hung over our heads like a terrible weight that we couldn't afford to let drop. Susan did her best to shield Ari from all these worries and concerns, not wanting her to have to live with the possibility of being taken away.

But Susan could not keep Ari in the dark forever. Eventually, Ari had her own concerns.

In 2016, on the fifth anniversary of the tornado, when Ari was eleven, she asked me a very pointed question.

"What happens to me if Nanny passes away?"

I assured Ari that no matter what happened she would always be okay, that her family and I would always be there to look out for her. But the truth was I didn't know for sure, and that's what I told her.

"I'll find out more," I promised.

Susan told me Ari had never brought up the subject with her. In fact, Susan had changed her will to stipulate that if she passed away, Ari should live with Susan's son Josh and his wife, Mandy, who had the same religious beliefs as Shane and Jennifer and who spent so much time with Ari that their young daughters were like sisters to her. But Susan didn't tell Ari about this provision, because she didn't want her to have to worry about such things.

I contacted a lawyer to learn more about how it all worked. The problem was that, while Susan was Ari's legal guardian, she was not her parent, and under Alabama law she did *not* have the authority to arrange Ari's immediate future for her in the event of her death. The court was obligated to *consider* Susan's wishes, but in the end would not be obligated to follow them. Once again, this left Ari at the court's mercy.

And yet, the lawyer explained to me, there *was* a way Ari could gain the kind of control and security and peace of mind she wanted.

She could have Susan legally adopt her.

This had not been an avenue Ari was interested in pursuing for a long time, because she saw it as a betrayal of the deep and loving bond she shared with her parents. As she often reminded us, her parents were *not* dead, they were just away—as if they'd gone on a long vacation to some faraway beautiful place. They were still her parents, even if they could not be with her right then. Allowing herself to be adopted, therefore, would be giving up something very precious and sacred to her. For many years, adoption was never even brought up.

"When Ari and I finally did talk about it, I was very clear about where I stood," says Susan. "I told her, 'I am not your mother, but I do what your mother would have done for you if she were here. A mother cannot be replaced. You can get someone to come in and do the things a mother does, but that's not the same thing. Jennifer will always be your momma.'"

Over time, Ari came to accept that, if she did go through with the adoption, it would not mean Susan was replacing her parents, but rather, in her own words, "just filling in." No matter what happened going forward, Shane and Jennifer would *always* be her parents, now and forever. That would never change.

Ari was also smart enough to recognize the chance she had to gain some real security for herself by becoming part of a legal family with Susan. If that came to pass, maybe Susan would be able to grant her permission to begin talking about Heaven again. The means to that end were not pleasant, but as Ari had done so many times in her short life, she would just have to square up and get through it.

"After a while, Ari was like, 'We just need to do it,'" Susan says.

Ari asked me to find an adoption lawyer for her, and I ultimately found an attorney named Sam McLure.

Sam practiced in Birmingham, which was some distance from where Ari lived. Which, for us, was a *good* thing—if Sam was able to get the court venue changed to Birmingham, we wouldn't have to deal with the familiar gaggle of court officials we were used to, *and* Sam could keep his fees lower by eliminating his travel expenses. Most of all, if the need arose, we needed a lawyer who would fight hard for Ari with everything they had.

With Sam, we found that kind of fighter.

When Sam was fresh out of law school, he and his wife, Mary Beth, adopted a three-year-old boy, Robi, from the Hungarian foster care system, sparking Sam's interest in the field of adoption and custody law, or what had long been known in Alabama as orphan field law. Sam was particularly motivated by a biblical passage, James 1:27:

Religion that God our Father accepts as pure and faultless is this: to look after orphans and widows in their distress and to keep oneself from being polluted in the world.

"Whenever family deprivation happens, it can lead to children without adequate protections, and people can maneuver in and steal a child's rights," Sam says. "Sometimes adoption is the only way to stop those kinds of assaults, or any kind of assault."

Years earlier, Sam and Mary Beth had also become foster parents and witnessed firsthand the horrific abuse that can befall children at the hands of some of their own family members or others. "Our eyes were really opened to the plight of children in our own country and how much physical and emotional abuse goes on," Sam says. "I had this idea to open an adoption law firm, and I asked other attorneys about it, and the most common response I got was 'Oh, that's sweet, but you'll never make enough money to get by.'" But one attorney, who served as Sam's mentor and was a partner at a huge law firm, recognized the need for such a law firm and also saw the moral imperative motivating Sam.

"He's the one that said, 'Go after this,'" Sam says. "So I did."

Sam called his new business the Adoption Law Firm.

As he explained it to us, in a situation where both of a child's parents pass away, the adoption process essentially turns the child into a new legal person with a new birth certificate. I know that sounds strange, but that is basically what happens—the adopted child will have a new, legal parent, creating a completely different set of circumstances for them. For instance, in Ari's case, having Susan legally adopt her would "make moot"—or completely wipe out—any custody or visitation policies put in place by a prior family court.

An adoption would mean that Ari's custody, at least, would no longer be at the mercy of the courts.

We arranged for Sam and Ari to meet so that she could approve of him and consent to going forward. Sam is a very kind and calm man, and a devout, heartfelt Christian, and he and Ari hit it off right away. They didn't talk about the case or anything like that, but Sam did make a promise to Ari to kind of seal the deal.

"Tell you what," Sam said, "if we win this case, I will walk down the whole sidewalk outside the courthouse on my hands."

I remember Ari looking up at me with a funny little smile as if to say, *Is this guy for real?*

In any case, we did seal the deal, and Susan took money from her retirement account—once again—and hired Sam, who agreed to keep his expenses as low as possible. Ari was on board. Sam was on board. Our team was in place. If it came to it, we were ready to fight.

Sam believed we had a strong argument, mostly because of the extremely close relationship between Ari and Susan. "Legally, it was a no-brainer," Sam says. "The court looks at who has the strongest relationship with the child, and Ari had been with Susan for six years, or basically half her life. That was very important."

The key to our case, Sam said, was changing the venue of Ari's adoption. "It was critical that we do that," he says. "At that point, Jefferson County [about eighty miles south of Arab] was welcoming cases from other counties and had the legal authority to take over the case. Ari and Susan just needed a break from the courts they'd been assigned to."

The most frightening unknown was whether or not any of Ari's other relatives would step forward and, for whatever reason, object to the adoption. "The only thing anyone could contest was if Ari having her grandmother become her legal mother was in Ari's best interest," Sam says. "I believe that would have been a futile argument to make, but you can never say for sure."

For that reason, we were legally obligated to make public notice of our court petition to have Susan adopt Ari, and specifically to mail notice to the couple that had petitioned the court for guardianship and custodianship of Ari. Then we had to get through a period of thirty days for anyone to respond to the petition. Sam filed all the necessary paperwork, and a hearing was set for May 18, 2017.

After that, all we could do was wait.

The waiting was achingly difficult.

CHAPTER TWENTY-FOUR

Three weeks before the hearing—and on the very day of the six-year anniversary of the passing of Ari's parents—something disturbing happened on the property where Ari and Susan lived.

They left their home together that morning, as usual, to drive to school. Later on, after school, they drove back home and pulled onto the property. As soon as they did, they saw it.

Long stands of old trees on each side of the twelve-acre property's borders had been chewed up and destroyed, leaving only mounds of dirt and mangled tree limbs.

"What?!" Ari yelled when she saw the damage. "It looks like a tornado hit my trees!"

It was true. Someone had used heavy equipment, probably a bulldozer, to plow through the long row of mature trees and tall shrubbery on both borders of Ari's land, and the debris looked eerily like the aftermath of the April 27 tornado. Many of the trees were completely down, but some had battered, torn-up trunks, and a slew of older trees had thick broken branches that dangled dangerously overhead. The wreckage was ugly and dangerous, and no attempt had been made to hide it or clean it up.

Ari and Susan, understandably, were taken aback. They walked across the field to get a better look, with Ari's dogs trotting behind them, but they didn't stay for long—it was all too upsetting.

"I will find out who did this," Susan told Ari. It was all she could think of to say.

"Ari used to play in those woods when she was young and she loved them," Susan says. "There was a little stream that ran through and filled up when it rained, and Ari and her cousin Lilly would take stuff in there and make a little playhouse or have a picnic. It was Ari's special place. And when we saw what happened from the road, we were like, 'What the heck? What happened to our trees?'"

Susan told me about the damage, and two days later I walked Ari's property and took pictures of everything. When Ari ran out to greet me she said, "Somebody made all my trees look like a tornado hit them." I warned her to stay away from the trees until we'd somehow cleared all the thick dangling limbs and debris. When Susan and I talked about it alone, Susan said she had called the sheriff, who told her the courts should handle it.

"We can't do anything because no one saw who did it," the sheriff explained.

Meanwhile, the courts told Susan the *sheriff* should handle it.

Susan kept pushing the sheriff while she did her own sleuthing, asking the road commission if anyone had applied to drive heavy equipment on the road that day. We both conceded that it could have been a coincidence that the damage was done precisely when Susan and Ari were away at the school, and precisely on the anniversary of the death of Ari's parents. But if it hadn't been a coincidence, the question neither of us could answer was:

What kind of person would do such a thing?

The entire summer passed with no answers and no cleanup. The deeply gouged holes in the woods collected water and drew mosquitoes, making it nearly impossible for Susan and Ari to be outside for long. The debris also attracted armadillos, who often met their match in Ari's dogs and got dragged out to rot in the sun, creating a terrible stench. Thick, ugly grass and weeds sprouted everywhere. It was a real mess.

Yet the usual problem persisted. Even with a reasonable offer from a contractor to clear the trees and debris and level the land, getting the steward to release any of Ari's money became a hopeless endeavor.

And, as usual, Susan got tired of waiting.

After trying for more than a year to get help, Susan drove to the local Walmart and bought a small chain saw for about $200 of her own money. "I'd never used one before," she says, "but I'd seen them used enough times." On her own, Susan went down to what remained of the woods and began clearing away thick branches and cutting through long tree trunks. She drove her little John Deere mower with a wagon attached, and she filled the wagon with debris and dumped it in an open part of the field and burned it when the pile got too big.

Then she'd start over and do it all again.

"Took me a while," Susan says, "but I probably cut through half an acre of tree parts and got them all in a pile and burned them."

In fact, it took Susan the better part of *four years*.

CHAPTER TWENTY-FIVE

The end of the thirty-day waiting period came and went, and even though Susan and I had fretted about it the whole time, in the end no one contested Ari's adoption.

I think we were all elated by that, but neither Susan nor I were ready to accept that the threat had passed. My fear was that someone could still simply show up at the hearing and disrupt everything, though I never shared that fear with Susan because I didn't want to make her any more anxious than she already was. Meanwhile, Susan was worried about the same thing.

As for Ari, she was preoccupied by something else. The day of the hearing, she was set to be inducted into the Beta Club at Arab Junior High. Getting into the club was by invitation only and limited to students with a B average and at least 17.5 hours of community service per semester. That day Ari would receive a special pin during the induction ceremony, capping what would be a very high honor for any student. But because of the hearing Ari would miss the ceremony, and she was worried she might miss the cheer practice that followed, too. This was Ari's first year as a cheerleader and the next day would be the first football game she ever cheered at. When it comes to cheering in the South, absences from practices are simply *not* okay, and missing one meant you'd likely have to spend the first quarter of the game up in the stands away from the squad, and no one wanted that.

The morning of May 18, 2017, my husband, Tom, and I met Ari, Susan, and Sam McLure at the historic Jefferson County Courthouse in Bessemer. Sam's law clerk excitedly told us this was her first adoption case. The hearing would be held in probate court, the part of the court devoted to wills, estates, conservatorships, and guardianships. In the dark brown wood-paneled courtroom, we were introduced to the presiding judge, Elizabeth North, a friendly blond woman in an elegant leopard-print blouse and black sweater. She seemed calm and attentive, and she had a lot of energy, even though this was her twelfth hearing of the morning. Sam assured us she was a fair and serious jurist and that she had already reviewed our case.

"She's always very tuned in to the weight of what she's presiding over," he said. "She's also a very nice person."

Sam further assured us this was technically an uncontested hearing, meaning it was too late for anyone to challenge the adoption. But as I said, Susan and I were shell-shocked from years of battling in the courts, and there was no way we'd let down our guards until the adoption was finalized, and maybe not even then.

For both of us, things just seemed to be going *too* smoothly.

The hearing opened with Judge North sitting down near us and not in her elevated judge's chair, which I found comforting. "I am a little bit less formal," the judge explained. "Especially when it involves kids. We just sit right here. The only time I go up there is when I'm going to argue about something. Everything else, I just sit down here."

Judge North asked Susan to describe the circumstances that had led to the hearing, and Susan took her through the story from the beginning, starting with the tornado and Ari's five days in the hospital and how Susan was with Ari all five days except for when she ran home to get some fresh clothes. The judge then spoke directly to Ari and asked her a few questions.

"Ari, tell me how many pets you have."

"I have, uh, four dogs," Ari said sheepishly.

"Four dogs? And do *you* take care of them?"

"Well, yeah, most of the time."

"She does pretty good," Susan confirmed.

The judge asked Susan about Ari's involvement in the community. "She goes to church," Susan said. "She's involved in gymnastics. She's a great gymnast. She loves to do that . . . she's done it ever since she was two years old. The coaches have told her that if she keeps it up that she will have a free ride to almost any college. She's done a lot of different sports since she's lived with me: softball, soccer, track. But gymnastics is what she really likes to do. *And* she just made cheerleader this year, too."

"Congratulations," the judge said, smiling at Ari.

"She's supposed to be inducted into the Beta Club today, but she decided to come here instead," Susan said, prompting some laughter in the courtroom. "This was more important."

"Will you still get a pin?" Judge North asked Ari.

"I will," Ari said.

"Well, sorry about you missing it."

Every few minutes throughout the hearing I'd steal a quick look at the rear entrance door to the courtroom. It hadn't opened yet.

"Are you ready to take this on?" the judge asked Susan. "The driving aspect? The learner's permit?"

"I've had three children," Susan said.

Judge North nodded. "So you know."

Turning to Ari, she said, "So this is what you want, too, right?"

Emphatically, Ari said, "Yes."

"You can't go back," the judge said to Susan. "She's yours forever, right?"

She turned to Ari and said, "She's yours forever, too, right?"

Susan and Ari were all smiles and nods.

"Y'all are going forward in motion," the judge went on. "Getting ready for all these exciting times. Ari, it sounds like you're going to be very busy *and* successful."

Ari lit up and smiled some more.

"Do you have anything else I need to know?" Judge North asked Sam. "We've covered all the bases?"

Sam told her that they had.

"Okay, then," the judge said. "I need the paperwork to get a new birth certificate. And I need to sign all these papers."

Part of me couldn't believe we'd progressed so quickly to this point—to finalizing the adoption. I took a deep breath and stole another glance at the entrance door.

"We've discussed this and Ari doesn't really want to change her name," Susan told the judge. "She wants to keep her name."

"Okay, so she is Arianna Hallmark."

"Yes, she had a wonderful daddy and she wants to stay a Hallmark. She is proud to be a Hallmark."

"Okay, that's perfect. Arianna Marlene Hallmark is her name."

Judge North signed the birth certificate and faced Ari.

"Okay, I signed it," she said. "This makes you official! And now you can get your picture taken up there in my big chair."

Ari giggled at the idea, but Judge North was serious. She motioned for Ari to go ahead and climb up behind the imposing judge's bench and into the imposing judge's chair.

"*Really*," the judge insisted. "Go on up there and make yourself comfortable. I've got a lot of papers to sign."

Ari made her way to the bench and hopped in the chair. The smile on her face was a mile wide. Out of the corner of my eye I saw Sam packing up his briefcase. *Could this really be the end of it?* I thought. *Did we actually win this time?*

Then the judge told Susan to go on up to the bench, and so Susan climbed up and sat down next to Ari. As soon as she did, Ari and Susan instinctively leaned toward each other and touched their heads together, an unconscious display of their closeness. They'd both been hurt so badly, and they'd both endured so much to get to this point. But somehow they had made it, together. And now my husband, Tom, snapped the photo I'd been waiting for—the first photo of Ari and Susan's new legal family.

Watching Ari in those moments, she seemed just a little bit lighter and brighter, as if a burden had been lifted, which it had. I can't say the moments after Judge North finalized the adoption were a celebration, because they weren't. It was, if anything, another somber occasion for Ari, who struggled so mightily with the decision to be adopted, and probably still wished she hadn't had to make it. It was not a time for a big party. But it *was* a moment in which we could all feel a bit of relief and comfort. There would be no more court-ordered visitations (only visits that Ari wanted) and no doubts about where Ari belonged.

As the judge said, she was Susan's, and Susan was hers.

"Do you like being on that side of things?" the judge asked Ari, looking up at her in the big chair.

"Oh, yes, ma'am," Ari said.

"Well, you look so official up there!"

"She does," I said to the judge. "She has that look, doesn't she? Like she could *do* this."

"Ari, you might grow up to be a judge," Sam told her.

"That's right, absolutely," said Judge North. "Ari, what do you think you want to do when you grow up?"

"Well, I'm not sure," Ari said, "but I think I'd either like to be a nurse or a lawyer."

The judge looked up at Ari.

"You can be both," she said. "I know several people who are."

Finally, Judge North thanked us all for coming and wished Ari well going forward. The hearing was officially over.

But Ari had one final bit of important business she had to handle.

"Will I need a school excuse?" she asked Nanny.

Ari was still anxious about missing school, not being at her Beta Club ceremony, and possibly missing cheer as well.

Judge North smiled, sat down, and wrote Ari an official excuse.

"I'm sorry you missed it," the judge said. "There will be other awards for you."

Outside the courtroom Ari accepted hugs and congratulations from everyone and finally gave her evaluation of the hearing.

"That wasn't bad," she said simply.

Coming from Ari, that was a lot. She just wasn't one to get too effusive about anything. Even so, I'm sure it wasn't lost on her that this time it was Ari who, quite literally, got to sit in the judge's chair.

This time, it was her wishes that mattered *most*.

We all posed for more pictures on the steps of the old court-house building while I held the manila folder with Ari's signed adoption papers tightly in my hand. Now there was only one more thing to do.

Sam McLure took off his jacket, rolled up his sleeves, tucked his tie in his shirt, and expertly walked along Third Avenue North on his hands. Ari giggled, Susan laughed, and Tom and I cheered while I videotaped the whole thing.

"I guess I was doing too much CrossFit in those days," Sam says now. "But, you know, I was just so happy for Ari."

CHAPTER TWENTY-SIX

By the time children are three or four years old they're capable of telling all kinds of stories, about themselves, or other people, or things they've seen or even things they may imagine when they're playing. And when most children are six or seven, they are no longer primitive storytellers but rather wonderfully expressive narrators of their own lives.

When Ari was six, she told the most unforgettable story I ever heard.

I've worked with so many children and I've seen how they begin to shape their views of themselves and the world through storytelling. I've also learned that children are very free and nonjudgmental about sharing stories of their experiences—they don't censor themselves, they accept the things that happen to and around them, and they relate these things with wonderful candor and directness (ask any kindergarten teacher). This childhood perspective changes as kids get older, and as adults we tell stories in entirely different ways and for very different reasons. The value of a young child's story, therefore, is in the purity and innocence of the storytelling—qualities that we lose all too soon.

This is why I believe that Ari's perspective of Heaven, and the way she has been so open, honest, and consistent in sharing it, is so useful to us. As Jesus says in Matthew 19:14 (NIV), "Let the little children come to me, and do not hinder them, for the kingdom of heaven belongs to such as these."

Ari has always shared her story in a very pure way. Even before the tornado, when she was five and being tormented by dreams of her parents dying, Ari told her story without worrying what other people would think.

All Ari could do, all she *knew* to do, was tell the truth about what she was thinking and experiencing. That's what children do.

She did the same thing after the tornado, starting in the hospital. There, she expressed the unthinkable pain she felt about losing her parents the only way she could—by screaming out. No words, just sounds, the only expression of her feelings she could summon. That, too, is something you will see young children do. They can get very frustrated when they don't find the right words to convey what's bothering them, and sometimes they release that frustration by screaming.

One of Ari's first interpretations of what happened to her also reflects a common childlike perspective. She spoke about how she and her family had "been so close"—so close to her mother being done with nursing school and becoming a nurse, so close to the fun family vacation they had planned and talked about and looked forward to, so close to the long summer in their new house. Getting that close, and having it all taken away from her, was, as Ari put it, simply "not fair." Children have a built-in sense of what is fair and what is not fair, and they are never shy about telling you when they get an unfair shake. Ari's reaction was normal, honest, and age-appropriate. Whatever else Ari's tragedy might have been, it was indisputably unfair.

Young children also often share unpleasant feelings and experiences that require higher vocabulary skills in ways that make it easier for them to talk about. When Ari first told me her full Heaven story over the course of several weeks at the school, she did not tell it in a linear way—instead, she hopped all over the place. It was a very free-form approach that depended on whatever was on her mind that day. She might begin by saying, *Look at my new white shoes!* and then talk about something a teacher told her, before sandwiching in something about her bad dreams or the tornado or her time in Heaven.

In this way, Ari took something that was impossibly difficult to talk about and shared it in a way she could tolerate. She took the hard things and mixed them up with the easy things. And yet she didn't leave anything out or avoid the painful parts—there was nothing about her experience Ari wouldn't talk about. In fact, I noticed she never showed any signs of distress when talking about the tornado, even the parts about her cousins' dog, Pepper, being locked out of the bathroom or her memory of being alone in the tornado with the doomed cows flying through the air all around her.

As long as Ari got to tell her story *her* way, she was okay. This, too, is a very common and appropriate facet of childhood storytelling. Children know what they want to express and they know how they want to express it. What they share may not be linear or orderly or even instantly decipherable. But in my experience, it is usually honest.

What's more, I've noticed that a child's recollection of an experience tends to feature more small and specific details than those of an adult. In one of Ari's first sketches, she drew the TV set she and her parents watched storm coverage on, with what looked like the word *VISA* written along the bottom of the TV. I asked her what "VISA" meant and she looked at me with pity and patience and said, "That's *VIZIO*. It's a Vizio TV." In fact, my own TV at home was a Vizio, too, but I'd just never paid any attention to it. Ari similarly recalled the indentation marks her father's glasses made on his nose that *weren't* there in Heaven, and the precise length of the dresses women in Heaven wear.

Children's recollections of experiences also tend to include far more pure *wonderment* than most adults can muster.

This wonderment reflects an early childhood perspective and is driven by *curiosity* and *inquisitive thinking*. Ari wondered if the stairs she traveled back to earth on with her angel were the same ones she watched her family go up. She wondered if maybe each family has their own set of stairs, and she wondered why the two angels were posted at each side of the huge doors to Heaven. When a child notices something that surprises or excites or baffles them, they can go on and on about it *forever*. Sadly, we lose our sense of childlike wonderment far too soon.

Only in the wonderful world of children would an angel in flight be described as looking "like he was standing up, but flying, too, not on his belly or anything." Had I experienced what Ari did in 2011, I surely would have described this detail and others in completely different ways, filtered through my adult experiences and perspective—and you would have *never* had as clear an understanding of the angel's flight as Ari's "belly" comment provided.

Ari's way of telling her story was pure and true to her frame of reference, which, to me, lends it more authority and credibility.

It's one of the reasons I've never doubted for a moment that Ari's Heaven story is not about a dream or a vision, but rather about an experience—something she *did* and *saw* and *felt* in a very *real* place.

∽∾∽

While the court took away Ari's ability to share her story of Heaven, they did not—and never could—take away her will to tell it.

"I think she *always* wanted to share her story," says Susan. "She really believes she can help people with it. She's *seen* it help people. But then these people didn't want her to talk about it, even though I believe it was her personal right to tell it. Even if she was a child, why shouldn't she speak her truth? Why would they try so hard to stop her?"

Most weeks Ari and Susan went to Old Brashiers Chapel Church on Kenmore Road in Arab for Sunday service. On occasion, Ari would see Susan stand up and share her testimony. Susan believed that giving her testimony was a part of standing as a witness of God, as well as a chance for God to use her testimony to help others and possibly change lives.

"I raised three kids and I went through a lot of things and sometimes we do things and we learn they're not the right things to do," Susan explains. "Then you feel the guilt and shame, and if you're a Christian you want to set things right and get back on track. I have testified about mistakes I've made, about my husband, about my journey to resurrection, and Ari would hear me do it."

Then one day, out of nowhere, Ari turned to Susan and said, "Nanny, I want to give my testimony, too."

"Do it," Susan said without hesitation. "Don't worry about it, just do it."

At the time Ari was part of the youth group at Old Brashiers, a nondenominational church that dates back to 1899. Every Wednesday evening a dozen or so teenagers gathered in the church's fellowship hall to hang out and talk about their lives and their relationships with God. Ari decided she wanted to schedule a Wednesday night to give her own testimony about her parents, her struggles, and her time in Heaven.

Susan called to ask me what I thought about Ari giving her testimony. Was there a risk in Ari talking about Heaven in the presumably safe haven of her church youth group? Susan didn't think it was too risky, and neither did I, but of course we couldn't know for sure. This would be Ari's first time telling her story to an assembled group since the court admonished Susan about letting Ari do something they deemed abnormal and unhealthy. But to deny Ari the chance to talk to her peers about what she went through—in a house of God, no less—seemed utterly ridiculous. I truly felt there was no way Susan and I should try to keep Ari from doing this. We agreed that if Ari wanted to do it, she should.

Ari chose the youth group as the place for her first Heaven talk in nearly four years because the kids in the group were all kids she knew well. It was about as comfortable a place for Ari to give her talk as there could be. Going in, she had only one condition—she didn't want Susan or me or any adult other than Pastor Josh and his wife, Mandy, to be there. This was Ari's moment, not anyone else's, and she wanted it to be just for her and her friends.

So it was that Josh drove Ari, Mandy, and their daughters, Anna-Claire and Addi, to the youth group the evening of Ari's testimony. That night, when Josh brought Ari back home, Susan pulled him aside.

"How'd she do?" Susan asked.

"Pretty good," Josh said in his typically succinct way.

And that was it. That's all we ever learned about Ari's testimony. That, and something Susan noticed about Ari right away.

"She was happy," Susan says.

Later in 2018, when Ari was thirteen, Arab's longtime veterinarian, Dr. J. Michael Brown, offered Ari the chance to tell her story again.

Dr. Brown is a kind of local hero in Arab. He took over the Arab Veterinary Hospital in 1983, even before he graduated from Auburn University, and he's been there ever since, helping care for thousands of beloved pets in his nearly forty years on duty. I knew Dr. Brown in the early 1990s, when my former husband and I owned a horse-breeding farm and Dr. Brown was our vet. There were many, many late nights during the winter and early spring months when he would make the ninety-minute drive to Florence to help us with our breeding operation and our stallions, colts, and mares. When I got pregnant for the first time, with Michelle, his wife, Susan, and I could sometimes convince Dr. Brown to use the ultrasound machine for horses on my belly to give us a little sneak peek at Michelle.

When I lost Michelle late in the summer of 1992, I lay in my hospital bed that night, wide-awake in the dark room at 2:00 a.m., distraught and confused and feeling just miserable. Suddenly, a nurse came in and said, "Um, there's a Dr. Brown and his nurse to see you?"

I smiled. I knew it was my friends Michael and his wife, Susan, who announced themselves as medical professionals just to be sure they'd be allowed to come in and sit with me. At that moment, they were angels from Heaven, lifting me up from the darkest depths. The

Browns stayed and talked with me until the sun came up, and it felt so good to be able to share with them some of the things that happened.

Who knew that the doctor I needed most that night was a veterinarian? But that's just the kind of people the Browns are.

Dr. Brown had been good friends with Susan and her husband, Mike, and he'd been particularly close to Shane Hallmark. Shane was in junior high school when he was stricken with alopecia and lost all his hair, and, as teenagers can be, the boys at school were really hard on him. They'd sneak up behind him and knock his cap off and run away with it, laughing. Things got so bad that Shane quit school altogether and began looking for a job.

It was Dr. Brown who immediately hired Shane to work for him as a handyman at Arab Veterinary Hospital.

Dr. Brown and his family were in Arab on April 27, 2011, when the Super Tornado Outbreak tore through the Ruth community. They hid out in their basement shelter (which was very close to the path of the tornado) and, throughout the long day, opened the shelter to dozens of neighbors and friends. Four years later, when some nearby property came up for sale, Dr. Brown saw the chance to fulfill a dream he'd had since the 2011 tornado. He bought a building on North Brindlee Mountain Parkway, added a roughly one-thousand-square-foot basement at the south end and turned it into a state-of-the-art storm shelter, with a bathroom, running water, a telephone, and TV and internet service. The basement was constructed to withstand an EF5 tornado, with enough space and seating for about thirty people.

What made the shelter truly distinctive, though, was that it had enough space and kennels to accommodate thirty pets as well.

Dr. Brown dedicated the shelter to the memory of Shane and

Jennifer and the others who died in Arab on April 27, and he decided to call it the "Hallmark Safe House."

The shelter opened unofficially during a frightening storm in March 2018, and quickly filled up with twenty-six people. "Those twenty-six people," says Dr. Brown, "brought along *thirty-six different animals.*"

Dr. Brown then asked Ari if she'd like to give a speech at the shelter's official opening and dedication on April 8, 2018.

Ari wanted to do it. Actually, she *insisted* on doing it.

By then, Ari's adoption had been final for nearly a year. Even so, we were hesitant. The courts were still in charge of so much of Ari's life and we could not be sure of what they might do if they perceived Susan was disregarding their admonition about Ari speaking. The invitation from Dr. Brown came some months after Ari gave her testimony at Old Brashiers Church. This time, however, she wouldn't be addressing just a dozen or so friends in a youth group; her speech would be for thirty or forty people from her community. What would happen if Ari's court-appointed supervisors discovered she was out there talking about Heaven?

Was this too big a risk for us to take?

At the time, Ari was close to turning fourteen, and, after her father reassured her in a dream, she began to seek a louder voice in determining her future. If the court had any issues with her talking about Heaven, Ari wanted to have her own voice in court. And she had a plan. In the state of Alabama, turning fourteen grants you additional rights as a minor. The courts generally give higher levels of consideration to the wishes of a fourteen-year-old. Ari was aware of this and, though she hadn't yet had to attend a court hearing, she felt it was time for her to begin speaking up for herself.

"I want my own lawyer," she told us one day.

She'd had more than her fill of lawyers, that was for sure, and she had certainly spent a lot of the money her parents left her paying a lot of different lawyers, but as long as they were going to play such a big part in her life, Ari felt she ought to have one who *she* picked out and who truly listened to her.

Susan and I talked it over, and before we signed off on the speech, I called an attorney named M. Chad Smith.

Chad was a small-town general practice attorney out of Tuscumbia, Alabama, the birthplace of Helen Keller. He handled child custody, divorce, domestic relations, and criminal matters, and he came recommended by my son Michael. I thought Chad might be able to help us win Ari the freedom to tell her story. I first went to see Chad weeks earlier, and as I waited for him in his outer office, I surveyed the room for any indication of what kind of guy he was. It's something I always do when I meet someone new, because I believe you can learn a lot about someone from their office and bookcases and walls.

Chad, for instance, worked out of an old historic home, which, despite its historic architecture, had a warm, cozy feeling and was set up in an informal way. He had pictures hanging everywhere of his wife and children, as well as several awards and photos that showed he was an avid outdoorsman. There was football memorabilia, too—Chad had been a player and was a big fan of the Alabama Crimson Tide. He belonged to the Fellowship of Christian Athletes, and I also noticed a commendation from a civic group, which showed he was community-minded as well.

So far, so good.

Then Chad walked in, and he was this big, stocky, linebacker-type guy, but he also had the sweetest, most boyish smile, and he wore trendy leather loafers, but without any socks, and his hair was just slightly mussed, all of which confirmed for me that he wasn't the pretentious sort. We sat down and I filled Chad in on the basics of Ari's story and gave him three binders with all the relevant documents.

"I promised Lisa I would look them over," remembers Chad. "That night I did and then I went to bed and I couldn't sleep. I couldn't stop thinking about what Ari was going through."

The next time I spoke with Chad, and before he agreed to come on board, I gave him an exit ramp.

"I've got to give you fair warning," I told him. "This is the kind of case that, if you get involved, will really suck you all the way in. Believe me, I know."

That didn't scare him away, and after Ari met Chad herself and liked him, he became Ari's lawyer.

Chad believed the court's prohibition on Ari sharing her Heaven story had no legal basis.

"It's illegal," Chad said firmly. "They can't enforce it. Ari, you talk about Heaven all you want to!"

Chad's confidence certainly made us feel better, and it was the decisive factor. Ari wanted to give her speech so badly, and we felt she was old enough and smart enough to make that decision. Perhaps if Susan and I believed we were going against our best judgment by letting her talk, or violating an actual court order, we'd have reacted differently. I was still worried the court might use the speech to confront Susan and make matters harder for them. But after hearing from Chad, and in light of the thoughtful plan Ari had devised for herself, we all agreed it was worth the risk. Ari accepted Dr. Brown's invitation.

She was ready to get back to her purpose.

I helped Ari create a PowerPoint presentation to introduce her story before her talk, showing photos of all the charity work she'd done over the years and her drawings of her time in Heaven. On the day of her talk, a fresh spring day, Tom and I met Susan and Ari in Arab and we all went down into the storm shelter for the dedication. Tom set up the technical parts and Susan laid out her scrapbooks and Ari's treasure boxes. If Ari was the least bit nervous, I couldn't tell. Ari and I sat on stools in the front of the shelter, while somewhere around forty people filed in and found places to sit or stand. There was a bit of formality to the event; it was, after all, a dedication of something that resulted from a very tragic event. I checked again to see how Ari was doing, and to me she looked as cool as ever.

Dr. Brown said a few words before we ran the PowerPoint presentation. Then it was Ari's turn. The packed basement shelter fell stone-silent as Ari, still this tiny little thing at thirteen years old, got up from her stool and stood in front of the crowd. I scanned her face yet again to see if she was uncomfortable in any way, but, once again, she just wasn't. She was poised and ready.

"I guess most of y'all have heard about my story," she began in her clear, strong voice and her twangy Southern accent, "but I'm here tonight to tell you about it *myself*."

What happened next was both ordinary and remarkable.

Ari stood in front of her community and shared her story for twenty minutes. It wasn't really a speech, it was more like her sitting down with a friend and telling them something that happened to her. Ari didn't rush through it, nor did she go slow. She never stumbled or lost her place or had trouble with a thought or a word. She just told her story.

After she was done, Ari stayed where she was as everyone in the shelter lined up patiently to say hello and meet her. I watched Ari as she spoke with every last person in line, and her poise was something to see. She looked everyone dead in the eye and engaged easily with them all, answering their questions about Heaven or just accepting their well wishes. And I watched the people's faces, too, as they spoke with Ari—people who likely had lost loved ones of their own, people who'd survived the 2011 tornado, good people of faith and charity, and what I saw in their faces was *gratitude*. As if they were saying:

Thank you, Ari. We needed that. We needed to see you're doing okay. We needed to hear your story of hope.

And as I sat slightly behind Ari watching the whole event unfold, I had a strange sensation myself.

I thought: *If I was Ari's age I don't think I could have done what she just did. I wouldn't have had her confidence or her authority, the way she was so straightforward with everyone. The way she was so calm and comfortable in that spot. I'm looking at someone who is wise—wiser than me in some unique way. I'm in awe of her.*

CHAPTER TWENTY-SEVEN

After her talk at the storm shelter, and another talk to a Bible study group, Ari let us know she was ready to give another speech at an even bigger venue.

I wasn't surprised. I'd watched Ari be filled with purpose and energy as she was finally able to share her story again. Ari had been right all along—people *did* want to hear her story, and she *could* help them by telling it. Ari's recovery from the tornado was their recovery, too, and hearing her speak so confidently about God and Heaven gave them strength in their own lives and struggles. Ari herself never doubted the power of her experience. I knew as I listened to her speak in the shelter that, if she wished to keep going, I would do anything I could to help her.

I told Ari I would keep my eyes open for just the right speaking engagement for her. This was in the time of COVID, which slowed things down, but eventually a wonderful opportunity found us.

It involved a very dear friend of mine, a pastor and licensed counselor named Tom Phillips (I usually referred to him as Dr. Tom). I first met him several years after my divorce, when my sons and I volunteered to help gather and distribute coats and Christmas presents for families in need as part of the Bethlehem Project, Dr. Tom's annual initiative through his New Beginning Church in Florence. Dr. Tom became a good friend and a kind of sounding board for me as I tried to help Ari through the aftermath of the tornado, and help Susan through the endless court issues. He was the person I called as soon as I hung up with Susan on the day Ari was screaming in the hospital. Even though he protested, I insisted on paying Dr. Tom for his time so I would feel comfortable asking him if the advice I was giving Susan and Ari was solid. "Is this the right thing to say?" I'd ask. Having someone I trusted counsel me like this was a true saving grace.

One day in 2021, Dr. Tom called me with an idea. He knew that Ari was intent on telling her story again, and in front of a bigger crowd, and he suggested she tell it at New Beginning as part of the church's annual kickoff dinner for the 2021 Bethlehem Project. So far, Ari had formally told her story to her youth group, a Bible study group, and forty people in a storm shelter. The dinner would be different. There would be more than a hundred people there, nearly all of them strangers to Ari. She would be all alone on a big stage with a microphone, in a city she wasn't familiar with. Everything about this speech would be new for Ari.

At the same time I believed New Beginning was a safe, comfortable space for Ari to continue her journey as a speaker. And, as I said, I completely trusted Dr. Tom. Susan and I brought the invitation to Ari who, predictably, jumped at the chance.

"That would be *great!*" she said.

The dinner was set for October 6, 2021.

Four days before Ari's speech, something foreboding happened.

Bad weather rolled into Alabama.

First there were rain showers, on and off, but mostly on. The previous months had been unusually rainy in the state, so more precipitation was not a welcome thing. The more water that stored up in soil and drains, the likelier flooding became. The rain showers gave way to heavy rains, and then to torrential rains, and then to severe thunderstorms. A steady procession of ominous weather forecasts continued for four days, leading up to the worst forecasts of all, for the later parts of October 6. The meteorologist James Spann predicted "strong thunderstorms across Alabama" and "a risk of severe storms across northern Alabama through the evening." Reports came in about heavy rains and the possibility of severe flash flooding.

The National Weather Service issued a tornado watch.

And all this fierce weather would be ratcheting up to its peak force just where Ari was set to be, just when she would be there—the town of Florence in northern Alabama, the night of October 6.

On the morning of October 6, Ari woke up, went to school, and had cheer practice, like any other school day. Afterward, she ran home and got dressed for her speech. There wasn't much preparation she needed to do. For her previous speeches Ari wrote some notes on a piece of paper, but she said she didn't want any notes for the charity dinner. She preferred to just get up and talk about what happened.

Ari, however, was very specific about what she wanted to wear that night. She wasn't a little girl anymore—she was sixteen now—and she wanted to dress more professionally. So she bought an elegant plaid blazer that she wore with jeans and high-heeled sandals, for a more formal but not overly serious look.

As for me, I went the opposite way. The venue was casual, so instead of one of my typical business outfits, I opted for a long vintage sage-green pleated skirt with brown sandals and an oversized white sweater. I was going for chic and casual, but my son Tyler said I looked like Jenny from *Forrest Gump*.

All day long, I worried about the weather. What if the ominous forecasts aimed right at Florence kept most people home and no one turned out for Ari's talk? What if they all showed up and the storm hit and trapped us all inside? Or what if too many people showed up and we stranded some of them outside in the heavy rain?

And what about Ari? Would she be okay? Would her drive into this potentially horrible storm, and the possibility of another tornado, remind her too much of April 27?

I unspooled a few unpleasant scenarios in my head before forcing myself to stop thinking about it. I will say that Ari herself did not seem worried about the storm *at all*.

That evening, Ari's new boyfriend, Trevor, a very nice young man, drove Ari and Susan from Arab to Florence, about a ninety-minute drive, in his roomy and sturdy pickup, just in case the roads got bad. Meanwhile, I drove to the church a couple of hours before the dinner to make sure everything was good to go. The event would be held in a large sanctuary room in which everything was moveable— chairs, tables, a stage. I noticed that extra chairs were stacked up in the back of the sanctuary, and extra dinner tables were set up in the entry area outside the big room. This meant they were planning on an overflow crowd. Apparently, a lot of people really wanted to hear Ari's story.

The sanctuary itself was filled with long tables covered in black tablecloths. In the front there was a stage with a drum kit and other instruments and amps, angled so that everyone in the room could clearly see it. The presentation following dinner had been planned down to the second, so Ari knew she had exactly eighteen minutes to share her story. I told her I would stand in the back of the sanctuary and hold up five fingers to indicate five minutes left, then three, then one.

The sanctuary began to fill with people. So far, the rains had held off and no one seemed too concerned about a storm. When Ari, Susan, and Trevor showed up, I led Ari and Trevor to an inner office, where they could wait while the crowd had dinner. Tom, my son Tyler, Susan, and some friends sat at a table in the front of the sanctuary. I looked for signs that Ari might be nervous, but there were none. She was cool and relaxed and joking with Trevor, waiting for her cue to get up onstage. Meanwhile, I was *very* nervous, both because this was a big, important coming-out party for Ari, but also because the microphones and technology involved in her speech were more complex than anything we'd done before.

And, of course, there was still the threat of a tornado.

Before Ari's speech, there were indeed technological glitches, but I told myself everything would be fine. It was around 8:25 p.m., and it was raining steadily in Florence, but the big storms had passed us by. Ari was set to go up onstage any minute.

Ironically, at that very moment, the worst weather of all was unfolding ninety miles away—right over Ari's hometown of Arab.

A massive swath of high pressure produced torrential rain and thunderstorms and unusually heavy rains in Marshall County. Some areas reported anywhere from five to ten inches of rainfall on October 6 alone, mostly from the evening storms.

The National Weather Service issued a flash flood emergency in the Arab area. The unrelenting rains created powerful, sudden runoffs that flooded roads, saturated homes, and stranded dozens of people in treacherous situations. A shopping center and a Piggly Wiggly in Escambia County were completely flooded. Police and fire departments mobilized to rescue twenty people trapped in their cars on the road and another eighty people caught in their rapidly filling homes. Raging currents of churning water submerged cars and blocked access to emergency services. Pedestrians waded perilously in waist-deep water.

Tragedy was not far behind.

In the town of Hoover, south of Arab, a young couple drove down a hill in their SUV in the Riverchase residential development, unaware that two lakes swollen with rainwater had merged into a single torrent, flooding Riverchase Parkway West and literally sweeping their SUV away. The vehicle went over a guardrail and flipped upside down into a creek, killing both passengers, each just twenty-three years old.

And in Arab, firefighters came to the rescue of a woman and a child clinging onto tree branches from atop their minivan, which had been washed off the road and into a creek. They were saved— but what one rescue worker called "the extreme conditions of the water" prevented firefighters from getting inside the minivan and saving the life of the four-year-old girl still strapped into her car seat.

Not too far away, on New Friendship Road in Union Grove—the very road where Susan, Ari, Josh, and Mandy have their chicken farm—heavy flooding trapped an eighteen-year-old woman in her car. Rescuers recovered her body the following day.

Arab, no stranger to tragedy, had lost some of its own again. Bad storms came, and bad storms would always come to this small town, and other towns and other states—that was the lay of the land. And the people of Arab, as they always did, would find solace in the Lord.

"For in the day of trouble He will keep me safe in His dwelling," it says in Psalms 27:5. "He will hide me in the shelter of His sacred tent and set me high upon a rock."

And as the worst of the rains pummeled Arab at 8:28 p.m. on October 6, ninety miles away in Florence I went onstage at the New Beginning Church and introduced Ari, who calmly came up, smiled at me, and took the microphone.

This was it. This was what we had all fought for—Ari's right to talk about Heaven, to share her experience, to let others benefit from what she went through. To testify to what she had seen and heard. This time, and for the first time, in front of complete strangers.

As Ari took her place on the stage, this little warrior who lost so much but kept her faith, my heart swelled with pride.

She was the one who simply refused to stop.

CHAPTER TWENTY-EIGHT

Wednesday, October 6, 2021
New Beginning Church
Florence, Alabama

I was six years old when this happened to me and my family. I had the perfect family. I was the only child. My mom and dad had trouble having me and they finally did, so I was their everything. I guess they were both wrapped around my little finger and I got everything I wanted. I was a total daddy's girl. You could not—*not*—keep me away from my daddy. So, I lived the life. That's all I ever knew, was my parents. As a young child, I learned that's not all you have in this life.

I was about five when I started having dreams. I just randomly had a dream one night that my parents died. That's not normal, some would say. So I went to kindergarten. I had tons of friends in my kindergarten class and I loved school. I loved going to school . . . until I didn't because of the dreams. I wanted to be home. My parents didn't understand why. I didn't tell them right off the bat that I was having these dreams . . . because . . . why would I do that?

So, at six years old, here I was, crying *every* day in kindergarten and no one understood why. I didn't even really understand why, either. Because, most of the time, you don't believe what you dream, but, for some reason . . . *I knew.*

It wasn't like any other dream I'd had before. I just *knew* that something was gonna happen. So I told everybody at school that my parents were going to die and that I simply just needed to go home. To know that they were okay and so that I could spend every waking minute with them. That's what I wanted to do. I guess I thought that, as a six-year-old, I could protect them somehow.

I did not understand why I couldn't go home and be with them. I sat down with my counselor at school. She gave me a dream catcher and told me: "If one of your parents dies, the other will take care of you." I told her, "No, you don't understand. I'm going to be here alone."

So at school I would spill milk on myself so that my dad would have to bring me clothes, so I could see him—so I could know he was okay. I would gag myself and throw up everywhere so I could go home.

My parents promised me that if I stopped crying at school, that they would take me to the Smokies, which is my favorite place on earth. I love it so much. So, I was like, "Okay, it's a deal." At this point, we didn't have much school left and I was like, "Okay, we can do this."

And then . . . April 27 happened.

As a kid, I didn't really understand tornadoes or anything like that. On Tuesday nights, every Tuesday night, me and my mom and dad would go to Huntsville to the movies and watch a movie and eat at Chili's. That was my mom's favorite place to eat, Chili's. And as we drove I always watched out for car wrecks. That made me super, super nervous that we would have one. But it made me feel better that I was *there*, so at least I could be with them if it happened. I wasn't worried about dying. I was worried about being left here by myself. That's so selfish, but, as a kid, you don't know.

So, April 27 rolled around and I went to school just like it was any other day. My mom was actually taking her final nursing exam early that morning. We got out of school and I was staying with my grandmother, and my dad was at our farm and he was hooking up generators and stuff like that in case power outages occurred, so we wouldn't lose any chickens.

It was probably about one o'clock that my mom and my dad took me home from school. We had moved into our new house ten days earlier, so my mom was trying to get pictures hung up and everything else. She was running around like a chicken with her head cut off, which was actually pretty typical.

My dad had mentioned that the weather was gonna get bad. It wasn't just like a threat anymore. It was *going* to get bad. So we had our little plan made out. We would get in the bathroom. At this point, I was not worried. I was like, "Okay, we're here. We're all together. Life's gonna be okay." Until it was probably about three o'clock, and my dad was trying to call my grandmother, his mom. And she never answered. So, as a man, he decided it was best that he go check on his mom and his niece and nephew, my cousins. They were seventeen months old. And when he said he was going, I pitched a little fit. You know, it just didn't make sense in my mind. "Why? Why would we go? Why would we leave home? We were safe here. Why would we leave?"

I *almost* had my mom convinced to stay home with me. Because, you know, that didn't make sense. But it's not what happened. So we all drove to my grandparents, who lived about three minutes away, at the most, from our house. On the way there we saw the tornado, in their backyard. And at this point, it was too late to turn around.

I can remember, we were getting out of the truck and, uh . . . you know, I was still okay, because I knew that we were all here *together.*

And I remember my mom dropped her phone and she was panicking, trying to pick it up, and I grabbed her and I was like, "Let's go!" It was all a mess. We had no idea what was about to go down. And we got in the house, literally just in time to be in the house, before . . . windows started breaking out and, uh, we were in the middle of the house, in a tiny bathroom, with no windows. There were nine of us in there. Next thing I know, windows are breaking out.

And I could hear doors falling in and, uh, I was sitting in my dad's lap. I was like facing his chest and I had my arms and legs wrapped around him. I don't remember a whole lot after that, but somewhere in between everything that happened I got to watch my family enter into Heaven.

What I saw was, I was in the middle of this field, and it was almost like a flashback that was happening right then. And I was in this field, and there was this *huge* staircase that was just never ending. There was not an end to it whatsoever. Even if you looked all the way to the top from the bottom, you couldn't see the top.

And I saw my angel. And people always ask, what did the angel look like. So it's not like a he or she type of deal. All I can say is that the angel was *beautiful,* like *so* beautiful . . . and like no model that you've ever seen here on this earth. It doesn't compare. The angel was *extremely* tall, way, way taller than anyone I've ever met on earth. It's strange and it's hard to describe them, because there's not really anything or anyone to compare them to here on earth.

So I was with my angel, and, you know, I didn't question my angel.

It's like I just knew what was going on. And at this point, I did not know that I was not dead. And I guess that's kind of strange to say, but I didn't. I just thought that this was where I was *supposed* to be.

And in Heaven it's not like you're standing there having a conversation. It's just like an understanding, like . . . you kind of know what they are saying and you understand it. You don't have questions, you don't emphasize anything, really, you just *understand* what you are supposed to do. And that's that.

And then I saw my dad. And my dad—he had a disease. It's called alopecia. He lost his hair when he was about thirteen or fourteen years old. So he had no hair *at all*. I'd never known him with hair. And all of a sudden in Heaven I got to see him with hair! I was *amazed*! I was like, "Where's your bald head?" And my dad always wore these thick, thick glasses and they always sat on his nose, in the same spot, and he would have indentions after he would wear his glasses all day long. I mean I never saw him without his glasses, and now I got to see him with no glasses and the indentations were gone, too.

And I saw my Paw Paw Mike. So, my Nanny, her husband passed away when I was about eighteen months old, maybe a little younger, so I never knew him really. I had heard a lot about him. I'd never even really seen many pictures of him, his pictures weren't just displayed around the house or anything like that. It was a very devastating thing when he died. So, my mom talked about him a whole lot, but I never heard a ton about him from my grandmother or anything. And in Heaven, I saw my mom just go up to him and hug him and I automatically knew that that was my Paw Paw Mike and this was who I had been hearing about. And he was so excited to see my mom! It was something so special and I'm so glad I got to see that, really.

My Paw Paw did not look old. In Heaven nobody looks old. Even if you die really old, you don't look old. It's just amazing.

People always ask me what people look like in Heaven. So, it's not like you look like your full body. But you're not like a *spirit*, either. I know your spirit goes to Heaven, that's understood, but it's not like you're a little ghost walking around everywhere. But it's not like you're in your same full body, either. It's like everybody just has the same young look, but you know who everyone is. In Heaven, everyone is equal and no one is judgy. And I think that's something that's really special and it would be a whole lot easier if that's how things were on earth as well! Everybody is just . . . In Heaven, we're all just the same.

And then we all just went up the stairs. I have no idea how long it took, but it seemed like in no time at all we were all at the top of the staircase, and there were these *huge* gates that opened into Heaven. And my family, they weren't confused. But *I* was confused. Because I got to watch my family go into Heaven, but for some reason I wasn't *with* them. I was away from them and I didn't understand why and it was almost like I wasn't allowed past a certain point. I just got to see in.

And what I saw . . . I saw streets of *gold*. And I say "gold," but the light that is in Heaven—it would *blind* you here. There is *no* light like it here on earth. And afterward, when I was in the hospital, drawing what I saw in Heaven, I was very frustrated because I had this little twelve-pack of Crayola crayons and they were *not* doing the job! And I was like, "Somebody has got to go get me some more crayons, 'cause this ain't it!" And they were like, "All they've got is a twenty-four-pack," and I was like, "Well, this ain't it!" There are *no* colors to describe what is in Heaven! There are *none*. Like, you can go and you can buy the *biggest* set of Crayola markers and they wouldn't do it justice. In Heaven, the colors are just *different.*

And I also saw all these magnificent houses. This is something that will always stick with me, no matter how many years go by—that my dad, he *loved* to build houses. I lived in three or four different houses within my little life span of them being here. He would build a house, sell a house. Build a house, sell a house, and on and on.

And in Heaven, my dad asked Jesus if there was anything that he could do. And Jesus told him he could build houses.

That's when I asked my angel, "Can I go in?" But then I understood that it was not my time to be here yet. That I had to go—I had to go back to where I was before. I didn't really understand that—why they got to stay, and they didn't say goodbye to me or anything like that. And that is one thing that I did *not* understand in Heaven—why I was not getting paid *any* attention whatsoever. I didn't like it, and I didn't understand it. But later on, as I got older, I realized—in Heaven, everyone is living their best lives! They aren't worried about anything on this earth, because they are in the best place that they can possibly be and they have *no* worries *whatsoever!* It makes more sense when you read a little bit more in the Bible about Heaven. Because *everybody* is happy in Heaven.

I get this one question a lot, and it's a good question—what was Jesus like? And what I can say is, He looks a little bit like some of the pictures you see of Him. Like the most common picture of Him, with the thorn crown on his head and the blood coming down, that's a little bit like what He looked like. But his facial structure— it's not like something you could draw. It's *so* unexplainable. And how *beautiful* Jesus is . . . like truly, *truly* beautiful. So the pictures are close, but not quite.

Okay, so, as a six-year-old, losing five of your immediate family members is something really, really hard to deal with. And to accept. It's hard for *anyone.* And I didn't really understand death. No one had ever died in my family that I was all that close to. My great-grandparents had died, but you know, it was time for them to go. They were very, very old and I understood that.

So I believe that God sent me those dreams to prepare me for what was going to happen. And because I *knew* something was gonna happen, eventually I was okay with it. And now I can say I am so, so thankful that I had these dreams, and that I had this experience of seeing my family enter Heaven. Because it took me the *longest* time to really accept that my parents were not here. I can remember even until I was about nine years old—and I never really shared this with a ton of people—but I did *not* believe that my parents were dead. I did not attend their funeral, so I never got to see them put into the ground, and I just didn't believe they were dead. I didn't. I'd watched them go through those doors in Heaven and I couldn't follow them, so in my mind it was like they had gone on vacation and left me behind!

Grief is a very strange, strange thing. I can remember that I was so angry for the longest time. I had a punching bag out in our garage, and I would just go to the garage and I would beat it. I really would. And it made me feel better. And then I would say my prayers every night and I would tell Jesus, "If I could just be there with them, I'd be okay." But over time, I was okay anyway. I mean, I got to see my family go into Heaven. What else could I ask for?

So now, I have made it my mission to share with as many people as I can that, just because you've lost someone, regardless of how you lost them, you are going to see them again. They are *not* hurting. They are okay, even *without* seeing you. And through me experiencing this, I have a lot of knowledge and a lot of wisdom that maybe most people don't, at least when it comes to a loved one dying. And talking about it now, it's something that I really, really enjoy doing now. Getting to help people, helping them to understand that everybody is happy in Heaven!

And I also tell them that you are going to be okay, too, and you are still here on this earth for a reason. I am still here for a reason. I'm sixteen, so I'm still figuring it out, a little bit at a time, day by day.

But I'll keep figuring it out, and it's taken me a long time to really be able to fully understand myself and embrace who I am. It has never bothered me to talk about these things, to talk about Heaven, at all.

It's just *who I am.*

CHAPTER TWENTY-NINE

After Ari finished her talk, we had fifteen minutes for members of the audience to ask her questions. Ari always loved that part. At first, people were a little shy about discussing the events of April 27 with her, but quickly Ari put everyone at ease. "There's not anything that I mind talking about," she said. "Go ahead, ask me anything."

After that, Dr. Tom said a closing prayer and Ari stood in a back corner of the sanctuary so anyone who wished to could stop by and say hello. We set the limit on the meet-and-greet portion of the evening to thirty minutes, explaining that Ari had school in the morning. Beforehand, I'd asked a technician to play a particular song as people were gathering to meet Ari. It was "This Is the Stuff," sung by Francesca Battistelli—Jennifer Hallmark's favorite song.

> *I lost my keys in the great unknown*
> *And call me please, 'cause I can't find my phone*
> *This is the stuff that drives me crazy*
> *This is the stuff that's getting to me lately*
> *In the middle of my little mess*
> *I forget how big I'm blest.*

I expected they'd play the song once and move on with the playlist I'd given them, but instead they played it on a loop the whole time Ari greeted people. At first I got irritated, before realizing the irony of that—I thought, *This is the stuff that drives me crazy* when I should have been thinking, *The important thing is the blessing of Ari graciously greeting all these people!* There was something beautifully appropriate about hearing Jennifer's favorite song nonstop as Ari shared her hopeful outlook with everyone. I just knew that up in Heaven, Shane and Jennifer were extremely proud of their daughter that night—and that hopefully Jennifer was rocking out a bit to the song she loved.

I also believe that Ari, Susan, and Trevor were protected as they drove back to Arab that night, into the worst of the storm, and were guided safely around flooded roads and downed power lines until they all made it home, hours later than expected, but, most important, safe.

Ari's poise and power as a speaker at New Beginning Church did not surprise me, but it did impress me all over again. It is not an easy thing to get up on a big stage all alone and tell a compelling story for eighteen minutes, and keep a hundred people hanging on your words, *with no notes*, but I had the feeling Ari could have gone on for another hour if she'd had the chance. The best way to explain it is to say that Ari looked like she was *precisely* where she belonged.

As Ari herself said that night, sharing her story of Heaven with others—doing what she can to *help* others—is just *who she is*.

I had a very distinct impression watching Ari that night, different from the awe I felt after her talk in the storm shelter.

My thought that night in Florence was—*Ari is going to be okay.*

CHAPTER THIRTY

The day I met Ari Hallmark back in May 2011, my life changed. It will never be the same again.

Ari and her story of Heaven taught me many valuable lessons and gave me a new perspective of so many things, that I am truly a different person than I was before we met. These are not specific things that Ari told me or taught me, because Ari never lectures anyone about anything—that is not her way. These are simply things I learned from being around Ari, and hearing her story, and watching how she acted. I could fill five hundred more pages writing about these lessons, and how life-changing they can be, but for now I would love to briefly share some of them with you here.

1.) Ari helped me learn that Jesus is always with us and that we are protected by angels in this life on earth.

I think of Ari's dreams before the tornado, and how some might consider them nightmares. But they weren't nightmares as we know them, with scary monsters or scary scenarios in them. In fact, they weren't even really dreams. As Ari describes them, they were more of a *voice*, soft and caring, helping prepare her for what was coming. The experience of the dreams did not frighten

Ari; it was the thought of what was going to happen—the thought of being left alone—that terrified her. And she carried the heavy, heavy weight of believing she could somehow stop what was going to happen to her parents—somehow save them by being with them—for six long months. But what lasted well beyond the tragedy was the *meaning* that Ari drew from that always soft, always caring voice:

We are never alone. We are always being looked after, loved, and protected.

2.) I now believe that our perspective of death—this thing we dread so much and that brings us so much pain—is simply not correct.

From Ari's perspective, and now mine, death is more of an instantaneous and truly beautiful transition than an ending. Here on earth we might see death as horrible and gruesome and unfair and painful, but what Ari witnessed—right in the midst of the terror and devastation of the tornado—was her parents going up to Heaven *in the blink of an eye.* There was no waiting period, no sustained suffering, just her family walking into a place that was beautiful and peaceful and indescribably *perfect*—sort of like the best vacation destination you could ever possibly imagine. A place with no worry, no anxiety, no judgment, no anger, nothing at all that isn't more beautiful than words can convey.

Ari's perspective of death changed with her experience on April 27, and it is impossible to be around her without sensing the peace and comfort and confidence this new perspective brought her. If you met her, you would see it is undeniable. I am lucky I got to know Ari, and her story changed my perspective of death as well. But what if all of us had this new and beautiful perspective? What would our lives be like then?

3.) Ari taught me that eternity is not necessarily something that is remote or far away, but rather something that is very *close*.

Ari talks about how the golden streets in Heaven look like they have mirrored lights coming off them. Ever since I heard that story, I have not been able to look at the sun reflecting on water in the same way. When I watched a sunrise at the top of Makapu'u Point in Oahu, Hawaii, it was Ari's description that ran through my mind. Now *all* I can see are beautiful mirrored lights shimmering on the surface of water—and this makes me believe that our lives on earth are connected and even intertwined with eternity. That eternity is reflected, for instance, in the beauty and glory of nature, in simple things like lakes and trees and hills. If we look around, I think we will find a *lot* of things that connect us to the idea of a blissful eternity. So the lesson I've drawn is to *pay more attention to the things around us that remind us of the things that are important and eternal.*

4.) Ari's experience made me realize that I know very little of what there is to know about existence.

Ari said something simple on the first day I met her, at the visitation for her parents, that I went on to spend many, many hours thinking about, and that I still think about. She said, "My parents can't be with me right now." At first, I thought, *What did she mean by that? That's not how we talk about death.*

But the more I've thought about it, the more I realized that *I have an almost complete lack of knowledge of how life works.* No matter what I've studied and learned so far, there is a nearly infinite amount of knowledge that remains out of my grasp. And it was Ari's simple explanation of her parents' death that made me realize how little I actually know. So the best thing I can do, and what I've started doing, is *to be less dogmatic and stay wide open to the everyday miracles of life,* because there is so much more we can all learn about the reality of existence.

5.) Another beautiful thing that Ari's story taught me is that we are all still deeply connected to the people we love who pass away.

Ari's parents and grandparents in Heaven were not sad about passing or worried about what came next. They were entirely at peace with and accepting of the process they were undergoing. Why? Because they understood that their connection to us isn't affected by time or space or dimension—they understood the bonds that connect us *endure* after our physical deaths. I've come to think of it the way I think of my two grown sons. They may be living in other states, and I may miss them, but I know where they are and I will see them again. The separation does not fundamentally alter our relationship. Even when they are away, they remain very much a part of who I am. Maybe death is something like that—evidence of how unbreakable our bonds of love really are.

6.) Sometimes, if our hearts are pure, we do the right thing, even if we don't know that we're doing it. It was Ari's parents who taught me this.

During the months that Ari had dreams of her parents dying, Shane and Jennifer never stopped comforting and reassuring her. They told Ari things like *We're not going to leave you* and *We'll always be a family* and *You'll always be our little girl.* And while they were mainly trying to assure Ari they wouldn't die, in the end everything they told her was absolutely correct. They promised never to desert Ari and they never did; they just went to another place where, as Ari says, she will join them soon enough. They promised they'd always be a family and they still are, in every meaningful way.

I now see Ari's dreams as the opportunity for her to grieve the loss of her parents *with her parents still there to hold her, and to help her grieve.* Think about what a precious blessing that is! And though they didn't quite understand what they were telling her, Shane and Jennifer did everything they should have done during a grieving process—they sat with Ari and listened to her and loved and comforted her.

They told her she'd always be their little girl—and if there's one thing in all the world that Ari knows is true, it is that she will *always* be Shane and Jennifer's little girl.

7.) Ari taught me that sometimes the most awful things in our lives are mixed up with the very best things in our lives.

Think of Ari's full experience on April 27. In a way, the tornado actually *ended* the devastating shock and fear and anguish that her dreams introduced to her life. What she saw in Heaven changed her perspective of everything that had come before, and that perspective would never change back to the one that brought her so much anguish. In the same instant on April 27, the worst thing that will probably ever happen to Ari was also the most *comforting* experience she will likely ever have in this life. Since then, I have been more aware of how events that strike us as terrible and hurtful can, at the same time, be nurturing and positive experiences—the best and the worst intertwined.

8.) This lesson may sound simple, but is actually quite profound— *pay more attention to your blessings here on earth.*

Another way to put this is *appreciate the people in your life.* I mean, *really* appreciate them. Think of their lives and their situations and all the things that may be affecting them. Early on after April 27,

Ari went through a lot of really difficult emotions: grief, fear, loneliness, anger, resentment. What I learned is that these emotions derived from the basic frustration of Ari's life—she could not have the thing she wanted most of all. Almost everywhere Ari went, she was around children who, unlike her, had both their parents with them. And yet these other children may not have seemed quite grateful enough for what Ari then understood was an immeasurable blessing. Perhaps they even seemed like they were taking it for granted.

I went through something like this with Michelle. All during the pregnancy I fully anticipated having a baby to take care of, and when I didn't have her, I was angry. And when I saw other mothers not paying attention to their babies, I couldn't help but feel irritated and think, *They do not understand what a blessing that baby is.* The truth is that it's easy for us to take the good things in our lives for granted, but Ari taught me to at least try to *always be deeply grateful for our blessings.*

9.) Ari made me understand that we all have a purpose here on earth, and that purpose is *to love and help each other.*

One of the things that most amazed me about Ari was how soon after the tragedy she began to comfort others. Perhaps because she grieved so much in the months prior to her parents' passing, and perhaps because Ari seemed satisfied and even content with the ending her experience in Heaven provided her, Ari began comforting others literally days after the tornado. At the visitation for her parents, Ari—still physically ravaged by the storm—walked down the aisle at church and hugged and comforted a crying man. How astonishing a moment that was!

Since then, Ari has never stopped loving and comforting others:

relatives, friends, orphans, here and in Kenya, people in nursing homes and church groups, parents and teachers at Sandy Hook, her Nanny Susan when she's feeling bad, and complete strangers she meets at events.

Ari's certainty about her purpose has taught me that in a very real way we *all* have the same purpose in this life—*to love and comfort others.*

10.) Ari's experience in Heaven made me realize an incredible truth— the things we often define as "real" are *not* what's actually real.

We spend so much of our lives focused on material things: our cars, our homes, our money, even our bodies. These are the things that we consider the reality of our lives. But Ari taught me that our lives here on earth are intertwined with what can be called a *Living Heaven.* She taught me that what is real are the things we *cannot* see.

Helen Keller once said, "The best and most beautiful things in the world cannot be seen or even touched. They must be felt with the heart." I believe this is absolutely true. Just as Ari could not see or touch certain things in Heaven, but still understood they were entirely *real*, we humans can't see the things that are most real and most meaningful about our lives. Love, for instance, is undeniably real. Thankfulness is real. Hope is real. Peace is real. Compassion is real. Kindness is real. Our bodies wither away, but what lasts forever is what's *inside* us—our soul or spirit or whatever you want to call it. Everything else is transitory.

That, perhaps, is why Ari's parents were so at peace in Heaven, and why they didn't seem to be concerned about Ari at all—because they understood that the only reality that matters is that life does not end when we die, and that they will all be together in Heaven before long.

CHAPTER THIRTY-ONE

Life in northern Alabama continued after the 2011 tornadoes—slowly, things returned to something like normal. Homes were rebuilt, churches reopened, roofs repaired, gardens replanted. But there were always reminders of what had been lost, and what could still be lost.

Reminders, too, of what had been changed.

Some people who survived April 27 had seen and survived other tornadoes, and believed they were hardened to the kind of devastation storms can cause. Charles Whisenant, a newsman who's covered hundreds of stories, wasn't as affected by death and dying as others who had experienced it less often. "I've watched cops pull bodies out of creeks, so the loss of life, as horrible as it is, was not that shocking to me," he explains. Yet even Charles wasn't quite the same after April 27.

"I'm still not scared of bad weather, but . . . I guess you could say I have more awareness of it now," he says. "More reverence."

Gary Beam, the mayor of Arab when the storm hit, says that eleven years later "my mind is still perfectly clear about what I saw that day. Just how vivid and monstrous this tornado was, how it picked things off the ground. I will never, ever forget those few minutes of my life that I spent watching that tornado."

For Gary, April 27 was also a powerful argument for the existence of God. "When I hear that someone is an atheist and they don't believe in God, I just think, that's the furthest thing from the truth. There is *so* much evidence of a living God. I mean, who laid Ari gently down in that field? Who could do such an unbelievable thing if not God?"

Some who witnessed the destructive power of the 2011 tornadoes now focus on how to keep people safe when the next one hits. Since April 27, which the meteorologist James Spann spent nearly the entire day on the air broadcasting updates about the relentless storm, one question has continued to haunt him—*Why in the world did over 250 people die in Alabama when warnings for all sixty-two tornadoes were so good?*

Spann spent several years looking into how meteorologists could not only make more accurate predictions but also reach more people with them and make them safer. But he was just as interested in another area of concern that he feels does not get enough attention—the mental health struggles of tornado survivors.

"I pretty much kept my mental struggles to myself during the first six months" after April 27, Spann wrote in his book about the storms, *All You Can Do Is Pray.* "Internally, I felt weak, guilty and defeated."

Jordin Putnam, one of the nine people who took shelter in Ann and Phillip Hallmark's home when the tornado hit, and one of the four who survived, understands those feelings. He suffered from survivor's guilt and other post-traumatic issues. "Right after the storm they had me on so many medications and antidepressants I was like a walking zombie," Jordin recalls. "I wound up taking myself off all the medication, but then every time I heard thunder I was a mess."

One night, Jordin decided to combat the terror he felt during storms by confronting them head-on. "I got a pack of cigarettes and I sat outside on my front porch during the next thunderstorm," he says. "I just sat there getting drenched and wrestling with my fear. I kept saying, *'I'm not gonna let you conquer me. I don't want to sit around in self-pity all my life.'* And I did it. I conquered my fear."

Other aftereffects of April 27 weren't as easy to conquer. Jordin suffered substantial injuries and still wakes up every morning in pain, especially in his back and foot. Once a gifted athlete who played football and basketball and ran track, he can no longer play any of the sports he loved. "Am I the same Jordin I was before the storm? No, the old Jordin is gone," he says. "The pain will always remind me of what I went through and I just have to learn to live with it. But the way I see it, I may not be who I used to be, but I'm a lot better than what I was.

"Time passes, and I am at peace with my life."

(Harold Buchanan, who was huddled next to Jordin in the Hallmarks' house when the tornado struck, survived the storm but badly injured his back and needed surgery; fortunately, he was ultimately able to return to his construction job.)

Jordin Putnam was far from the only one transformed by the storm. One resident of Arab had been separated from his wife for two years before April 27, 2011. Afterward, they got back together, and eleven years later they are doing just fine. Another man who told me he was once a "pretty heavy drinker" was on his way to fetch a beer from his outdoor fridge when the April 27 tornado swept him up and seriously injured him. He survived and later told me, "That was my very last beer."

Susan Garmany—who was too focused on Ari's care to ever dwell on her own well-being—was profoundly changed by the storm, too.

"Losing the only daughter you ever had makes a big difference in your life," Susan says. "Jennifer would have taken care of me in my old age. She'd already picked out a bedroom for me in the new house. So there's a kind of permanent sadness that just lays on top of your life."

On a wall near the dining room in the house Susan shares with Ari, you will still find the slightly warped metal wall-art piece, stamped *Trust in the Lord*, that Shane muscled flat on the morning of April 27, to get it to hang properly. "Shane, Jennifer, and I stood together in that spot by the wall for five minutes while he wrestled with that picture," Susan says. "It was the last time the three of us were ever together like that."

Even so, says Susan, she can still find the humor in it all. "I used to tell my husband, Mike, that raising Jennifer was going to be the death of me. She was so independent-minded and so full of energy. And here I am raising Ari, who is basically a mini Jennifer. In a way, I feel like I'm raising Jennifer twice."

In the end, maybe all tornado survivors have to go through intense personal battles like these, whether it's sitting outside during storms or studying ways to make people safer or just learning how to trust the world again.

As James Spann notes, all the preparations in the world, all the warning systems and Doppler radars and high-tech alarms and homespun signals, might not protect you from a powerful tornado if it comes down your street and makes a direct hit. We may know quite a bit about tornadoes—how they form, where they tend to hit, how strong the winds are—but ultimately tornadoes are not something we can fully explain. We cannot explain, for instance, why a tornado turns two feet to the left and destroys an entire family, rather than two feet to the right where there are nothing but trees.

Tornadoes, in the end, are not ours to fully comprehend.

In a way it is like Ari's time in Heaven.

Ari saw colors she could not describe. She recognized people she had never met. She saw hair on her father's head she could not explain.

These were things that were just not hers to fully comprehend.

But that did not stop Ari from believing, with all her heart, that everything she saw was real. She did not *need* to understand all the things she experienced in Heaven. It was enough for her to have faith that Heaven exists, and that the loved ones we have lost exist there, too.

Perhaps it all comes down to faith.

I always go back to what her aunt Cindy told Ari to help her stop crying at school. "If something is going to happen," Cindy said, "it's bigger than you. The only thing you can do is make the best of every moment that you have with your parents *right now.*"

The tornado was bigger than all of us. And all any of us can do is make the best of it. Life goes on. It just looks a little different.

Ari's court battles continued—the battles to get her out of the conservatorship and gain her independence.

There were a lot of reasons why Ari wanted the conservatorship to end. She was fifteen now, and she felt she was more than capable of making decisions about her own life. (The court, on the other hand, was entitled to remain in control of Ari's finances for another four years, and, if they so decided, possibly even longer than that.)

One of the most helpless feelings for all of us was seeing how much money was being routinely drained from Ari's inheritance by the bureaucracy of her conservatorship and by the steward. When Susan was conservator she was permitted to be compensated for her time, but she declined to take any money from Ari at all. That was not true of the person who took over for Susan. But that alone would not constitute a legal reason for removing the conservator. A violation of the applicable Alabama Code was needed to create sufficient "cause" to remove a conservator, and Susan and I spent years presenting the court with what we believed to be more than sufficient cause in five different areas.

Yet the court never wavered from its position. As one official declared in an earlier hearing, the court continued to believe it was the best arbiter of what was and wasn't good for Ari. "Ari is growing up," the official told a judge. "She's turning into a little flower, and we have to be careful with her and continue to nourish and protect her." That same official even told Susan that her adoption of Ari was not legal because of technicalities, and the court was "looking into the matter." Anything we thought was certain and settled was, the court made sure to remind us, still in their power to change.

In September 2020, we found ourselves in court for the fifth time to dispute the fiduciary management of Ari's estate by the steward, and to demonstrate legal cause to remove him. We did not go in with the highest of hopes. Even our lawyer, Chad Smith, wasn't optimistic about our chances.

"The odds of winning the case were thirty-seventy against us," he says now. "Removing a conservator is just a very difficult thing to do."

It all came down to this one hearing that, in a surprise move that very morning, the judge limited to just two hours.

At one point in the hearing, the judge decided to take a short recess and speak to Ari privately in her chambers. Twenty minutes later, a very angry Ari emerged. She told us the judge informed her of the impossibility of winning her freedom from the conservator. *Did Ari want to continue wasting all her money on a fight she couldn't win?* the judge asked her. (In fact, we only fought in court during routine hearings the court scheduled, we used *no* money from Ari's account, Chad basically donated half his time, and Susan and I paid the other half.) *Or didn't she just want to get on with her teenage life and be like all her other friends?*

"*It cannot happen,*" Ari was told. "*He cannot be removed.*"

For the first hour and forty-five minutes, things could not have gone worse for us, leaving us precious little time to accomplish anything. Things got so tense that I noticed that Ari had curled up in her chair and shut down, absolutely miserable, while Susan was literally bleeding from nervously picking her fingernails. I could not bear to see either Ari or Susan suffer this way, and I almost leaned over to Chad and suggested we just get up and leave and end the whole thing immediately.

But I didn't, and Chad rose up from our table for one final, last-chance round of questioning of the steward.

This is what I have in my notes about what happened next.

Chad told the court that the steward did not balance any of Ari's accounts each month or even quarterly, leading to significant errors and even negative balances in some accounts.

"I review the statements," was the steward's defense.

"And charge Ari for that?"

"Yes, I do."

"Are you a forensic accountant?" Chad pressed him.

"Sometimes."

"But are you considered to be a forensic accountant?"

"I look at accounts."

It was a frustrating back-and-forth, but Chad was not deterred.

"Are you a *certified* accountant?" he asked again.

"I went to college," the steward replied.

"Do you have a degree in accounting?"

"I have a minor."

"Are you a CPA?"

"I'm not."

"You charge Ari a lot of money for accounting. It's the biggest portion of your charges. Do you do all your own accounting work?"

"I don't."

I was surprised to hear him say that. It never occurred to me that someone else might be doing the accounting that the steward charged Ari for. Chad did not follow up right away; instead, he let those words hang in the hushed courtroom for a nice, long while.

"Do you do *any* of your accounting work?" Chad finally asked.

"I pay someone to do it for me."

"How much do you pay them?"

"I don't recall."

"You don't recall? Just generally, *approximately* how much do you pay them?"

"You'd have to ask her. I just have a girl in the office who does it."

A girl in the office? I thought. What did that even mean? Did he really not know how much he paid this girl to do his accounting work?

"She just tells me how much to pay her and I do it," he explained.

The steward had cracked open a door. Chad barged through it.

"Do you charge Ari the price of the contract labor, or do you charge her your fee of a hundred and fifty dollars an hour?"

"I charge what my fee is."

Finally, a court attorney called "the girl in the office" who did the actual accounting work for the steward and put her on speakerphone. The attorney asked her directly how much she was paid to do the steward's accounting work.

"Twenty-five dollars an hour," she responded.

At that moment, I felt something shift in the courtroom.

"So," Chad went on, drawing out his words, "you pay a girl in your office . . . twenty-five dollars an hour . . . to do the accounting work that you charge Ari a hundred and fifty dollars an hour for?"

"Yes," the steward replied.

"And you think that's okay?"

"Yes, I do."

In that moment, everything changed. I felt everyone in the courtroom stop *breathing*, caught up, as was I, in the steward's casual admissions about his practices. The judge closed the hearing by saying she would consider Chad's closing argument requests that the conservatorship be immediately returned to Susan, and that Ari's estate be reimbursed for all the accounting work she was overcharged for, going all the way back to 2013. The judge said she would announce her decision shortly.

More than three months passed without a word.

In January 2021, we filed a motion for another hearing to press the matter. Just one day before the scheduled hearing, we heard from the steward's lawyer and another representative of the court.

They proposed that, in exchange for postponing the hearing and not pursuing our request for reimbursement, they would accept *all* the terms we presented in a proposed draft order—and restore Ari's conservatorship to her grandmother Susan.

We had won.

In July 2021, Susan drove to the courthouse to pick up the actual piece of paper that declared she was Ari's principal conservator, which in effect restored control of Ari's life to Susan and Ari. Shane and Jennifer's wishes for their daughter had finally, finally been honored. It was all over.

"He reveals the deep things of darkness," it says in Job 12:22, "and brings utter darkness into the light."

CHAPTER THIRTY-TWO

It took Ari nearly ten years of her young life to fight through all the complications and aftershocks of the 2011 tornado, and to arrive at a place where, at the very least, she was finally free to lead her own life and share her own story. They had been hard and painful years, and in that time Ari changed quite a bit. She was not, as she often said, a little girl anymore.

She was grown up now.

"Ari has really matured in how she deals with things," Susan says today. "I think she put things together, and she came to understand why she had those dreams about her parents, and when she understood that, I think it helped her find her purpose in life."

As Ari puts it, "When I was younger I didn't understand what God was doing. But as I got older, I understood more. I realized God wouldn't do me like that. God has a plan."

Something that greatly impressed me about Ari is her consistency and steadfastness in sharing her story of Heaven. In all these years she never wavered in her conviction to tell it, never wandered from the pure message of her story, never worried that people might think she was making it up. She just stood tall and, when the opportunity arose, told the world what happened to her and what she saw in Heaven.

Not long after we finished Ari's little book, I remember the editor of a local paper asking eight-year-old Ari if her Heaven story was "real."

Ari just looked up at him with infinite patience.

"If it wasn't true," she said, "I wouldn't be putting it in a *book*."

Ari had a way with skeptics, that's for sure.

Recently, I asked Ari—who turned eighteen in 2022—if she thought she would continue sharing her Heaven story all her life.

"I've thought about that a lot," she said. "It's kind of hard for me to answer right now. In the future, when I have kids, I don't know how it would affect them to have me talk about it. Eventually I'll want to have my own little family and leave what happened to me in the past. But I'll always minister to any stranger who needs help. That won't change."

In so many ways Ari is just a typical Southern teenager living a very busy life. She was awarded a two-year scholarship to attend Snead State Community College—but she isn't quite sure what she wants to do or to be, other than knowing "it will be helping people in some way, like my mom did." For now she's a cheerleader at Arab High School and is looking forward to graduating.

Lately she has taken up off-roading with her boyfriend, Trevor, in his Razor ATV and she doesn't at all mind coming home covered in dirt and mud. She also spends a lot of time mothering her brood of dogs—Foxy, a Christmas present for Ari when she was three; Poppy, the rescue who loves sneaking off to chase cows (which he knows he's not supposed to do); and her newest dog, an Aussiedoodle, a cross between an Australian shepherd and a poodle. (Ari got this one after Goober, her little black-and-white mutt and her mother Jennifer's favorite of them all, passed away from cancer.) She named her newest pup Stetson, after the cowboy hat brand.

"My dad got me a Stetson when I was a little girl and there are all these pictures of me wearing it, and I still have it," Ari explains.

In the summer of 2022, Ari sent me a text late one night. "We had to say goodbye to Chloe today," she said. "Chloe was a good friend when I felt alone." Chloe, the alpha of the bunch, the orphan puppy born on the day of the 2011 tornado and anonymously gifted to Ari soon after, arrived in Ari's life at about the same time I did. I saw that Chloe was always right by Ari's side—*always*. She helped Ari to heal and, many years later, also became a faithful companion to Susan. (As Ari became more independent, I think Chloe sensed that Susan needed her a little bit more.) Chloe snuggled with Ari as she endured physical and emotional pain that first summer, she went on adventures with her over the years, she protected her from all strangers, and she loved Ari deeply, and Ari loved her just as much. Chloe was with Ari in the days following the passing of her parents all the way up to the time that this book, which delivers Ari's message to the world, was completed.

She was a dog with a purpose.

There are also times when Ari really misses her parents, and on some sentimental days—their birthdays or an anniversary—Ari will imagine talking to Shane and Jennifer, saying hello, asking for advice or just checking in (once when she visited the cemetary, she happily sang her mother's favorite song, "This Is the Stuff," to her).

"It does get really frustrating sometimes," says Ari, who broke up with her first boyfriend several years ago and suffered her first heartbreak. "It was a very sad breakup, and I would have loved to be able to talk about it with my dad, but I couldn't," she says. "That was hard."

When I watched Ari give her talk at New Beginning Church in Florence, I had the strong feeling she was going to be okay. That is not to say that I believe her life will always be easy, or that she has some magical power to conquer adversity. I expect she'll face all the same hurdles and setbacks and defeats we all face, as well as all the little miracles and happy mercies and wonderful bursts of love that make life such a blessing.

What I mean by "okay" is that I think Ari has a sense of purpose that she is now free to pursue, as well as a resolve that will give her the strength she needs to face whatever life brings her. There is something solid and stalwart inside her, a brightness to her heart and a boldness to her spirit, that I think will make her stand out no matter what she chooses to do. All I hope is that Ari will always feel the great love that surrounds her, always know how special she is in our eyes, always understand that when we thought we were rescuing her, she was really rescuing all of us.

I asked Ari if she believes her parents are proud of her in Heaven.

"I mean, just like any teenager I've made mistakes and I'm sure there were times when I made them roll around in their graves," she said with a laugh. "But yes, I do know they are proud of me."

CHAPTER THIRTY-THREE

Late in the summer of 2020, Ari decided she wanted to meet with Kenny Casey, the man who saved her after the tornado. She hadn't seen him since the visitation for her parents in 2011, when she was six.

We arranged to meet Kenny at the barren field in Ruth where he found Ari nine years earlier. There, Ari presented him with a new premium-steel Case knife and a new red sweatshirt, to make up for the shirt he took off his back and wrapped around her head the day of the storm. Ari was resolute through the whole meeting—she'd never really heard the story of how Kenny found her and carried her to the road, and she genuinely wanted to know more details about what happened that day, and what it was all like for Kenny. She asked him to walk her through the field and point out where he found her, and where he found her parents and grandparents, and she asked him hard questions and didn't flinch at any of his answers.

Then Ari asked Kenny a particularly pointed question.

She knew her Paw Paw's body had been found still holding on to her young cousin Julie, who survived the tornado. That meant Paw Paw held on to Julie through the entire storm, never letting go despite being picked up by the raging 150 mph winds and thrown nearly one hundred yards.

Her question to Kenny was—why hadn't her own father held on to her just as tightly? Ari had been thrown over two hundred yards and was found far away from her father, Shane, which meant that, at some point, Shane must have let go of her.

"I don't get that," Ari said. "He would have held me just as hard as Paw Paw held Julie. I know he would have."

Kenny took a pause and looked down at the ground. Then he looked straight into Ari's eyes and told her something he hadn't told anyone before.

"When I found your father in the field, I saw that some debris had torn a big hole straight through his stomach," Kenny said. "If he'd still been holding on to you, whatever tore through him would have torn through you, too, and you wouldn't be here."

Ari didn't say anything. She just thought about what Kenny said and nodded slightly.

Later that day, when Ari and I spoke about our time with Kenny, she explained her thinking to me.

"My dad *did* hold me tight—so tight that nothing could have made him let go," Ari said. "And he *didn't* let go. But then my angel came down and took me out of my daddy's arms and took me up to Heaven and then set me back down in that field."

I told Ari I thought she had it exactly right.

Acknowledgments

There are many important people in my life who have chosen to put up with my obsession with getting Ari the freedom to tell her story, and then write this book. These special people have continued to support me throughout the long and somewhat messy process. I'd like to start with two very important Toms.

To my husband, Tom Reburn, who I met in person exactly three weeks after the April 27, 2011, tornadoes and who has never flinched at all the hours I've spent on being involved in Ari's and Susan's lives and in writing this book—thank you from the depths of my heart. You *always* encourage me, from bringing me milkshakes, to buying me adjustable height desks and ergonomic rolling chairs, to rubbing my shoulders and, when I get frustrated, reminding me that this is exactly how God made me—someone who loves a huge project. You call me your "pretty girl" and you are my perfect eHarmony prize! I would accomplish much less without your love, support, and seemingly never-ending belief in me. How lucky can I be?

I also want to acknowledge my dear friend Tom Phillips (Dr. Tom), a pastor and counselor. He gave me advice about Ari before I even met her and he was always there to help me work through the unusual complexities of Ari's and Susan's lives. His deep wisdom, gracious spirit, optimistic and humorous outlook still make me smile. Dr. Tom passed away unexpectedly only months after orchestrating Ari's first large speaking event. It seems a fitting tribute to his strong belief in the importance of Ari's message for our world and her purpose on this earth that he squeezed us in—at the very end of his time here.

At the end of Ari's event at Dr. Tom's church on October 6, 2021, just before his closing prayer, I passed the microphone to him and I teased my very bald friend (off mic) about liking Ari's recollection of people getting their hair back in Heaven. Not to be outdone, he took the microphone and told the guests, "Well—I've heard a lot about the hope of Heaven, but this is the first I've ever heard about the hope of hair. . . . Let us pray." Dr. Tom, I miss you greatly.

An enormous thank-you also to the silent team who brought Ari's story together. They are the foundation and the scaffolding that made my work possible and built this book. Bill Guggenheim, coauthor of *Hello From Heaven!*, heard Ari's story in 2012. He contacted me and became Ari's self-appointed champion. Bill never wavered over the next ten years in his belief that the world needs to hear Ari's message. Without him, you would *not* be reading this book. Gail Ross of Ross Yoon, our literary agent, waited for seven years for us to be able to allow her to guide us through this complex process. I love her no-nonsense, get-it-done attitude. We began our time with Gail at FAO Schwarz in New York City, in the baby doll section, and now we are bringing it to a close as Ari graduates from high school. That's perseverance.

Thank you, too, to the incredible team at Simon & Schuster. During our 2014 trip to New York City, Ari, Susan, and I stumbled across the Simon & Schuster headquarters in Midtown Manhattan, and Ari and I posed for a quick picture in front of it, just like we might have in front of a movie star's home, never believing that one day we might actually have a chance to work with anyone on the other side of those glass and brass doors. The Simon & Schuster team never made me feel like an amateur (which I am), but took all my requests to heart and worked together with me to keep Ari's story pure (as she made me promise to), while still delivering a polished and professional final product.

A special thank-you to Priscilla Painton, who took a personal interest in Ari's story and showed great purpose in making this book happen; to my editor, Lashanda Anakwah, who brought invaluable insight and patience to the writing process and was an absolute joy to work with; and to the art, copy, and legal teams at S&S, who all played huge parts in creating this book you now hold.

I'm so grateful to my coauthor, Alex Tresniowski, for all he's taught me. From the moment I first met him, waiting for me inside an upscale restaurant in Manhattan, squeezed between a wall and a column in a space much too small for his towering frame, I knew I liked him. He looked exactly the way I thought he would, the personification of a New York City professional writer and author: tall, dark-framed glasses, salt-and-pepper hair. When I arrived late (I walked two blocks in the wrong direction), carrying my typical oversized purse and juggling two large gift bags, he surely must have had a clue about what he was in for, as I enthusiastically exploded, "Hey, Alex!" and attempted to hug him across the tiny table already full of hors d'oeuvres. That day, he made me feel "at home"—and that's one of Alex's best gifts. Alex took my many clunky words and shaped them into this beautiful story. He taught me to "say it with less words" and "keep it moving," and I'll be eternally grateful that he taught me about the "invisible threads" that connect us to each other on this earth. Thank you for everything, Alex! *You're the best!*